DOWNWARDLY MOBILE

Travels with Mavis

Ray Canham

Downwardly Mobile
Travels with Mavis

Copyright © 2018 by Ray Canham

All rights reserved. This book or any portion thereof may not be reproduced or used in any manner whatsoever without the express written permission of the author, except for the use of brief quotations in a book review.

downwardlymobile.weebly.com
downwardlymobilebook@gmail.com

Dedication

This book is dedicated to James, Matt and Dom, for being our light during the dark times, and also to the memories of Owen Williams and Donald Alfred Canham.

CONTENTS

Downwardly Mobile 1
Contents 2
Foreword 5
Introduction 6
Chapter 1 7
Chapter 2 10
Chapter 3 17
Chapter 4 24
Chapter 5 36
Chapter 6 38
Chapter 7 44
Chapter 8 51
Chapter 9 64
Chapter 10 69
Chapter 11 72
Chapter 12 76
Chapter 13 79
Chapter 14 89
Chapter 15 91
Chapter 16 106
Chapter 17 109
Chapter 18 120
Chapter 19 128
Chapter 20 132
Chapter 21 135
Chapter 22 143
Chapter 23 150
Chapter 24 156

Chapter 25	163
Chapter 26	169
Chapter 27	178
Chapter 28	184
Chapter 29	188
Chapter 30	192
Epilogue	195
Acknowledgments	196
Notes:	198

Ray Canham

FOREWORD

By Ro Williams

I am doubly honoured to be asked to write the foreword to Downwardly Mobile, firstly because I was instrumental in bringing Ray and Alison together and secondly it is good to know that something positive can come out of tragedy.

Ray approached me because he wants the proceeds from the book to go towards a cause in memory of my son Owen, who was Alison's cousin and who was taken from us suddenly in July 2014 at the age of just 39. Alison told me that Owen's passing was one of the reasons that she and Ray decided to change their lifestyle so dramatically and to live their dreams. In recognition of this they wanted to do something that could, in some small way, honour his memory. Owen was a DJ and he was beginning to build his profile on community radio and at clubs in East Anglia. I am delighted therefore that the proceeds from every copy of this book sold raises money to help budding DJs at South Street Studios in Ipswich in his memory. The studios are a not-for-profit organisation and their target audience is people with special needs, young carers, young offenders and other hard-to-reach groups.

I followed Ray and Alison's adventures on their blog and awaited each episode with anticipation. I love the humour in Ray's writing, the vivid descriptions and the memories that their travels unlocked. Reading Downwardly Mobile made me laugh and cry, made me think and then made me want to sell our house and buy a motorhome, a plan that was only thwarted when my partner caught an estate agent measuring up our home. I recommend it to anyone who's ever harboured a longing to travel and to downsize their life, or even if you just want a bit of a giggle and like reading about people's adventures, and misadventures, as they grapple with a completely new way of life.

And by the way, please remember while you are reading this book that I drive an Audi!

INTRODUCTION

Thank you for purchasing, borrowing or stealing this book, if you intend to read it, so much the better. I am Ray Canham; I married Alison in September 2015 and on our honeymoon, we decided that a conventional life wasn't really for us anymore. We'll reveal more about ourselves as our story develops. Just a few words of warning before you plough on though. This book started life as a blog and what you now hold in your hands is an edited version with some additional material. I have taken a few liberties with the sequence of events where it helps the narrative but otherwise all of the twists and turns, rants, nostalgia, opinions, humorous observations and descriptions are interwoven; just like they were in real life.

When I started, I thought it would just be a record of our day to day travels, but the more I wrote the more personal in nature it became. Eventually I gave in and wrote it in the first person, largely with my thoughts, feelings and memories to the fore. That isn't to diminish Alison's role or experiences; it's more a reflection of the limitations of writing it in this way. I hope that I have done justice to what was an incredible year exploring the country in a motorised box on wheels, working at festivals and wrestling with domestic appliances.

As we travelled around, I recorded our thoughts and feelings about the places we visited and things we did. Sometimes these may not chime with your own views or experiences. If that is the case, then I suggest that you buy extra copies and give them out to all of your friends and neighbours so that they too can be offended.

Before you proceed you may like to check out the exclusive area on the Downwardly Mobile website that contains a photo record of our adventures and a few other titbits reserved for people who have purchased the book. Check out the acknowledgements page at the end of the book, at the bottom you'll find details on how to access it.

With those provisos out of the way let us get on.

CHAPTER 1

'Getting downwardly mobile opens your eyes to really living'[i]

Early one morning at the end of February 2016 I woke with a start. I'd been married for almost six months and had just handed in my notice at work. I'd bought a motorhome using a loan that strictly speaking I wasn't entitled to, our house was sold, and we still had two cats to rehome. In a months' time my wife and I would be homeless, jobless and leaving our hometown forever. I couldn't have been happier.

This book chronicles our adventures when we spent the summer of 2016 travelling around the UK searching for somewhere to settle. Thanks to contacts we'd made over the years the plan was to break up the sightseeing with work at small music festivals and gatherings. Along the way we would test the tolerance of friends and family around the country who were foolish enough not to pretend they were away, and would therefore be lumbered with two under washed nomads on their doorstep and a motorhome the size of an aircraft carrier on their drive. We'd also test our relationship and tolerance of each other by living in a space the size of an average bathroom with barely enough room to swing a cat.

It became both a physical and a spiritual journey; one we undertook with precious little planning and no safety net. There was soul searching, looking back, reconnecting with estranged family and confronting of our demons. It's also a love story; a tale about two people who are very much in love with each other falling in love with the country, with the open road, with the freedom to live a simple life, to laugh, cry, love, get cross, swear at Audi drivers and to search for a place we could call home.

* * *

Alison and I were married in September 2015 after meeting at a friend's camping trip in 2011. Between us we have approximately three grown up children and two cats. We share a passion for the great outdoors, hiking, camping, music and coffee. We've both worked all of our lives, Alison predominately in administration and me as a nurse for people who have a learning disability, and then in social housing in a series of jobs with increasingly long and bewildering titles.

Our prime years, the ones between wondering what to do with our lives and wondering where they went, could have continued in the same pattern, endlessly rebounding between home and job, paying the mortgage, performing jobs of negligible significance to anyone, saving for holidays in the sun where the stress of work would eventually fade two days before the flight home. Retirement would follow, shoved out to pasture, left to measure fading years by the ticking of a cheap clock on a chilly mantelpiece.

Then one day in July 2014 Alison received some shocking news that made us really think about the direction of our lives. Her cousin Owen passed away suddenly. At only 39 years old his death was devastating to everyone because there was no forewarning, no chance to prepare, for him or his family and friends. A sudden bereavement robs friends and relations of the opportunity to get ready and face the inevitable. I'd known Owen as Alison's cousin, an acquaintance from camping trips and as the DJ at family functions and I felt the shockwave. For his family the second the news came, the moment that the shockwave hit them, their world stopped turning.

Slowly it started spinning again but it would, could, never be the same. Each sun rise would be a reminder that Owen wouldn't call, at every family gathering there would be someone missing. As the routine of everyday life returned everyone close to Owen would feel a pang of guilt as they shared a joke or enjoyed a day out without him. Sitting next to me as we drove away from Owen's funeral, Alison wiped her tears away and reflected on the suddenness, the unexpected ending of a young life. Here one minute and gone the next. On that short journey we vowed to find a way to live our lives as fully as we could.

As two people who spent a long time single and raising children we both harboured a longing to travel, to take off, abandon our worries and to live life in the moment. Of course, reality, in the shape of work, children, debt and mortgages scuppered any progress until one day the thought occurred to us that actually there was nothing preventing us from living our dream – except us; our children had left home, work had become a way to pay debts and house prices were edging ever upwards, meaning we'd be in a position to sell up, buy a motorhome and have enough to exist on for a while.

So that's why we closed the front door of our home one last time on a chilly morning at the end of March 2016, stuffed the remnants of the previous night's pizza into our neighbour's bin and, armed with a road map, a fancy satnav that we hadn't worked out how to turn on and a note book, we set forth.

CHAPTER 2

Breaking Away

We put the house up for sale on Boxing Day 2015. This was the time to test the market, as the shiny estate agent put it, and see if we could attract viewers. If we found a buyer our plan was to try to complete the sale in April. First though it meant a Christmas of frantic cleaning, touching up of paintwork, gardening and general maintenance until the house sparkled. I was forbidden to touch anything and was encouraged to eat outside. The customary family visits over the festive break were preceded by us removing a crust of dust and paint from our skin and frantic rootling through boxes to find clean clothes. Nevertheless, after a succession of viewers, from the monumentally bored to the ridiculously enthusiastic, we received an offer for the asking price. This was it. If we accepted, then the journey would be on. There would be plans to make, finances to panic over, a vehicle to buy and countless other obstacles to terrify us. This was make or break time, a final do we or don't we discussion, a sleepless night and then, over breakfast we both said yes. We spent the day in a daze, rapidly assembling our rough notes and ideas. We had just given ourselves three months to sell up, buy a motorhome and hit the road. It sounded easy said like that.

I'm not one of life's planners but fortunately Alison likes to think ahead. She assembled the skeleton of our strategy for the coming months while I trotted off to work. I returned home one day to find a glossy map on the wall with pins stuck in to show where we had festival work lined up. These were joined up by wool in straight lines as every effort to get a ball of double knit to follow roads had failed. It made our living room look endearingly like a secret nuclear missile control centre. We added the places we'd both consider settling down, some other places we wanted to visit and drew up a rough itinerary. We'd started adding the meat to the bones of the plan.

I had a few of my late father's old maps but Alison vetoed their involvement in our preparations after I casually let slip that the map I was using for work didn't have the M25 marked on it. These maps formed an essential part of our family holiday planning when I was growing up. My father's approach was to get out his extensive collection of dog eared charts that together covered most of the British Isles, study them on and off for a few days and then triumphantly declare that we were going to Norfolk…again. Just like last year and the year before that. His map of Norfolk was probably the most recent in his collection, many of which were older than he was. Holidays for me as a child would mean puttering along roads with grass growing down the middle, even though a bypass had been built sometime in the years since his map had been published. More than once he had to reverse, grumbling, out of a farm track or exit a lay-by that had formally been an A road. I still have in my possession his Suffolk road atlas that shows elevations for cyclists and 'automobiles of limited power.' But whatever route we took it seemed to end up in Norfolk anyway. My mother's theory was that we always went to Norfolk because he had travelled far and wide in the Navy and the fact that he could get killed was a risk worth taking for seeing the world at someone else's expense. Now he was on terra firma the accountant in him had clearly worked out that Norfolk was cheap and as a bonus we were unlikely to come under enemy fire.

We started buying motorhome magazines. Well, in truth Alison did. I tried it once and was engulfed by a wave of dread when I went to the newsagents. For a moment I was back to being a spotty hormonal teenager, standing in a bookshop in SOHO that had a discreet adult section downstairs. Once I had plucked up the courage to shuffle down the curiously sticky stairs I was confronted by racks of dubious delights, from the relatively benign girly magazines to hard core ones that brought tears to my eyes, and presumably to the eyes of the unfortunate farmyard animals featured on the cover too. I effected 'sauntering around' like a seasoned pornography connoisseur, although I'm sure I looked exactly like what I was; a blotchy frustrated hick with a glowing face. Somehow, I eventually purchased a copy of Hustler and snuck out, afraid that in a city of 6.5 million souls I'd bump into one of the two people I knew.

Back in 2015 I returned from the newsagents with a copy of Motorhome Monthly Magazine (MMM) discretely hidden in the pages of Record Collector, made an excuse and dashed upstairs before remembering that it was only a useful guide to all things motorhome that I'd purchased. Unless you have a particular fetish for manmade fibres and grey hair you'd be hard pressed to find anything to divert you from articles about interesting walks, the best ways to fill up your water tank, how to connect to the electricity supply and many others of varying use. As I mentioned I'm not the planning part of the team, but Alison devoured them from cover to cover, made notes in the margins and rapidly filled a note book full of hints and advice.

We visited a couple of motorhome dealers armed with a checklist of dos and don't's culled from the pages of MMM and fell in love with an ex hire 2013 Dethleffs Sunlight, built on a Fiat Ducato base. Well, fell in love after eliminating all the luxury homes out of our price range, machines with odd shaped beds or toilet/shower/kitchen combos, groaning engines, rusting hulks sold as 'vintage' and vans too big for UK roads or two small for 6 months or so on the road. After pretending to negotiate, for forms sake, we agreed to purchase her just below the asking price. Because six or more months in a confined space could test even the best of relationships, we opted for something on the roomy side and ended up with a six-berth home. We christened her Mavis after one of our favourite singers Mavis Staples, a member of the legendary Staple Singers.

With a huge motorhome now blocking the sunlight to our neighbour's house our next task was to consider the contents of our home. We lived in a three-bedroom house in Colchester; an anonymous semi in an anonymous street in a largely anonymous town in Essex. I'd lived there for close to 30 years, through marriage, children, divorce, crippling debts, depression, a career change, Alison moving in, getting engaged, getting married and buying Mavis. With two adult children just moved out and Alison and I combining homes the house was full and the garage bulged at its seams. When I eventually got around to sorting it I was ashamed to find festering bags of old baby clothes, toys, three quarters of a cot, some mouldy medical text books from my days as a student and among the detritus a box of almost pristine records, ones I had long since given up hope of seeing again. Thus Alison came home one day to be greeted by me bursting from the garage like an excited puppy waving a pile of 7" singles, and a notably empty skip. Once I'd rescued the vinyl the saving grace was that the rest of the contents were a putrid mess, and so we just heaved it all into the skip.

As the clear out and packing started in earnest the first of many car loads of books and bric-a-brac was taken to charity shops. We issued an alert to friends and family giving fair warning that if they had ever lent us anything the chances were that they could buy it back from Oxfam in Colchester if they were quick. We then arranged for the remainder of our possessions to be placed into storage at one of those big shiny warehouses that have sprung up on the edge of most towns; brash, colourful and loaded with the crap we've all craved and sweated for but don't have room to keep. We took the first few loads ourselves but the big stuff we left until we were recommended 'a man with a van', who actually turned out to be two young men; one whippet thin, constantly chattering, calling us love and mate and who told completely inappropriate tales about 'birds' he'd known, and his surly companion who only spoke to affirm his mate's tales or to answer a direct question. It was like they had a finite amount of words between them and they weren't sharing equally. I accompanied them to the storage unit to ensure our furniture was packed appropriately while Alison sorted stationary, having altogether too much fun arranging paper into size, hue and weight, checking pens still worked, grading paper-clips and getting oddly sentimental over erasers. When I returned from the second of several trips she accosted me and enquired in a stage whisper how they were doing. I affirmed that to date nothing was actually broken but it was as well that one of us was around; I found a heavy box of precious records on top of a garden chair balanced on a leaning wardrobe. When chatty boy said *'me dads got lots of vinyls…'* I winced and made a mental note to reduce their tip. When they left we re-sorted everything to our satisfaction.

After all this we were left with a house that echoed, with bare walls and a mattress on the floor. It had been a whirlwind, with hardly any time to think about how we had come to the conclusion that selling the house and buggering off with only a sketchy plan was a good idea. We sat exhausted, excited and terrified and reflected on our path to this point.

* * *

In September 2015 Alison I were holed up in a remote village in The Peak District. The cottage had solid stone walls, fortification against the winter gales that can whip up out of the valleys and smack the exposed dwelling with force. At that moment though it was warm outside, the air still and dry, the thick walls and small windows providing a cool refuge from the glare of the sun.

I was eating dinner seated opposite Alison. We'd been married for four days and were on our honeymoon. I'd been trying to describe how I felt, and failing miserably. It wasn't just the heady rush of love; not the glow of our wedding day receding into a warm memory, nor was it joy at the thought of 10 more days of work free holidaying that I was trying to describe. It was something else, a safe, warm and tranquil sensation; an impression that our future belonged to us alone and not to work, family or friends. I noticed that my head wasn't buzzing, but was awash with space, with a consciousness that was entirely focused on us enjoying the here and now. I tried all sorts of explanations to express my feeling, words that gradually faded out in the face of Alison's knowing smile. She gently took my hand, looked into my eyes and whispered…*'you're relaxed.'*

And there it was…I *was* relaxed. No background stress from work lying in wait to ambush me in a quiet moment, no nervous glances at my phone for a message from someone from my past kindly pointing out my faults and no excited tension for the wedding…will it go okay? (It did) …will Shirley say anything to upset Bob again? (She didn't) …will the weather be okay? (It was glorious). And there was no worry about the honeymoon; it was just a cottage and us.

I looked down at my plate and realised that for the first time in weeks I had not started my meal by making sure that I had a morsel of each type of food on the plate on my fork, because I thought the first bite had to include a taste of everything all in one go. Quite how this ritual developed is anyone's guess, but it had been around for a while, flaring up and receding with the rhythm of my anxieties. I've had a tendency since my teenage years, possibly even before that, to take comfort in ritual as a way of coping with stress.

I must have been a troubling child. Quiet to the point of reclusiveness, I'd hide from other children, avoid adults and cry in corners at parties. All guaranteed to earn me chastisement from my mother for *'grizzling'* and generally being a wimp. I learnt to cope and drifted through school, made friends and ran free over the fields of Hertfordshire. Then when I was 11 years old my father changed career and we moved to Suffolk. We took root in a rambling old house in an alien market town. I felt completely alone; my Home Counties accent didn't fit in with my peers, the school was a strange old-fashioned place full of bullies and fierce teachers who taught a different curriculum to the one I'd left. The cane was used occasionally and we lived in fear of it. I never received it, but it was a constant threat in this bewildering old-fashioned world I'd been parachuted into, foreign to a boy brought up with an informal 1960s education in leafy suburbia.

At some point my mind started to exert control in odd ways. Ritual, a term I'm using because it works for me, became important. Bits of my day were taken up by repeated actions like touching the four corner posts of the drinks cabinet in a certain order 4 times. There were a few of these rituals that had to be conducted at particular times every day. I would usually settle once they were completed, but sometimes odd thoughts would interrupt me at other moments during the day and I'd focus on doing something meaningless, like touching each finger with the fingers of my other hand and vice-versa four times; always four. It became significant and I thought of it as my lucky number. I'd count in fours, eat four baked beans at a time, and touch whatever I was fixated on 4 times. I'd switch my bedroom light on and off four times every night. The neighbours must have thought I enjoyed a very brief disco before retiring.

It's a strange comfort that comes from performing an action that you recognise is patently absurd, that you know has precisely zero effect on anything and whose non-performance results in absolutely no effect whatsoever. Yet somehow it is important, it's built up inside your head to become a way to make the bubbling anxieties, the insecurities, doubts and stress physical; something tangible to be manipulated and controlled in a way that the mind alone isn't able to do. At times I would fight back, fearful of some bad luck befalling me but determined not to comply with the interfering voices echoing around in my head. Gradually the rituals subsided, only to flare up in times of pressure. Usually they were controllable and generally not disruptive to everyday functioning. Nevertheless, a trace of ritual was always lurking, a suggestion that doing things in a particular way was important. After all, when I had, for example, a big presentation at work looming what harm could it do to start a meal by making sure I had a morsel of each type of food on the fork?

Alison fought her demons too. Finding herself in an emotionally abusive relationship in her late teens she struggled to free herself from its bonds. Courage came with motherhood, the realisation that she wanted her son to have a mother that he could respect instead of a quivering wreck. Extricating herself physically was one thing but the emotional wounds were deep. Struggles to keep a roof over their heads and her battle against debilitating bouts of depression took their toll.

And then we found each other. We revealed our fears, worries, hopes and dreams to each other. We shared a home, went to work, went to gigs, had friends over, got engaged, laughed, went on long walks, talked and hatched plans, got married and went on our honeymoon. We did those things newlywed couples do, we went around with wide grins and soppy eyes, walked arm in arm even when it became uncomfortable, and generally lost ourselves in each other. For maybe the first time ever nothing from my job seeped into my head to worry me while away. I knew that there would be hundreds of emails waiting when I got back, questions and queries, spats to iron out and the usual baggage that is a middle manager's lot in life. But sod it, this was our time, our little world and the rest could wait. I could relax. Not just chill out or switch off for a while but function at work and at home without the need for any rituals. I found that I didn't need to suppress them anymore. Something had changed.

We decided that enough was enough. We could seize the initiative as a couple; mutually dependent and independent, as we should be. One of the things that we bonded over was our shared sense of escape. Alison, a single parent since the age of 21, has a spirit of resilience; outwardly determined and stolid despite her past struggles. For a long time she had entertained a desire to jump into a campervan and flee, to take off and find peace and to leave behind the negative people, the debts and worries, the depression, the responsibilities that belonged to others but were placed upon her shoulders; to be permitted to be herself.

I too had thought of absconding. I was also a single parent and although I had shared responsibility, raising two boys while maintaining the pretence of normality took its toll. Driven to take on more stressful jobs to service the debts and support the family, depression and anxiety bit hard. I was stolid and showed little emotion, keeping the dark times in my head, a mass of writhing negative emotions squirming around. I had every intention of seeing the boys securely into further education and then finding work abroad, where I might be free to start again. No more struggling to keep a roof over our heads, no more working in positions it was hard to morally justify, no more anxieties borne out of demands on our time and good will. Supposing we just quit work and spent the summer pursuing our passions for music and travel from the comfort of a motorhome while looking for somewhere to build our nest. So we found a way to leave the rat race to the rats and live our dreams, a summer on the road without the safety net of a home or jobs.

CHAPTER 3

The South

We left home at midday on Wednesday 30 March. After a hectic morning there wasn't much time left to reflect on what we were leaving or on the adventures we were about to embark on. A tortuous drive to Cambridge included two traffic jams with two loud and impatient cats. We eventually introduced them to their temporary home with all four of us in a slightly frazzled state. Pausing only to pass on the most rudimentary of instructions about which end food goes in and which end it comes out of we hit the M11 heading south - and into more traffic chaos. The journey to Canterbury took us 4 hours longer than it should have and we finally arrived at 10:30pm where the site owner restored our faith in humanity by greeting us with a smile and a flask of hot chocolate. With chocolaty moustaches we sat down, exhausted but happy. We were actually doing it. We had no home except Mavis, no jobs to worry about and a summer stretching out ahead of us full of opportunity and hope.

After the trials and tribulations of our first day on the road we started Day 2 with a trip to visit the world's most forlorn motorhome supply shop. Astonishingly the owners hadn't thought to include anywhere for motorhomes to park, so I slung Mavis over their neat grass verge while Alison popped inside, was ignored by the surly staff and came out again empty handed so we took great delight in ignoring the Keep Out signs and reversed over their carefully manicured gravel drive. Delighted though we were with this minor act of passive aggression the real joy came when we returned to the campsite and walked into Canterbury. The town centre is a UNESCO World Heritage Site, with the Cathedral the main focus along with the charming streets surrounding it. The Cathedral itself is the seat of the Archbishop of Canterbury, the Primate of the Church of England; a title that has a refreshingly Darwinian twang to it. It also has something of a bloody history. I'm sure most people are at least vaguely aware that Thomas Becket was murdered here on the orders of Henry II and martyred in 1170. Back in 1012 the then Archbishop St Alphege was murdered by Danish raiders after they sacked Canterbury, captured him and he refused to be ransomed. I assume they got the right man, since St Alphenge seems to have been known variously as Ælfheah, Elphege, Alfege and for some reason Godwine. Then in 1381 Archbishop Sudbury was beheaded in London during Wat Tyler's Peasants Revolt. Incidentally his head is still kept at the church of St Gregory at Sudbury in Suffolk. Two further Archbishops, Thomas Cranmer and William Laud were executed in 1556 and 1645 respectively, after which the killing of Archbishops of Canterbury seems to have gone out of fashion.

Aside from being careless with the lives of its Archbishops the city charmed us both immensely. Entering the town via the Westgate Tower its allures are plentiful, with a variety of independent shops, fine parks and a real jewel in the magnificent Beaney House of Art and Knowledge. It's a museum, gallery and exhibition space attached to Canterbury Library and is exactly as a museum should be; compact, engaging and varied, with exhibits from ancient Egypt rubbing shoulders with a collection of swords, stuffed animals, portraits and a fascinating collection of dolls house furniture among the many curiosities. Even more impressive was the helpfulness and enthusiasm of the staff, who even at 5.30pm on a Thursday were eager to help, especially the young man who encouraged us to handle various Roman objects and explained about each one. I'm not sure where enthusiasm crosses into obsession but he appeared to be skating cheerfully between the two.

Waking with slight hangovers, a legacy of visiting an old work colleague of mine in nearby Whitstable the evening before, life in a cramped space started to take its toll and we soon vented our frustrations. Firstly, the power in Mavis was acting oddly, the 12V supply seemed to be temperamental and we were having doubts about the leisure battery, although we were too technically incompetent to know exactly what was wrong. Secondly, living in a space smaller than most kitchens required mutual understanding and a degree of empathy we would need to adapt to. For example, if one of us was standing at the sink the other became trapped at whichever end of Mavis they happened to be in. A sort of dance then occurred as we squeezed around each other, only for one person to realise they'd forgotten some essential item and the dance began again. After clearing the air we escaped into the wide open Kent countryside for a long hike, following part of the Crab and Winkle Way – a disused railway line running between Canterbury and Whitstable – before tracking off to dip in and out of a nature reserve and across fields back to Mavis who immediately seemed spacious and homely.

The next day we decided to attend the sung Eucharist service at the Cathedral. I considered wearing a tie; I had one with me somewhere but then I remembered that ties are stupid. I've never really understood the purpose of a tie. I concede that it can look smart, adding decorum to a gentleman's attire for formal occasions, but as everyday wear it seems odd, like a fabric arrow pointing to one's willy or in my case a kind of formal bib. In an office environment the wearing of ties opens a window to the soul of your colleagues. You get the plain, sombre tie wearers, the fashionistas with their huge or skinny knots as fashion dictates, the work experience lad with his nylon school shirt and a tie he's borrowed from his dad with a pattern like 1970's wallpaper. Then there's the old boy in accounts who's worn the same suit for the last two decades, and who every year dusts off his racy Christmas tie with the sad little faded reindeer and 20 years' worth of mince pie stains. And then, worst of all is the office worker who wears silly ties with comic book motifs, little cars or Disney characters on to show he's a bit of a laugh and not the sad sack of disenchanted frustration with an unrequited crush on Sally in Finance that he really is.

So, avoiding anything more formal than a cycle helmet we broke out the bikes for the journey which was entirely downhill from the site, making it far more fun going in than coming back. After a coffee at a French cafe we alighted at the Cathedral for the service. Alison put it into words afterwards, saying, *'I'm not part of the high church tradition but I loved the pomp and majesty of the ceremony and hearing the choir just took me beyond myself. The sense of being part of what is a vibrant worshipping community with a real local church feel, and following in the footsteps of worshippers and pilgrims who have shared in prayer and praise since the first century actually moved me to tears. Sitting here now in glorious sunshine, admiring an incredible view I am filled with a real sense of peace and wonder.'*

After the service we were invited into The Chapter House for drinks which provided a more parochial feel to counter the formality of the service. One of us even managed to spill tea on a minister. After hasty apologies we were left to our own devices and wandered around the Cathedral, basking in the splendour of the building, the sun shining through the stained glass lending a purple hue to the magnificence of the architecture and its adornments.

After exploring some of the city centre we took the steep climb back in our stride like the athletes that we are, and walked most of the way. We tidied Mavis up a bit and, based on our growing experience, changed things around inside to make more space and ensure things like clothes were more accessible. It also gave us an opportunity to personalise her a bit and so we woke up with glowing faces from the previous day's sunshine in our *home*, rather than in just a motorhome. After packing up we headed off to a site near Hastings, a tranquil spot nestling in mature woodlands.

* * *

Lulled into a false sense of security after yesterday's cycling exploits we decided to head into Hastings by bike, only to divert to Pett Levels and the coast when we realised what the gradients were like. At one point Alison was actually rolling backwards. Somehow we did manage to climb one enormous hill of the sort that ordinarily requires crampons and ropes, then free-wheeled downwards for about 3 miles to enjoy a hasty sea view before struggling back to the campsite.

Is there a better way to greet the day than sunlight dappled through the trees accompanied by the birds singing? Of course every silver lining has a cloud, and in our case it was to open the curtains to our neighbour, a gentleman of ample proportions wearing shorts, surgical stockings, white England socks and open sandals while enjoying a good swear at an uncooperative barbeque. He really was an unpleasant chap. When they had arrived the day before he swore copiously at his wife and daughter and spent the best part of 24 hours erecting the awning to their caravan accompanied by much profanity and blaming of his family. He greeted me with a cheery *'Hallo mate'* every time I stepped outside Mavis. Why he couldn't be civil to his own kin, who appeared meek and on edge around him, I don't know. I tagged him as a bully, an inadequate lump of a man dragging his long-suffering wife and children down with him, their esteem worn away by his fragile domineering ego. Then again, I could be completely wrong. Bullying is something I'm sensitive to after some fairly miserable experiences as a child. The juvenile school yard bullying was generally manageable until the teachers joined in. When the adults you trust question your masculinity or ridicule you then the only escape route, the one the posters and leaflets tell you about, is closed. Nothing I can write now could possibly describe the haunting solitude of being your own best friend for the 6 hours or so of the school day, so I tend to hate bullies and hoped for the sake of this guy's family that we'd just caught him on a very bad day. Failing that I hope he fucks off out of their lives forever and they have the confidence to build a better life without him.

We realised that we had now spent one whole week on the road and Mavis was beginning to look more homely as each day went by, or more untidy as Alison likes to put it. To celebrate we drove into nearby Rye where we discovered one of the frustrations of this lifestyle is the lack of car parking suitable for a vehicle of Mavis' ample proportions. We ended up in the coach park at Rye station desperately hoping that there wasn't some despot in a high vis jacket lurking behind the fence eagerly rubbing his hands together waiting to pounce.

Rye is a charming little town, built on a pimple of raised land in the middle of reclaimed marsh and it is particularly picturesque, in a chocolate box kind of way, with cobbled streets and plenty of exposed beams. We couldn't help noticing that they delight in taking a particularly literal approach to house naming. The house opposite an old pub is called The House Opposite while further down the road is The House with a Seat - which, you won't be surprised to read, has a seat outside and likewise the first house in the road was christened with the carefree abandon they exhibit around here as The First House. There are also several 'viewing points' dotted around Rye but these just meant you could see a long way from them. You couldn't see anything of interest unless you have a fascination for expanses of flat green landscape, in which case Rye is a special treat.

* * *

The next morning Alison became poorly on our journey so when we arrived in Littlehampton (west of Brighton, geography fans) she immediately took to bed while I remembered all my medical training and made myself lunch. I went to dispose of the various items of waste we'd accumulated and found that I had to re-sort everything into a bewildering array of dustbins, variously labelled for general waste, card and paper, glossy magazines, glass, food waste and so on. I wouldn't have been surprised to find an assertively typed list of severe penalties for the misplacing of refuse. I understand why they do this, but I've always viewed petty rules with suspicion. Some clearly make all our lives better and safer; all driving on the same side of the road or not shooting people for wearing socks with sandals for instance. Caravaners at some of these sites do seem to like a rule though; often I fear it's to save them thinking for themselves. Their world, and I realise I am unfairly generalising, is one of black and white. I imagine severe punishment is encouraged for minor infringements, like driving at 1 mph over the site speed limit or not having a Waitrose loyalty card.

A letter to the Caravan Club magazine recently decried falling standards because people were walking to the shower blocks in their dressing gowns. I'm really not making this up. What sort of petty small-minded blimp thinks that is worthy of a letter? I imagine some retired Major spluttering into his cornflakes as another Winceyette clad bosom bounces past his immaculately kept caravan, causing stirrings he's fought long to suppress. Of course, not everyone is like this, but the rules of each site do sometimes verge on the unnecessary. Keeping noise down between 11 pm and 8 am should just be a common courtesy, but presumably because a few dolts with shoe sizes bigger than their IQ don't possess common sense it's now enshrined in camp site law. The list of infractions is plentiful, from how to park your 'rig' to showering in the correct fashion, avoiding the grass, and of course the complicated lists of what exactly constitutes 'mixed recycling', and here I confess I got confused disposing of several bags of Alison's vomit. Fortunately, we left the site before the DNA results came back.

Meanwhile, back from my adventures in recycling I made up the sitting room bed and Alison spent the rest of the afternoon asleep under the quilt like a tiny mountain range gently rising and falling. She rose in the early evening and we strolled into town, enchanted by the local tradition of liberally sprinkling dog shit all over the pavements to welcome visitors. It turned our walk into a lively game of turd hopscotch, which was less fun than it sounds. The town looked a little rundown, but the good folk of Littlehampton are clearly not to be defeated and there was some sympathetic redevelopment around the harbour area and a charming coffee shop attached to a civic building overlooking the final stretch of river and out to the sea beyond. The only downside is someone obviously thought calling it The Look and Sea Centre was a good idea. It describes itself *'as a fun and interactive attraction that has a newly refreshed Heritage Exhibition now focused on the history of the river, harbour and seaside of Littlehampton.'* Today though the fun interactive attraction was clearly outside where a cluster of people gathered in an atmosphere of tense anticipation to watch the local lifeboat launch. Far from the adrenaline fuelled near chaos we expected it all seemed to be a cheerfully benign affair, with laughing and joking, leisurely finishing of cigarettes and banter with the waiting crowd until the last crew member scurried around a corner to a modest cheer and the boat was finally lowered into the sea by tractor. It bobbed up and sped off in a plume of spray into the open sea.

The Royal National Lifeboat Institution is a marvellous charity. In 2015 their lifeboats launched 8,228 times, rescued 7,973 people and saved an estimated 348 lives. They put to sea 124 times in winds above force 7. That's a 'moderate' gale, wind speed up to 38 MPH. On land that equates to effort needed to walk against the wind. Imaging having to lean into the wind to walk while your lifeboat is tossed around like a twig, balancing against rolling waves and at the same time trying to draw close enough to a vessel to take a wounded sailor off or to fix a rope for towing. Now imagine that at night. Over 3,240 launches were in darkness in the same year. They often risk their lives for fools who drift out to sea on inflatable air beds, inner tubes or rubber boats sold alongside the 'kiss me quick' hats and saucy postcards. Not long after we were in Littlehampton six people died around the British coasts in a single weekend; that same weekend one woman had to be rescued three times in four days by the RNLI. It was understandable that the RNLI reportedly *'gave her a comprehensive safety briefing.'* Hopefully that included a promise to deposit her on the moon if she ever strayed within 10 metres of anything deeper than a puddle.

The following day we had a date in nearby Brighton to meet up with my eldest and his girlfriend. Lulled into surrender by good food and wine they foolishly agreed to be guinea pigs for our first attempt at entertaining in Mavis the next day. I'd left them with a map of the route from the station to the site with the main features, like the supermarket, railway crossing, and with turds hastily drawn on, which was obviously of use as they arrived for Sunday lunch fragrant and in good time. We'd been learning the art of 'top cooking' on two gas rings, and if their visit was anything to go by it was coming along well; everyone was polite, ate up all they were offered and we've had no reports of ill effects. Fond farewells exchanged we waved them off at the station and prepared for our next adventure, heading onwards to Weymouth and a few days exploring the Dorset coast.

CHAPTER 4

South-West-East

We headed away from Littlehampton in squalling rain which cleared enough for us to get a clear view of the imposing Arundel Castle and the spire of Chichester Cathedral in the distance. While driving long distances we've found simple distractions to keep our interest and this day's offering included the wince inducing locksmiths van 'Surelock Homes', a splendid radio controlled mowing machine keeping the verges of Hampshire neatly trimmed and a beguiling sign for Monkey World Tank Museum, which I'd rather hoped was dedicated to primates fighting in heavy artillery, but we later discovered was two separate attractions in need of some punctuation.

We passed from rain to watery sunshine and into the New Forest with its pallet of browns, purples and lilac before the run in to Dorset and thence to the outskirts of Weymouth. We pitched at an impressive site with stunning views over The Fleet Lagoon. Of course you already knew that it's England's largest lagoon, which is a much sought after title I'm sure. It was most enchanting, and we took an early evening ramble via Fleet Old Church, a comely little place only two pews deep thanks to most of it being washed away by a flood in 1864.

After the site at Littlehampton, with the railway, busy road and the sound of children playing, the site at East Fleet had a quality of silence that we have seldom experienced before. It was almost tangible. Alison described it as '*a silence where you can detect the sounds only of nature; the hum of a bumble bee, the song of a robin and the lap of the almost still water as it gently kisses the shore. In the depth of this silence I feel, not as I expected, an interloper, but rather it connects to a peace within me that transcends the here and now, that speaks to the most primal part of me, that remembers a time where nature reigned unchallenged and human beings were more intimately linked with the seasons, the tides and the rhythms of creation.*'

Next day, after we were rudely awoken by the banshee-like squawking of a seagull we reflected that we have both been experiencing a sense of guilt at enjoying our new leisurely lifestyle. It's as if after working our whole adult lives something inside thought we should still be beavering away in pursuit of...well I suppose that's the point really, in pursuit of what? Money maybe - but as the saying goes *'some people are so poor all they have is money'* and we already felt enriched by the gentle pace and ever-changing sights of our new life. Maybe it was some deep-rooted protestant work ethic that drove us to feel we should be contributing in some way. Of course, until now our lives had been spent doing just that and paying our taxes like the compliant citizens we are. We were living off our savings and taking no state handouts. If all that sounds like self-justification, then I suppose it is. Still, the sun was shining, Hank Wangford played a dour waltz on the stereo and Alison had just found a bottle of Jack Daniel's Apple Punch we had stashed and had forgotten about so sod it we thought, let's live.

And live we did, first by walking in sunshine into Weymouth for a pootle around. And let the record show that on the basis of our one visit we thought Weymouth was a super place, with a busy harbour, lively high street, restful gardens, stunning views and all set on an expansive sandy bay upon which children played, dogs frolicked and we ate fish and chips from a box. Maybe the sunshine helped but it really was everything you could want from a seaside town.

Modern Weymouth is made up of the old port of Wyke Regis and its neighbour Melcombe Regis, which were united in an Act of Parliament in 1571. Maybe they had a ceremony and exchanged vows or something. Anyway, this union slowly swallowed up at least 7 more villages to form the modern town, although they may have had cause to regret letting Melcombe Regis join as it is believed to be where the Black Death came into England in 1348. The unified town of Weymouth became one of the UK's first tourist destinations after King George III took his summer holidays there. If it prospered from royal patronage, and it certainly seemed to, then together with its neighbour Portland it flourishes today from more proletariat holiday trade, to the value of around £105.2 million in 2013, according to the local authority's figures.

After the seaside charms of Weymouth we spent a day in the more tranquil beauty spots of Lulworth Cove and Durdle Door further along the coast. Making the most of glorious sunshine we had a paddle, avoided yappy little dogs and excitable children, ate a cream tea and climbed the hill from Lulworth to Durdle Door, where we watched a young man trying to impress a girl with an increasingly elaborate series of handstands with varying success and where small children ran excitedly towards the sea, put one foot in and raced back to avoid the chilly waters. We let the views sink in as we wandered, lost in the balmy day and spectacular scenery. A special mention for the staff in the tidy little tourist café and gift shop back in Lulworth, who were closing up but let us avail ourselves of the lavatories and show ourselves out via the staff exit. Unless their boss happens to read this in which case they most assuredly abided by the rules and none of this really happened.

After the usual morning ablutions and changing of the gas canister with only minor swearing we asked at the site shop about the charge on our leisure battery. It didn't seem to want to charge from the hook up, but charged when the engine was running. All sorts of unintelligible technical language was exchanged with the man in the shop which resulted in Alison giving a local specialist a call. Well, let it be proclaimed now that Sean at South Coast Auto is a prince amongst men, although we suspect his forearms are more heavily inked than most royalty. Not only did he arrive within 10 minutes, he was charming, diagnosed the fault almost immediately and didn't want payment for his trouble. We did of course make sure he didn't leave empty handed.

Buoyed up by the tattooed spirit of human kindness we walked towards Portland, a journey which somehow contrived to start and finish at sea level yet be considerably more uphill than down. We caught a bus across the causeway that joins Weymouth and Portland and stayed on it as it chugged around Portland - circuiting the forlorn settlement of Southwell, which from appearances as bus passengers appeared to be nothing more than a large and grim estate, and then into Easton where we alighted for coffee before visiting a local church. St. George's Church has two central pulpits and each of the boxed-in pews faces towards them rather than the altar as they do in most churches. Joy of joys, we had our own guided tour from an ex-quarry worker, who even let Alison ring the church bell and then went on to tell us about the Easton Massacre.

Press gangs were rife around these parts and the Navy's gangs were considered a legal recruiting method. Permitted by a magistrate's warrant, groups of men led by an officer would roam the streets and taverns of a town using violence and coercion to enlist men. Conditions in the Navy were harsh and pay low so willing volunteers were in short supply, hence the often desperate means employed by the gangs. Port towns were particularly prone to press gangs as an experienced seaman needed less training. The gangs were rewarded on a commission basis for men enlisted so their incentives were high and rules, such as they were, were often ignored. In 1803 navy frigate The Eagle, or maybe The Aigle, sources vary, docked at Portland. The captain led 40 or so men on a dawn press gang 'raid' into the settlement of Chisel. Armed with a warrant signed by the Mayor of Weymouth they chased residents into Easton Square where they seized a local man. The townspeople fought to rescue him and in the ensuing skirmish 3 local men were shot and killed and two more, including a local woman, Mary Way, were wounded. Mary later died from her wounds and her grave is in St. George's churchyard. The Captain and two lieutenants were tried and acquitted. It was a stark reminder of the unforgiving way of life on Portland. The quarries provided tough backbreaking work, fishing was dangerous and young fit men honed by a hard life were prized by the press gangs.

Walking on we reflected that despite Portland's many charms and stunning views it still bore its industrial heritage like a permanent scar; even the disused quarry where valiant attempts to enliven it with sculptures made from the local stone was sullen and clearly used by locals to exercise their dogs, or at least to dispose of their waste. The prison, as bleak and foreboding as you'd expect, loomed over the west of Portland, casting its long shadow over the surrounding countryside and the homes built to house the prison staff was utilitarian and charmless on the outside. Maybe on a brighter day and with more energy we'd have found more to lure us. Descending for a reviving cuppa on the beachfront we then climbed to the town of Fortunewell, which appeared somewhat neglected and peeling, its tight steep lanes grim and monochrome under a heavy sky.

The next morning we surfaced at the crack of 9am to hammering rain and with the lingering thought that only yesterday we had remarked on how lush Dorset was. What hadn't occurred to us then was that the reason for the lushness was the rain that now looked set to feature for most of the day. Undeterred we set off to find the newer of Fleet's two churches sitting squat and retiring among tall trees in a dark vale. From the outside it looked gloomy but inside it was bright, airy and most welcoming in a Spartan 'let's get down to business and forget all the pomp and baubles' kind of way.

As we were already wet we decided to follow the footpath over the fields and back to the site, after all how much worse could things get? We soon found out as we headed across a gentle stream and up a steep incline, the wet mud making us feel like we were walking up the down escalator. Undeterred we crested the hill and joined a path sandwiched between a paddock and hedge that slowly narrowed to the width of a person, and after a sliding decent turned into the local stream, which with a deftness that can only be described as accidental, we successfully forded and emerged onto the Fleet Road. We were as wet as it was possible to get without actually swimming but as we followed the field path opposite the rain got heavier and the ground stickier but we trudged on. As we rounded the last hill we both agreed it was terrific fun. And we meant it too; a great morning and back to a warm shower and a cuppa.

On a whim we decided to visit Westbay and Bridport on the rather splendid X53 Jurassic Coast bus service. The journey was bumpy and at times tortuously slow uphill but the views were spectacular, especially around Abbotsbury from where you can see the whole of Fleet Lagoon and Portland in the distance. We sat upstairs on the last remaining seats among what seemed to be a rather jovial Saga trip. Alison was delighted to be the youngest person aboard. If the bus driver had cause to brake sharply I'm fairly sure that a pile of false teeth would have clattered to the front and no doubt the other passengers would have had a great time sorting them out. Among our fellow travellers were a few who insisted on pointing out what I like to think of as 'the bleeding obvious'. Every mile or so a clarion cry would erupt from someone with *'Ooh look, that house is for sale'* or *'there's cows in that field'* or some similar inanity and we soon realised that a for sale board could keep an animated conversation going for ages, or at least until a gently ruminating bovine came into view to draw their attention.

Eventually we left the faint smell of lavender and aftershave that has a picture of a ship on the bottle and alighted in the busyness of Westbay. We took a stroll under cliffs that are eroding at an alarming rate then back over the cliff top coastal path. Sandwiched between eroding oblivion on one side and the mind-numbing oblivion of the golf course on the other we shared a chuckle as someone attired head to foot in designer golf apparel took several practice swings then immediately sliced the ball about 12 yards into the undergrowth. He repeated this several times as if it was going exactly as he intended, maintaining an air of nonchalance throughout the whole spectacle. Eventually we started to look conspicuous so we walked on and eventually into Bridport. It seemed a fine town but our bus was due and we didn't linger as we had arranged to meet an ex-colleague of mine who per-chance was staying at the same site as us. So that evening convivial pints were downed with her and her husband while we swapped tales of the road. They were planning to circumnavigate the UK in their motor-home Bessie and we wished them every success and drank far more than we should have.

* * *

In the morning when we were confident the beer was drained from our systems we left Fleet along the Jurassic Road, which was less bumpy in Mavis than the bus the day before and she took the hills in her stride. The views were striking and ever changing as we moved from the rugged coastline and steep slopes of Dorset to the rolling patchwork of Devon's hills with their regular strips of rich russet soil among the greens and golds. The journey enchanted us, so much so that Alison described the ever-changing views as filling her soul to overflowing...and retaining the poetic theme she even managed to alliterate a rant at an Audi driver who cut us up. It was like travelling with a sweary Wordsworth. Eventually we turned into the narrow lanes of Stoke Gabriel, near Totnes. After the usual unpacking routine we took a stroll into the settlement, which we took to immediately, with its multi-level houses tumbling down steep hillsides to the pretty harbour on the River Dart and tide fed mill pond. The town and the woods were resplendent and welcoming in the late evening spring sun.

Next morning I happened to choose a shower cubicle that had a fixed height shower fitting. Whoever thought this would be a suitable arrangement should be lightly tortured and then have their Caravan Club membership revoked. I'm presuming it was set for Mr. Average so it just pointed steamy water at my eyes rather than, for example, towards what's left of my hair. The icing on this particular cake was that unhindered by my grubby pink flesh it directed the water neatly under the shower curtain and into the drying area, where my shoes started bobbing around in the surf. I tried taking the shower off the wall but couldn't coordinate the shower gel as well, so I ended up liberally spraying the cubicle, my clean clothes and the person two cubicles down. Ten lively minutes later, with freshly polished eyes and soapy hair I emerged in a mood sufficiently improved to traipse gaily to the twee shop on site and purchase some fresh eggs for breakfast and a walking map of the area while Mrs Canham continued her ablutions unhindered by such trivialities.

Armed with the map we took to the local green lanes for four undulating miles into Totnes. These lanes are technically public highways but unsuitable for all but the most robust of 4X4 motor vehicles of the sort that you can hose down inside and out, not the shiny type used to drive precious Jeremiah and Rupert 1/2 a mile to school. The walk turned out to be a marvellous experience on tracks so eroded by the passage of countless feet, human and animal, that they carve through fields in private moss strewn gullies, at times up to three feet deep. Fleet Mill, now a private residence, marked the halfway point and from there we ascended steadily into the bungalow fringed estates of Bridgetown before descending sharply and up again into Totnes itself.

Totnes sits on the river Dart and rises up in a refreshing parade of independent shops, including rather a lot of butchers for some reason. We ambled around the town for a while, had a peek in the church and amused ourselves as one does by window shopping and generally getting in the way of people with better things to do. The Green Cafe sold excellent vegetarian scotch eggs so deserves a special mention. They also had a box of knitting needles and wool by the counter so that customers can knit a square towards blankets for an African orphanage. You can also donate to a scheme to help local people who are homeless. It was all done without preachiness and by cheerful and friendly staff. A mention too for the drivers of Totnes who seemed to be unfailingly polite, waving people across roads where in other places they'd pretend they didn't see you. Refreshed and rejuvenated by its air of responsibility and politeness we retraced our steps along the green lanes and back to Mavis. The only downside was that after all the exertion and general muddiness I had to face the showers again.

We noticed that, rather like Rye, they do like a literal place name around here. Great Tree, White Rock and the rather splendid Windy Corner to take three examples that form a little triangle West of Paignton. I'm assuming nearby Garden Centre is a more modern addition. I suppose if a way marker on your journey is a great big tree the name sticks. *'Turn right at the great big tree for White Rock Bob, you can't miss it, it's a great big tree...come to think of it you'll know when you get to White Rock too...'*

Nearby Tweenaways sounds like a 1970's children's TV programme about young scoundrels on an estate who nevertheless solve mysteries and help old ladies across the road, Glampton like a resort full of pine camping pods, and the good Burghers of Dittisham clearly got bored so settled on Dittisham, Higher Dittisham and Lower Dittisham with what looks on the map to be commendable accuracy if not imagination. Just north of where we were staying it was so bereft of population the map even names individual barns. We'd passed Millcombe Barn on our walk the day before which turned out to be a handy navigation point, more so than if we were looking for Ham Barn as there are two marked on the map a 1/2 mile or so apart. My favourite though has to be the local tradition of naming individual clusters of trees; Rypen Clump, which sounds like a member of the Dutch football team circa 1978 and the less than enigmatic Windmill Hill Clump.

Having exhausted all the fun of local place-names we boarded the Number 25 bus into Paignton. A special mention for the driver who cheerfully steered us around the snug retirement bungalow strewn outskirts of Paignton with ease, slaloming her way around parked cars, road works and loose children. She was the friendliest soul aboard, even stopping to let little old ladies burdened with shopping off as near as she could to their destination, disregarding the official bus stops in the name of doing the right thing. This cheered us immensely.

Paignton Harbour is twee and strangely remote from the town it serves, but busy with industry nonetheless. The promenade filled up slowly with people who've reached the age where man made fabrics in pastel shades become appealing. Walking into the town we ran the gauntlet of countless amusement arcades where the one thing missing seemed to be amusement. Nobody in these places looked happy; they all wore a fixed, expressionless air of defeat. Set between the amusements were various snack and drink outlets where the customers all sat with similar grim expressions, sharing tables with their significant others but not communicating, just staring numbly ahead as if salvation from holiday purgatory could be found in the pound shops and rock emporiums on the opposite side of the street.

We picnicked overlooking the sea, were mildly diverted by two amorous seagulls, strolled on the beach and wandered the promenade where they were painting over the winter rust and replacing bulbs in the illuminations in preparation for the summer season. Back at the harbour we were gratified to get the same bus driver home and took great comfort in her cheery demeanour, more so than the drivers behind her who had to repeatedly wait as she stopped to exchange pleasantries with locals and dropped people willy-nilly around Paignton's suburbs. Bless her.

* * *

In the morning we took to the road for an overnight stop in Bath. We walked the 2 miles or so from our site into the city via Victoria Park and the famous Georgian Crescent where we lingered next to a guided tour long enough to glean some interesting background information without attracting suspicion. For all its grandeur it really is just a bendy row of apartments, so we moved on and into the city itself.

The Abbey was a joy; cheap (suggested donation of £2.50 and no pressure), with a beautiful nave featuring impressive architecture, particularly the ceiling, a magnificent great window which depicts 56 scenes from the life of Jesus and it boasts many friendly and knowledgeable guides who were keen to help and explain without being intrusive. From them we learnt that Edgar was crowned the first king of England here in 973 and that in fact the Abbey is a parish Church nowadays.

Bath wears its alumni on its sleeve so you get plenty of Roman and Jane Austin memorabilia, but if you look past the commercial side it's a fine place, stately and accommodating to the ceaseless tourists and full of interesting alleyways and byways, enticing views and interesting shops. Even so after a couple of hours we grew tired of Olde World Tea Shoppes and walked back, where I managed to trip over a speed-bump because my attention was diverted by reading the 'Beware Speed Bumps' sign.

The facilities at the Bath Marina site were more rudimentary than the Caravan Club sites, but ample for our needs, although I had my customary tussle with the shower which seemed to have two settings, face melting scald or Arctic blast. Eventually I found a delicate position where the two merged and thus enjoyed temperate ablutions while pondering how long I'd have left it before asking for assistance. About 10 years I decided. As a bloke, asking for help doesn't come naturally, or indeed at all. I could cheerfully set off from my former home in Colchester to East Mersea, a journey shy of 10 minutes and be somewhere around Bristol ring road before asking a stranger for directions, and only then if there was a reasonable chance that I could abduct them and leave their remains at a remote spot so word didn't leak out that I had required assistance.

Alison suffers no such insecurities, she will leap out of the vehicle and happily enquire about the route and return 15 minutes later knowing not only the way but also where a good place for a meal is, the exact ages and idiosyncrasies of their children, their favourite brand of oven chip and what their Doris said about Bob at Julie's wedding. Addresses will have been exchanged and promises of Christmas cards made and talk of a reunion. In the middle of a crowded concert many miles from home Alison will spy someone she met while waiting for the bus in Beeston in 1996 and dart off to catch up where they left off 20 years ago. Meanwhile her husband and I will exchange nods and venture an embarrassed grunt or two about the inclemency or otherwise of the weather.

Maybe somewhere in men's evolution the gifts of introspection and meaningful communication were less essential than naked bravado. Preparation for raiding your neighbour's settlement for a few bushels of corn, a couple of oxen and maybe a new wife or two wasn't helped by reflections on mortality or fostering a deep understanding of your neighbour's hopes, fears and anxieties. Meanwhile the women of both sides would probably be sitting down together sharing a brew and letting their men folk get it out of their system. Anyhow it's a talent I envy.

With such thoughts out of the way we packed up and enjoyed the journey out of Bath and onto the A4 through the city where the traffic was obligingly slow enough to let us enjoy the splendour of Bath's historic buildings. Our journey took us away from the crinkly bits of the West Country and onto smooth Cambridgeshire where we pitched up in Comberton on the outskirts of Cambridge.

* * *

We had set aside a couple of days to see friends and family and the first order of the day was to walk to Alison's parents, a distance of about 6 miles. The downside of this arrangement was carrying two loads of washing. Determined to do it anyway we headed off like two packhorse's up Comberton's Long Road. This is well named. Although not long compared to, say, the A1, it is dead straight and soul destroying to trudge along on a Saturday morning, into the wind and facing the oncoming traffic. Cars would either skirt us by driving as far away as possible or whiz past a hairs breadth away, so it was a relief to discover that alongside part of the road the Parish Council had negotiated a permissive path, which was all very pleasant until we were faced with an abrupt end on a footbridge where an angry sign declared PRIVATE - KEEP OUT. Quite why the landowner withdrew their permission is a mystery, but it forced us to traipse sluggishly back to Long Road and thence on through a network of paths and pavements to emerge at the busy Girton Interchange on the M11/A14. This is one of those junctions that look like a clover leaf on maps and our path took us under grim tunnels strewn with litter and graffiti and across busy carriageways. It was reminiscent of the 1980s video game Frogger, where the sole purpose was to successfully cross continuous ribbons of traffic by avoiding oncoming vehicles. Once across and spurred on now by the adrenaline rush of surviving the crossings we walked into Girton along a country lane and met our knight in a shining VW, Alison's father, at our agreed rendezvous point for a lift the rest of the way and a convivial afternoon with much exchanging of news, fine food and sneaky looks at the football scores by the gentlemen present.

Moving-on days are distinct from others as there is a procedure of stacking, storing and stowing away to be done to make Mavis ready to roll on to the next site. Mornings start with the usual muted exchanges of a couple living in close proximity...'What time is it?' - 'Where's my other sock?' - 'Is this your bra or mine?' - 'Was I snoring?'

The correct answer to this last one by the way is always *'no dear'*, in defiance of any evidence to the country. Given the confines of motorhome life we've established that jobs are best divided into inside and outside tasks, otherwise we meet amidships laden with stuff to poke into cupboards with no feasible way of passing each other. The alternative is for one of us to remain seated but neither feels comfortable seeing the other scurry around, effectively doing nothing except watch; although I tried to make a virtue of writing our blog while Alison ambled by laden with pots and pans and a determined look about her. Hatches battened down and suitably refreshed from our morning ablutions, and my now customary wrestle with the utilities (today the shower snatched a late victory from what looked like a certain 0-0 draw when I discovered it had been craftily showering my clean pants with an errant jet of water the whole time I was washing) we set off for Mersea Island.

* * *

Mersea is an island because it is connected to mainland Essex by a causeway that floods when there is a particularly high tide. It has a long history of occupation, including an ancient burial mound we passed on our way in, and was an important settlement in Roman times, where they established the still flourishing oyster trade. It's a special place for us as it is only a few miles from our former home in Colchester so we have several friends who live nearby. We were staying on the Seaview Holiday Park, which, to be fair, is an accurate description as we could indeed see the sea from Mavis as we pitched right on the sea front. In fact we were the only people on the touring park, the rest of the site being taken up with an extensive estate of elaborate static caravans. Some of these were positively palatial judging by the little we could see, with tiny but immaculate lawns and ornate fences. There was also an abundance of KEEP OFF and PRIVATE signs suggesting that the temporary citizens of this little suburban home from home are intent on protecting their little piece of this green and pleasant land. Wandering around it is all rather surreal, not unlike a film set where everything is just a little too 'real'; colours too vibrant, windows sparkling, lawns manicured into perfect green submission and paintwork fresh and unblemished.

The facilities in this little oasis of middle England were the most rudimentary we had encountered so far. Upon arrival there was a brief ceremony where we were handed a key to the toilets and showers in exchange for a £20 cash deposit. All well and good but the single key is the gateway to four little havens of ablutionville. Firstly, for men's and women's toilets with wash basins and shaving points, presumably the later more generously provided for in the former. Then the same key for the adjacent men's and women's shower blocks. By now you will already be seeing the intrinsic difficulty in, for example, accompanying each other for a morning comfort stop, when one of us has to unlock the door for the other. Now imagine that having finished said comfort stop the person without the key wants to use the showers, they have to rely on the other person returning to unlock them, which of course is unlikely as they are now merrily singing away in warm soapy bliss unaware of Mr Stinky shivering outside clutching his towel and soap-on-a-rope. All this is manageable after a bit of practice for two people but imagine if you had children or grandma along too?

Oh, and now we're warming to the theme; the gents had a door sprung so hard it could propel a small child into the next field, the taps are on press down self-timers so short you don't get a chance to manoeuvre your hand under the stream before it stops, which is mute anyway since all the taps dispensed only cold water and the hand dryer was so feeble it was like having your hands sighed on by a pixie. And why, and I ask this in all seriousness, does the gents have a toilet brush in every other stall? What are you supposed to do if it's busy? Peer over the wall with an *'excuse me, I seem to have made a bit of a mess, do you mind just passing me the toilet brush...Oh, and I see you've got today's paper - how did Albion get on last night?'*

After a night dreaming of warm water and my own toilet brush I awoke to discover that it was my birthday. I've experienced a fair few in my time but this one was the first on the road. And it was splendid, with presents and cards smuggled in, including a very complicated furtive exchange in Brighton that George Smiley would have been proud of, and then Alison took the opportunity to pop in to see her former work colleagues in Colchester. 'Pop in' by the way, is Alison speak for any time just shy of 60 minutes and probably a bit more - and when she finds you standing outside under a blanket of snow with a parking ticket stuck to your forehead and asks if you've been waiting long for some reason you will hear yourself say *'on no, just got here honey-bunch, light of my life.'*

Anyway, everyone was hunky dory, so with a cheery farewell we went off to a motorhome and caravan supply shop for even more stuff, some LED bulbs for the 12V system so that we can live longer off grid and some of those supplies you never know you need until you see them, like adjustable rails, cup holders and some added security, which I then measured up using the time-honoured method of spaghetti broken to the correct length to check if outside and inside fittings matched. They did.

Our first festival of the season was approaching fast and we were experiencing a combination of excitement and anxiety that inevitably accompanies a new experience. Mostly though we were eager to hear some new music played live. Music has been a constant companion through both of our lives and was the first thing we bonded over. Our first date was at a concert in Cambridge by the Welsh singer/songwriter Martyn Joseph and since then attending and organising gigs, listening to our latest purchases and volunteering at music festivals has occupied a large portion of our leisure time. One of the greatest treasures of music is its ability to bring people together to share the experience. For us it has always been as much about the social side as the music itself and is why we started the Queensland Live house concerts, which saw a succession of acoustic artists playing sessions for a carefully screened audience in our living room. One of the downsides to selling up is that we are not able to put gigs on ourselves and share that intimacy with friends. But our chosen lifestyle has plenty of benefits and we made coffee, grabbed some biscuits and sat on the sea wall in the sunshine as the waves lapped the shore. A wherry in full sail drifted by on the horizon and a dog let off its leash dived into the water and played in the surf for the joy of it, lost in its own happy world. It was all most becoming and in the sinking sun we reflected that 4 weeks and 1,188 miles into our travels we're only just starting our adventures.

We left on a grey morning with the sun hiding behind heavy clouds, teasing us by shining out to sea. We were off to the Cosmic Puffin festival where we were about to make a grand and unforgettable entrance onto the site.

CHAPTER 5

Cosmic Puffin Festival

Cosmic Puffin was started in 2008 almost by accident when the young daughter of a friend of the organiser spent some time in a critical condition in intensive care. A benefit gig was arranged to raise money for the COSMIC (Children of St Mary's Intensive Care) charity at the hospital. Drawing on the talents of many bands and with about 100 paying punters they managed to make a small profit. It has had its ups and downs since then but in recent years has grown in size and ambition. More charities now benefit and the festival attracts artists and customers from all around the UK and from abroad to a relaxed, easy going festival raising money for worthy causes. Incidentally the name came from combining the COSMIC charity with the Puffin ward at the hospital where the young girl was transferred to convalesce.

* * *

We arrived on site at 5pm and after being given 3 different sets of instructions by 3 separate stewards we elected to plonk ourselves in the motorhome and caravan area, which seemed eminently sensible right up until we heard the tell-tale sound of spinning wheels. Stuck in 3.5 tonnes of Mavis we thought we were staying put for the duration until a trader with a Landrover was found to pull us free. We were going to recommend his stall but we had a look and it was mostly cheap festival shit so we won't bother, but anyway he was lovely.

After a hurried pitch up on more solid ground we scurried over to the crew and band catering tent where we would be working for the weekend. Predictably Alison knew the person in charge and so suitably briefed we set about helping to set up the kitchen, cook and serve hot dogs and get to grips with washing up 40 litre pans. After our shift we slept fitfully, thanks mostly to gale force wind and rain and partly because we had to be up at 6am scrubbed and ready for our next shift.

We started our early shift groggily but our cheerful colleagues and the bleary but always friendly and appreciative crew and bands coming in for breakfast soon raised our spirits and we settled into serving, prepping and washing up like the enthusiastic amateurs we were. After work we mooched around the site, Alison had her hair braided and we made friends with our neighbours who came armed with Willow, the world's bounciest dog.

Officially we had a day off on the Saturday, so we walked along the beach into Mersea to demand tea and biscuits from friends who probably hoped we wouldn't be back in the area quite so soon. News and hugs exchanged the afternoon was spent napping in Mavis and the evening watching the bands. Another 6am start the following morning and we walked through the camp site to the now familiar smells of bacon and hash.

After our shift we explored the now buzzing festival site in the breeze and sunshine before catching more live music. One manic front-man made an impassioned speech on the environmental impact of eating meat which was greeted by a cry of *'what a wanker'* from a lady dancing enthusiastically with a corned beef sandwich. She did however take up his offer to accompany them on tambourine later – as did Alison whom, let the record show, uttered no disparaging remarks related to him eating or indeed beating his meat.

Sunday night blended fitfully into Monday as the encampment of one particular band decided to party, chat and otherwise play noisy buggers all night. My inability to understand anything more technically advanced than a plate also meant that my 7am alarm went off at 6am, just as the band in question had walked to the beach. Alison, little Miss Sunshine herself, leapt out of bed radiating early morning good will to all in a delightfully profane way. At least we arrived in good time for our final shift in the kitchen.

Cosmic Puffin was ramshackle at times and maybe parts of the organisation could be improved, but order eventually emerged from the chaos and it all seemed to work because people wanted it to and mucked in to make sure it did. It was a great atmosphere and the people, paying customers, crew and bands alike were some of the most engaging, interesting and personable people we could have met. It was a privilege to work with them. From the drunken man ricocheting off dancers being gently guided to a seat to the young man with learning disabilities dancing with careless abandon in an arena where no one worried what he did so long as he enjoyed himself; from the duty first aider wearing pantaloons, headband and glittery beard who arrived on a Harley with inflatable flamingos sticking out of the saddlebags to the heavily tattooed woman with 6 young children in tow who were all unfailing polite, gentle and wise beyond their years, our first festival of the season confirmed that the path we'd chosen was definitely the right one.

Stopping only to surreptitiously switch off the power to the van containing the band who kept us awake all night we left for Woodstock. Fifty years too late and in the wrong country but hey, the details aren't important, it's Woodstock!

CHAPTER 6

Travelling North

We arrived at Woodstock in Oxfordshire tired, smelling distinctly agricultural and in need of rest and relaxation. The site we were on lay within the Blenheim Estate and close to Woodstock village, to which we took a stroll once we'd set up. It was very pretty and interesting in a picture postcard middle England kind of way but seemed to take its twee-ness a little too seriously. The pubs, and it's certainly not short of them, make much of their food's provenance and emphasise how local it is. It's all very well knowing that my asparagus has only travelled four miles to be on my plate but at the prices they charged I expected to have a personal introduction to the farmer and to be offered a tour of the farm as well. Maybe the fatigue was affecting me and it would look better tomorrow when we planned to visit the vast edifice that is Blenheim Palace to see where the old bulldog Winston Churchill was born into abject poverty.

Fortuitously our campsite receipt granted us reduced entry against the not inconsiderable entrance fees to the stately pile that is Blenheim. Built by the first Duke of Marlborough as a statement of his wealth and power it stands in striking formal grounds, thanks in no small part to the work of Capability Brown. Look over the estate in any direction and the view is always framed by trees of different hues and shades, giving a rich (in every sense of the word) texture to every scene.

But the first stop for us was the Palace so, promenading down the grand gravel driveway, we duly presented ourselves at the entrance for a briefing, which consisted of being told we had two options, right to tour the formal house or left to see the 'interactive' history. We went right and straight into the Churchill exhibition. Old Winnie was born at Blenheim two months prematurely; in fact so unexpected was his arrival that the family had to borrow baby clothes from a local shopkeeper. Well, I say borrow, but as they're in the display cabinet the thieving sods obviously didn't return them.

The exhibition was very interesting and humanised Churchill's life. Although privileged and possessing a clear sense that he was destined for greatness he still struggled at school, only scraping into Sandhurst at the third attempt. He was also an incurable romantic and apparently besotted by at least three separate women and proposed to them all. One even rejected his advances for the pragmatic reason that she needed a fortune that Winston didn't possess. Maybe because he was so used to rejection, he almost missed his chance when Clementine, or Kat as he called her, came along. She nearly left for London in frustration because he took so long to get around to popping the question. Eventually he plucked up the courage and so they came to be married on the 12 September 1908. Coincidently the same date as us if a good few years earlier, which endeared the old Pug and his Kat to us enormously. Well, that and the fact that Churchill took to wearing one piece 'Romper Suits' of his own design, with capacious pockets and matching monogrammed slippers. Some of these were even available in pin stripes which he wore without apparent shame.

The exhibition glossed over some of the more unsavoury aspects of Mr Churchill's life. A believer in racial hierarchies and eugenics, he wasn't exactly shy or sensitive in his opinions. There are plenty of examples of his insensitivity, and that's putting it mildly. According to John Charmley, author of *Churchill: The End of Glory*, Churchill saw himself and Britain as being the winners in a social Darwinian hierarchy. He thought white protestant Christians were at the top, above white Catholics, while Indians were higher than Africans.

'I do not admit for instance, that a great wrong has been done to the Red Indians of America or the black people of Australia. I do not admit that a wrong has been done to these people by the fact that a stronger race, a higher-grade race, a more worldly wise race to put it that way, has come in and taken their place.' He told the Palestine Royal Commission in 1937.

He was prone to being selfish, grumpy and inconsiderate too. Clementine is reputed to have seriously considered divorce at least three times. I suppose leading the country to victory takes a certain character that comes at a price. You don't have to be a nice guy.

After the Churchill rooms the rest of the house was all a bit staid. Impressive though it was, and the entrance hall, the library room and the state rooms were very fine indeed, the place didn't feel warm and vibrant in the way that, say Chatsworth in Derbyshire does. Chatsworth continues to add art, modern as well as old, to its collections and benefits enormously from them. By contrast Blenheim felt like a museum exhibit frozen in time. The building itself is spectacular but when you get down to it that's just a load of bricks stacked in a pleasing fashion. They trade on Churchill, only ever a guest at Blenheim anyway, rather than the delightfully louche Marlborough family whose talents seemed to be for losing slightly less men than the French on the battlefield, gambling and philandering. Still, we had the interactive exhibit to look forward to.

The so-called interactive display told the tale of the building of Blenheim and of some of its more colourful characters with animated mannequins and talking pictures, in a fun and informative way; or in an ill-conceived amateurish and boring way if you're over 10 or brain dead. It started promisingly but soon ran out of ideas. One room consisted of sitting backstage in a replica of the Palace's theatre listening to the servants acting and discussing...well we're not sure what but if we found it confusing, the party of four Chinese tourists accompanying us looked positively bemused. There was nothing to divert your attention if you had come here to spend your hard-earned Yen and couldn't understand actors voicing generic rural accents. Other exhibits were mildly distracting; I found a room where I discovered what I thought was a cash machine but turned out to be a touch-screen map showing me how The Duke of Marlborough won a decisive battle, as far as I can recall by arranging to have most of his soldiers slaughtered just after half time. Anyway the lovely and much more generous of spirit Alison wishes it to be known that she enjoyed the interactive experience and thinks I was being an old curmudgeon.

We stopped at one of the three eateries Blenheim has to offer where we were confronted by a paltry selection of pre-packed sandwiches, crisps and pies. The only difference between this and a motorway service station was the surroundings, and here clearly Blenheim saw an opportunity unavailable to Moto or Roadchef and hiked up the prices accordingly. So you can enjoy a £1.95 bag of ordinary crisps and a £5.60 baguette in a converted stable while reading advertisements for other overpriced crap. The only redeeming feature was that they called the chocolate brownie a Capability Brownie. Maybe we've been members of the Caravan Club too long, but we found that amusing.

The afternoon was spent wandering the gardens which completely entranced us. Walking in the sunshine admiring Capability's, err...capabilities was most becoming. The garden was full of carefully thought out touches that appear completely natural. For example, the waterfall he designed to drain one lake into another is hidden from its approach by trees, so you hear it first and build a sense of expectation. When you do see it you don't realise that it is an entirely man-made construction that has rocks artfully placed to maximise the sound and drama of the cascading waters. We saw a Grey Crane swoop low over the water, a duck in a tree and another busy defending his mate against other drakes, of which there seemed plenty, and all manner of small wildlife. What most impressed us though was the amazing vision of Capability Brown who was designing parkland and gardens that would be at their best long after he was gone and whose beauty he would never see.

Feeling in need of further sustenance we found another cafe and paid £2.10 each for tea we had to dispense into a paper cup ourselves. Much grumbling in a quiet British way later we left for Woodstock to collect provisions. It was more becoming today; the Cotswold stone seemed radiant in the sunshine and brought the place to life. On our way back to Mavis we were gratified to see a herd of asparagus being driven up the high street and into the Widget and Firkin by Nigel the farmer.

We wandered into Bladon in the evening and chanced upon a group of splendidly attired Royal British Legion gentlemen milling around the churchyard. Alison being, well, Alison, was soon in animated conversation with a heavily be-medalled gent and thus discovered that May 4 marked the anniversary of the liberation of the Netherlands in 1944, and that the Legion meets at 8pm on this day every year to place a wreath on Churchill's grave. After a quick peak at his grave and the well-tended Churchill family plot we left them to mark the occasion in private and walked back to Mavis in a reflective mood. As the sun set over the tranquil streets of Bladon we watched the lambs frolic in the adjoining fields and planned our next stop. Tomorrow we'd be heading north to the Lake District.

* * *

The less said about our journey the better. Suffice to say it involved considerable delays, diversions, simmering tensions and the satnav packing up just when we needed it. Nevertheless, we reminded ourselves that unlike many we weren't missing deadlines or running late for appointments and neither were we the unfortunate people involved in the accidents that caused the delays. In particular we reminded ourselves how lucky we were to have a toilet on board Mavis and made full use of it as our morning coffee took full effect.

We were delighted to find that the site in Kendal was simply stunning. We pitched among trees, next to a babbling stream and in fading dappled sunlight, with the aroma of wild garlic and the trill of songbirds for company. The site was a former gunpowder mill and ruins dripping with moss poked out of the undergrowth and neat little bridges spanned old water channels. We wanted to come back here as 10-year olds to explore with the careless abandon and wonder of childhood. It was all most bewitching and the cares and frustrations of the journey melted away.

After a comfortable night we walked out of the site and across a narrow cable foot bridge that spanned the broad river Kent. We followed the river for a while in the mid-morning sunshine before we joined the path of the disused northern section of the Kendal to Lancaster canal. This section of the canal was closed in 1955 because of persistent leakage due to fissures in the limestone. Although some of it had been filled in it was easy to trace the route, and the former tow path made for agreeable and level walking. Most of the original bridges were still in place, marking the canal's path like sentinels from another age. It's hard to imagine these remote structures that now cross meadows and pastures, spanning busy waterways alive with industrial traffic and packet boats providing a passenger service.

Now sheep litter the landscape with their busy lambs in tow, in turn both curious and nervous of our presence. We walked with the sparkling river below us weaving around the green rolling hills, the rugged foothills of the Lake District in the distance and the sun shining on our backs. After an hour or so we left the course of the canal and descended into Kendal, pausing for a cheeky al fresco cream tea overlooking the river. We went on to explore the town, which was a delight. We were particularly taken with The Yards; narrow lanes that run at right angles off the High Street. They are similar to Edinburgh's Closes along the Royal Mile, except in Kendal no one tries to sell you tartan flavour fudge or shortcake with a hairy cow on the tin. What we expected to be offered was mint cake but the only place we saw it for sale was in a supermarket in the centre of town. Odd, as the mint and sugar confection, apparently invented after a batch of peppermint creams went wrong and formed a 'mint cake', is one of the reasons that Kendal is known; at least to us.

We sought refuge from the sun in the church, with an ornate font lid; a towering wooden sculpture that lifts up by way of pulleys to reveal the baptismal font below. We didn't linger to find out more as the organist was clearly learning a new hymn or, more accurately, wasn't learning it and there are only so many false starts and bum notes one can take before muttering language that ill becomes a place of worship.

We set off early the following morning to venture north to Glasgow via Windermere. We took the Kirkstone pass on the narrow A529 and alongside Lake Ullswater to join the M6 at Penrith. What a glorious route it was. As it was early Saturday morning traffic was light and we played leapfrog with a French motorhome as we each vied to get into viewing spots large enough to accommodate us. With rare foresight we'd prepared breakfast for the journey so 10 minutes out of Windermere we parked up under Red Screes looking across the path to the ridge beyond and down into the valley.

It was a beautiful spot to stop. Two ewes, each with a tiny lamb in orbit kept us company. We ate rolls, drank coffee and lingered a while to breathe in the spectacular views. Rocky outcrops wore wigs of moss and grass, rivulets ran down lonesome hills and trickled into the streams below and it was all wrapped up in a myriad of greens and browns dotted with battleship grey sheep and runners in dayglo panting their way over fell and dale. Further away some of the higher peaks still had a capping of snow. It was all very fetching, and the stop meant we could drink in the surroundings without running the risk of scraping Mavis down a stone wall or flattening a cyclist. It also meant Alison was spared my running commentary on sights she'd just missed. The French motorhome whizzed by us as we'd cheekily made sure there wasn't room for it in our little haven and thus truly satisfied in mind, body and inter-racial rivalry we sped on. The next spot was nabbed by our rivals in a haze of Gallic smugness but at the ample Kinock Pass car park we made our own détente by the universal language of motorhomers - the slightly shy wave.

Coming down from the Pass the road followed Lake Ullswater along its western shore. With the sun out it felt like driving through the French Rivera in a 1960's film featuring Sophia Loren. Ullswater was just coming to life, with canoes and small dinghies being launched and an air of busyness about people striding around the narrow pavements. For a while we kept pace with a steamer chugging along the lake before we branched left, away from the lake and onto the M6 towards the border.

CHAPTER 7

North of the Border

Our first night north of the border was in Strathclyde Park on the outskirts of Glasgow. The park has its own loch, some water sport facilities, the remains of a Roman Fort and bath house and M&D Amusement Park, which boasts that it's Scotland's first theme park. It looked very compact and rather dog-eared but then we were seeing it from outside, the wrong side as it were, and judging by its popularity over the weekend it must be doing something right. Earlier while parking at the site we had one of those restrained disagreements couples have where neither party wants to upset the other. The reason was our inability to understand the others parking instructions. This was largely because we'd never bothered to explain what all the frantic arm waving and odd pointing the other party could see in the rear-view mirror was intended to convey.

With that sorted and not wanting to waste a breezy but dry afternoon we walked through the park and headed uphill towards the suburb of Bellshill to get some groceries. The route led us into an estate where stick thin teens in mismatched tracksuits lurked, pudgy toddlers trailed busy mums and stern-faced women wearing quilted jackets and determined looks marched along exchanging news. We passed a grim, forbidding pub where serious drinkers nursed pints behind chicken wire covered windows and walked by cheerless armour-plated shops. In these drab surroundings the local school was a riot of primary colours secured behind heavy-duty fencing. Nevertheless, everyone we encountered was friendly, so I threw away my book of estate clichés and went shopping.

We walked back by a different route through well-trodden informal parkland. It made a refreshing change from formal Victorian parks favoured by many cities. The path wound through glades of gorse, straggling briars and mature trees. At one point a railway viaduct seemed to burst out of dense foliage and over a deep gorge where far below the river made its tumbling way into the loch. At times we felt as remote as one can in a city the size of Glasgow and returning to Mavis we relaxed with the now obligatory cuppa.

Waking from our first sleep north of the border our intention was to get the bus into Glasgow city centre. When we thought we had missed the first one we took coffee in a restaurant connected to the amusement park to wait for the next one. It arrived with a small yellow cube alongside the cup that we thought was cheese, and remarked that maybe coffee with cheese was a quaint Scottish custom we'd yet to encounter. It turned out to be vanilla fudge which was altogether more pleasing to the palate. The bus arrived late due to a fault and the kindly bus driver took us in for free by way of compensation, although I did wonder if we were there to help push if it finally broke down. Happily, we arrived safe and sound in the city centre and walked along Buchanan Street away from the generic high street shops down to the bars and seedier end where the M8 motorway thundered through the city.

Turning left we walked beneath the motorway to the banks of the Clyde where we picnicked in the sunshine, away from the roar of the highway. Lunch done, the riverside walk took us to the curiously Parisian looking Glasgow Green, with its stone archway, tree lined avenues and resplendent winter gardens. The park wasn't crowded, even on a balmy Sunday afternoon, but informal games of cricket and football were being played, toddlers wandered about in that tottering bumpy way peculiar to the under 3's and couples promenaded along the walkways or sat in hunched conversation on the lawns. It was a timeless scene from any city anywhere when the sun comes out and people can grab a few precious moments to relax away from busy streets and hectic lives.

We chanced upon Celtic football supporters returning from their fixture against Aberdeen. As we walked against the tide of green and white every person appeared dour and serious, engaged in earnest conversation with the person next to them. All this we took as a sign that their team hadn't performed well so it came as a surprise to read later that Celtic had in fact just won the Scottish Premier league.

Climbing gently past the massive Tenants brewery complex we entered the necropolis, which looks down on the rest of Glasgow. It's higher than the nearby Cathedral and every bit as imposing and atmospheric as you'd expect a city of the dead to be. The stonework of the monuments and tombs had the rough blackened look of a lot of Glasgow and was arranged in a higgledy piggledy fashion on steep uneven slopes, with little byways and overgrown paths branching off the tarmac walkways. John Knox's monument took pride of place, looking down onto the Cathedral at the highest point and was well worn by sightseers, although it wasn't clear if that was because of the vantage point his commanding position gave for pictures or from people paying homage to the father of the protestant reformation in Scotland.

Back in the city centre we were reunited with our friendly bus driver who again refused to take payment. Apparently, the bus was laid on for visitors to the theme park and the fare was redeemed against the entrance fee and thus it would be unreasonably pricey for us. Even the inspector who was chatting to the driver said he hadn't seen us, ushered us onto the bus and bade us a good day. So we returned to the site in good spirits, refreshed by the good folk of Glasgow and eager to down some cold beers in the fading May sun, which we did with due ceremony with a toast to the Public Transport workers of Glasgow.

* * *

The next morning as the sun broke through we left the site and immediately entered Glasgow's motorway system. On the one hand it is very useful to speed through a city and out the other side without the congestion of somewhere like London. On the flip side the map looks like someone's spilled spaghetti on the page and navigating it resulted in dialogue along the lines of:
'Was that junction 7?'
'I don't know, I think it was 18b'
'But according to the map that's in Leeds...Oh look there's the Cathedral again.'
Once safely in the hands of the satnav we headed out of a city that looks to be building in every available space. All along the route new houses were going up, each one a carbon copy of its neighbour. Painted green they'd make ideal houses for a giant game of Monopoly. We reflected that whatever Glasgow's other charms its people were the stars for us, polite, helpful and giving of themselves in a kindly fashion. If only they'd speak a bit slower I could take an active part in discourse with them, a problem that didn't seem to afflict Alison who is updating the Christmas card list as I write.

We headed north from Glasgow and wound our way through the Trossachs National Park to the Western shores of Loch Lomond. The mountainous fringes of the eastern shore, at first hazy and indistinct slowly revealed their colours of greens, browns and purples as the day wore on. Small islands hugged the shore, with tufts of erect trees sprouting above stony shores. At the southern end the Loch was azure blue, gently rippled by the breeze but further up it took on the colour of rich peat, slightly golden like a well-aged whisky.

So entranced were we that we stopped to paddle on a small, isolated beach. Well Alison did while I fiddled around with the camera. She returned with blue feet, maybe because it was cold or perhaps she'd trodden on a Smurf. Either way, photos taken we scrambled up the bank, crossed the almost deserted highway and cruised ever upwards keeping the loch and its rugged backdrop to our right until, in a moment of spontaneity we decided to spend the night at a site at Ardlui on the northern most point of the loch, where the river Falloch feeds it.

We had a spot overlooking the small marina, sandwiched between peaks on either side, some still with traces of winter snow. We took an evening walk out of the site, but everywhere seemed to lead to narrow stretches of road strewn with crumpled Tenants cans and other detritus, presumably from passing motorists, so we contented ourselves with watching the setting sun cast playful shadows over the peaks and troughs of the steep loch banks. We saw sparrows giving themselves dust baths and then hopping over the grass as if it was red hot, swallows swooping down over the waters to hoover up insects and a duck proudly fussing over her ducklings and rounding them up when they drifted off too far. We heard a cuckoo's lonesome call, somewhere upstream a goose honked in that slightly cartoonish way they have, and a lone robin trilled an evening song. Our neighbour joined in with bursts of van rattling snoring, deep resonant snorts and wheezes that cleared the trees of birds so we retired inside to Mavis where his nocturnal symphony was suitably muffled.

The following morning we treated ourselves to breakfast at the hotel adjacent to the site, and very good it was too, setting us up for the day, not just because our stomachs were now lined with a full fried breakfast but because they only charged us for two *'wee kiddies' meals'* as we didn't have any cereal or juice. Only because we didn't realise that we could have helped ourselves to them but it felt disingenuous to mention that to our kindly waiter.

* * *

We retraced our steps southwards and away from the loch onto the A83. This must be one of the prettiest driving roads in the UK, if not the world. From the top of Loch Long every twist and turn revealed another view more breath-taking than the last. Craggy peaks burst from forests of deep green pines with strands of bright new growth unevenly woven in. We traced a stream of iron coloured water tumbling over sun bleached rocks and stopped to breathe in the silence under the towering edifice of Beinn Ime. It's odd how the absence of any sound can become an almost physical presence, like a weight placed around you that muffles the outside world and heightens the splendour of the landscape, or as Alison described it, *'like being enveloped in a cocoon of silence.'* Further on we dropped down to the salt-water Loch Fyne which we crossed at its northern most point and drove down the western shoreline. The poet in Alison surfaced again as she described exactly where the driver who overtook us on a bend could stick his car.

Thankfully the calming influence of the scenery worked wonders and we drove on sandwiched between bluebell woods and sun kissed loch. We paused at Inveraray, a small settlement with a picture postcard high street of white painted shops, a neat little harbour and the former town jail now doing brisk business as a tourist destination. The Castle had the appearance of a child's drawing; squat with a fairy-tale turret at each corner. The village green overlooking the loch was scattered with tourists and locals basking in the sun. It was serene and lazy under the midday sun, no one seemed to hurry, least of all us, but reluctantly we moved on. Out of town and through vibrant green trees to areas where great swathes had been felled, leaving hillsides strewn with the debris of hurried logging reminding us that for all its attractiveness this is a working landscape.

At the splendidly named Lochgilphead we entered broad flat farming land with fields of cattle and sheep grazing on the inhospitable slopes with their playful lambs. We stopped outside the village of Kilmartin. You probably haven't heard of it, we hadn't until we chanced upon it in a guide book, but it is one of the most important pre-historic and early history sites in the world. Around Kilmartin Glen, in a radius of about six miles there are at least 800 recorded ancient monuments; standing stones, burial cairns, rock art, forts, carved stones and duns (old forts). As well as this richness it's also home to Dunadd on the river Add. This was reportedly a royal centre where Scotland's earliest kings were inaugurated.

A pleasant way-marked stroll led from our stopping point by the river to Kilmartin village via some of the pre-historic sites. We stood among standing stones, some with ancient carvings or cup and ring marks as they are known; neat circles carved into the stone for unknown but probably ceremonial purposes. The stones stand in a quiet glen with nothing but sheep and the occasional curious tourist like us for company. Especially bewitching was a single stone, alone in its own daisy carpeted field. A reminder that whole civilisations have risen and fallen, countless wars been fought, species have become extinct, men have walked on the moon and these stones have stood in the same spot, silently oblivious to the passage of time.

Nearby were stone circles, some of which mark graves. These areas have been re-purposed over time, so that what may once have been a grave site became a ceremonial site, a meeting place for tribes or a place for trade, with evidence of iron from Ireland and deep black jet jewellery from Yorkshire among the finds. There were three main burial cairns left (a fourth was destroyed in the 1800's) that were aligned with the stones. A separate smaller and well-preserved cairn sat near the standing stones with a grave, apparently of a child, on its outer ring. A lot of the rocks placed over the cairns were used by locals for building and even in Victorian times when their importance was widely appreciated and serious research was being conducted, quarrymen still carted off barrow-loads of stones. Now they are preserved and cared for. You can go inside one of the cairns and see the grave within including its cup and ring marked stone lid. After nearly falling backwards into the grave Alison then wondered if the markings were actually made by someone who was clawing to get out. On that cheerful note I led her out for some fresh air and a cup of tea in the village.

Kilmartin Church sits overlooking the Glen, with an unusual stepped graveyard encircling the hill it sits on. The graveyard holds a collection of intricately carved medieval stone grave markers which, like the rest of the attractions we visited, had bold, informative information boards, were well tended and completely unguarded. To top it all there was no admission charge. The Scots do seem to appreciate that they are custodians of this history rather than owners and they take that role seriously, but without assuming any self-importance or propriety over it. If someone like English Heritage got their hands on Kilmartin Glen they'd charge you admission, erect a hideous multimedia centre selling overpriced crap and have expensive cafes and huge car parks. You'd be prevented from actually wandering up to and around the attractions and would have to content yourself with a peek from 500 yards away and an interactive experience where you could see a plastic copy up close. The National Trust, to choose one example, charge you to visit the forts at Hadrian's Wall – but if you just want to walk the wall its free, as long as you promise not to look at any archaeological remains along the way. There is a sign halfway to one fort instructing you to close your eyes unless you've paid. I may have made that last bit up about the sign but I wouldn't put it past them.

At the small Kilmartin museum there was a shop selling local art, books and postcards, a cafe run by a local young entrepreneur and toilets you could use whether you were a customer or not. As you can probably tell we were quite taken with the place and we reluctantly wandered back to Mavis, who we'd left shaded by trees and parked for free in a car park with an area set aside for motorhomes.

Now rather weary after our journey and wanderings we headed further north to the town of Oban where we pulled up at a site just south of the town. The views from our pitch were splendid; we looked over the Sound of Kerrera to the island of the same name, with the peaks of the Isle of Mull rising behind. As it was still light at 9:30pm in early May we took a walk out of the site through bluebell carpeted woods to the shoreline. As the sun set over Kerrera and with the gentle breeze wafting the scent of wild flowers and pine out to the ocean beyond we shared one of those perfect moments of utter stillness and calm, a magical end to a special day.

Next morning we walked to Oban from the site, a distance just shy of 3 miles but we took the windy scenic route up and along the hills. Once we'd negotiated the boggy bits and steep ascent we were rewarded with stunning views to Mull and over the quiet tranquil waters around Oban harbour. We passed a bleached sheep skull, and found quite a few other bits of it as well scattered over a few feet. We concluded that it had either been prey to something or its parachute hadn't opened. On our decent into town we met some serious looking walkers, kitted out in khaki shorts, waistcoats with multiple pockets, hi-tech walking hats and every other accoutrement the eager shop keeper could sell them. In-spite of their gear they were navigating from a map that was essentially an oval marked out in red dotted lines on a piece of white paper that had Oban written on it. There was no indication of heights, distance or landmarks. Nevertheless they were jolly and intrepid and after seeking directions from us set off in completely the wrong direction with a jaunty determination in their stride.

Oban isn't the most picturesque town, clustered around its busy port that ferries people and goods to the nearby islands but in the sunshine the waters sparkled and people went about their business with a lethargic gait that a blazing sun encourages. We had our obligatory post walk cuppa in a bakery shop where we watched a woman using tongs to painstakingly move individual cakes in the display cabinet as she took great care to ensure that no flesh came into contact with the tiniest morsel. She then took a step back, eyed them with a critical look and brusquely rearranged them all by hand.

Our neighbours on the site were a couple in their mid-60s who had been civil but dour and monosyllabic for the two days of our stay, but as we packed up ready to hit the road they morphed into Willie and Margaret from Perthshire, the world's most talkative couple. Married for over 40 years they seemed content and relaxed in each other's company, comfortable in the silent routine that couples develop over time. Willie was originally from Glasgow, a Rangers fan, and for *'a wee while'* he played professional football, turning out for Sunderland until life took him in other directions. Nowadays he's a doorman at a famous Scottish Hotel, where he's met many a celeb, but is most proud of his picture with Sir Alex Ferguson. Margaret worked in retail but is now a self-employed gardener and has worked on some big estates. She took great and well-deserved pride in showing us around their caravan. Enjoyable though our time with them was we needed to get going. I excused myself and got busy doing little jobs by way of a hint, including running the engine in Mavis for a while. Eventually I dropped a sack over Alison's head and bundled her into the back of the van before speeding off. You can tell that last sentence was a lie because I'm still alive to write it.

CHAPTER 8

Prangs and Puffins

Once under way we joined the A82 again for the trip up to Glencoe. People have told us this is a spectacular place, so we were immensely excited. Sadly, not far into our journey some dolt in an American style motorhome took a corner too fast, and just as we were both saying how he was on the wrong side of the road and travelling too fast a loud crack startled us and our driver side wing mirror scattered over the tarmac. Being on an already narrow road and with traffic piling up behind we did the only thing possible and carried on until we could safely pull over a mile or so further on. I carried out some running repairs, salvaging the wiring and generally trying to look butch and like I knew what I was doing. Once over the shock and with dangling wires secured Alison bravely took the wheel again and we ploughed on to Glencoe.

Shock slowly turned to annoyance at having to sort it out, as well as the inevitable cost and the fact we'd no idea about the other party. We hoped that they'd learned a lesson, and if not that they met every single midge Scotland had to offer. After a stop for a cup of tea (we are English after all) the scenery started to calm us as we drove across the broad and foreboding Rannock Moor, between mountains glowing green and gold in the sun or menacing and rugged in the shade. Our base for a couple of nights was the Glencoe Mountain Resort. It is a centre for skiing in the winter with a chairlift leading up to The Basin, a plateau half way up the mountain from where ski pulls and another lift take customers up to a variety of runs. It also has a couple of mountain bike tracks and does a healthy summer business taking hikers, mountain bikers and those just curious to see the views from 2,300ft up.

Once pitched up we made some calls and were directed by a garage in Fort William to one in nearby Ballachulish, as they were concerned they were a bit too far away and a local garage would be easier for us. Cheered by their decency we duly presented Mavis for inspection and let the record now show that Lochside Garage in

Ballachulish is a rare gem. After gently showing us the cost of a replacement wing mirror on his notepad with the kindly manner of a doctor imparting grave news, the proprietor bade us return the next day when he would fit it and we could resume our travels.

Buoyed by his helpfulness we stopped off at the Glencoe visitor centre, which was making every effort to close early, so we didn't linger but instead stopped further on and explored a bit of the Glencoe scenery up close. Fed by waterfalls and streams that bring snow melt and rain from the mountains down narrow tree lined gullies, the waterways cut through the rocks, slicing through the high valleys until they reached more level ground where they became shallow, scree lined streams that meander through the lush valley floor, seemingly in no hurry to meet the River. It was all most refreshing and we returned to a battered Mavis in a better frame of mind, although we still really hoped the midges were biting at wherever the other motorhomers were headed. With that thought we retired for the night.

* * *

On a crisp, bright morning we took the ski lift to The Basin. This forms the main ski area in season and although patchy snow was left in the crags and higher slopes all the other ski lifts, pulleys and other paraphernalia were closed and the area looked rather shabby and neglected cleared of its icing of snow. Clouds were obscuring the higher peaks and at this altitude the wind whipped around and into every loose seam and flapping cuff. We'd left the valley floor in tee shirts but now waddled about like polar explorers in as many layers of clothing as we could carry up. Our reward was magnificent views across the bleak looking Rannoch Moor with its twinkling lochs and the A82 slicing through in a straight line. We rambled about taking in the views with the sharp bright smell of snow in the air. Eventually we descended to the footpath and made our way down the steep path made of loose scree and rocks that moved alarmingly when you put your weight on them. It was worth walking down though as we tracked alongside the stream tumbling over numerous waterfalls on one side and the mountain bike route on the other. Occasionally we were rewarded with the sight of heavily armoured bikers humming past and taking off over frightening jumps in their pursuit of the ultimate adrenaline rush. As fellow thrill seekers we went for the high-octane option of lunch in the cafe before heading back to Ballachulish to get the wing mirror fitted.

With a bit of time to kill while the garage worked on Mavis we wandered into the visitor centre and cafe. We had seen signs for a Folk Museum at nearby Glencoe village but I vetoed this on account of my father having dragged me around many such attractions in my childhood. I found no fun in displays of old farming implements, corn dollies and sinister looking mannequins. I doubt my father actually liked folk museums either, but they gave shelter from the rain and were usually free. He was firmly of the opinion that if you had to pay it wouldn't be worth the price of admission. He was born to accountancy in the same way fish are born to swim. Thus Canham family holidays were characterised by long walks, sandy picnics and on rare occasions when money reluctantly changed hands, a round on the crazy golf course. As we'd inevitably be holidaying out of season in gale force winds we risked decapitation by the whirling blades of the windmill and at holes facing the wind your ball would be blown back to you as soon as it came to rest. I suspect this was a ploy by my dad to maximise value for money.

On one memorable occasion he received a small parking fine for marginally overstaying our allotted time. So incensed was he that the rest of the holiday was spent trekking from free parking spots out of town, carting a day's supply of food, bucket and spade, wind break and waterproof clothing from villages a few miles inland. We'd then have to divert by a car park so he could tally up the amount saved in his notebook. Consequently, we spent a fortnight hiking through Norfolk until, on the last day, he could triumphantly declare that we'd recouped the amount of the fine and could return home with our heads held high. When I returned to school they sent a note home worried that I had lost so much weight and my mother had to explain that I'd been on a walking holiday.

Back at Ballachulish the garage did Mavis proud. They charged a bare minimum for labour and then gave us loads of helpful advice on where to go and what to do in Scotland, which we would have done sooner if they hadn't spent so much time telling us about the array of attractions their country had to offer. Still, they were great ambassadors for Scotland and we eventually managed to bid them a cheery farewell in our pristine new wing mirror as we pulled away.

On the journey back, Alison reflected on the accident and that apart from the shock and the expense, she felt bitter that it had stolen some of the joy of driving from her. It was a knock to her confidence and she was wary of vehicles on the busy road with lots of other motorhomes and lorries. She then shrugged, indicated right and swung Mavis into a parking space that the average Smart Car driver would baulk at, and brought us to a stop overlooking the Three Sisters range at Glencoe Gorge. We set off to walk up a very steep path. Upon reflection, to use the word 'steep' is to miss an opportunity to use the words 'near vertical'. The route took us up towards the snow topped Bidean nam Bain Mountain following a rocky path that zigzagged up to the left of a deep gorge that carried fresh snow-melt waters to the river below.

Heading up we paused and spied 3 young male deer silently grazing below us. They were clearly aware of our presence but carried on eating with occasional glances in our direction. It was a privilege to share their territory and we climbed on with renewed vigour after our encounter. The path led on to an impressive waterfall and small hidden pools in a tiny high valley, but our shadows were swiftly lengthening and the sun was soon to fade from view as the path's steep walls cloaked it. Choosing a lone rock as our target we clambered up, exhausted but very happy. Here we looked up towards a majestic snow-capped peak with its waterfall tumbling into a lean and noisy young stream and we traced its path down through its broader more sedate middle section to where it joined the main river in a stately meandering fashion. Presently we started the climb down.

You may think it curious of someone who loves mountain walks and was recently on a ski lift, but I have a lifelong aversion to heights. It is a physical reaction and usually easily managed. Mostly I ignore it, occasionally I have to give myself a stern talking to and very occasionally I have to wrestle it into submission. Today was a wrestling day. Coming down over the same cliff hugging path, I carefully felt for each step and held on to anything more solid than air. Edging my way along the scree I got about halfway when my foot slipped, only slightly but enough to cause me to freeze. I felt a chill and the beginnings of involuntary spasms in my calf muscles, a characteristic of my dread of heights. I froze for what seemed like minutes but was only a few seconds, until Alison's calming words got through and expelled the intrusive fears. With a hearty cry of *'sod it, I'm insured'* I lurched forward for the next solid rock and continued crab-like to more solid ground, where Alison gave me a hug and reminded me that I'm not insured any more so would I please try and be careful, at least until I am. The rest of the descent was characterised by us plodding carefully down uneven stones to level ground where secretly we knew our descent was akin to two graceful mountain goats skipping gaily from rock to rock with careless abandon, even if it looked ponderous and ungainly to the untutored eye.

* * *

We woke to find that the exertions had taken their toll on us. Physically we had stiff legs and aching joints. Emotionally we were tired and tetchy. Driving through to the village of Glencoe we tried a car park but although there was a suitable space it was covered in broken glass and we disagreed upon its suitability. Irritably I pulled out and intended to go up the road to find an alternative. However we found ourselves on the B863, which essentially runs in an oval around Loch Levin. Well, this little road was simply wondrous and as we undulated around the slopes, through strands of pine and along the loch side our troubles receded. The sun sparkled on quartz exposed by many turbulent streams. We stopped and climbed beside a waterfall of crystal clear waters and pure white stone to look back over the deep blue of the narrow loch. On this fine spring day the views appeared almost Alpine. We lunched beside the river at Kinlochleven, on the eastern tip of the loch. It's a becoming little town, isolated by at least 6 miles from Glencoe and further via the northern shore but it boasted an Ice Climbing centre, some shops and a modern but frayed building hosting The Aluminium Story, which we avoided. The fact it was closed was only one of the many reasons we could think of to bypass it. Presumably the settlement prospered around this industry and its closure must have taken its toll on such an isolated community, so it was refreshing to see it, if not thriving then at least heading in the right direction.

In better spirits we now headed to Fort William, where every property alongside Inverscaddle Bay seemed to offer bed and breakfast. As the town serves as the finish, or start, of the West Highland Way presumably they do good business with walkers, and every so often heavily laden sweaty people would trudge by in a determined fashion. The town was pleasant enough but it was the first time we'd really been faced with so many shops selling tacky Scottish merchandise. There were only so many tartan hats, tea towels, Nessies and models of Scottie dogs that we could take but its saving grace came in the unlikely form of a supermarket selling vegetarian haggis, so we forgave it everything, bade farewell and swung Mavis into Glen Nevis where we pitched up in the shadow of the mighty Ben Nevis. We sat outside under blossoming trees as the sun set, lost in our own private worlds just listening to the river gurgling over stones and the birds singing while we worked out how to cook the haggis without use of an oven.

* * *

Glen Nevis forms a long L shaped valley that cuts through mountains that include Ben Nevis and the tongue twisting Aonach Beag and Sgurr a'Mhaim. All are over 3500 ft. high, with Ben Nevis the mightiest of them all at 4406 ft. We set out to explore the valley in the shadow of these mighty peaks starting out along a logging road in the Nevis Forest, striding through crowded pines where sunlight peeked through the foliage. In the shade of the dense woods the air remained distinctly chilly but where logging had cleared the forest we walked in brilliant sunlight that washed the detail out of the mountains. In these cleared areas gorse had taken hold, glowing bright yellow and fragrant in the still air. Gorse, and in particular its sweet woody smell always reminds me of family holidays taken on the east coast; my mother and father wandering on ahead with the dog in tow and me moping along behind. I was usually lost in my own little world, one that didn't include endless drizzle, dank holiday chalets and parents who thought linen sheets were an extravagance. From some unknown source my father requisitioned paper sheets for our holidays. These were advertised on the packet as strong enough to last for a fortnight's holiday and ceremoniously distributed to me on the first night, when I was reminded that we only had one set each. By day two they were inevitably ripped. After the third night it was like sleeping in ribbons of fibreglass. By the fourth night I'd dispensed with them altogether and slept under a coarse army-surplus blanket that was only marginally more comfortable than sleeping in a gorse bush and most certainly less fragrant. But I digress.

We followed the road down to the glen floor at Achriabhach and had a picnic at Lower Falls, an enchanting waterfall in the Nevis River that splits around orange rocks into two gushing noisy courses, where they are joined by gentler falls in a steep sided gorge with deep, crystal clear waters and exposed smooth red rocks. While eating we were entranced by a small bird that took to landing on rocks in the stream, diving in and swimming around before fluttering out, having a good shake and then finding a new spot to dive again. In the clear waters we could watch it swim smoothly under the water, every bit as graceful as it was in the air. I christened it the Lesser Spotted Marsh Tit Nibbler. Fortunately, Alison can be relied upon to fall into conversation with anything more sentient than a tree and on this occasion it was a sprightly old lady, who informed us the bird was a Dipper, because it dips into the water, which just goes to show that Ornithologists have no imagination.

We struck out on the path to the south of the river, following its course through boggy fields and tree lined river banks until we emerged at Paddy's Bridge. Here the main path crossed the river and joined the small road up to the glen's head. We however continued along the track we'd been walking on and picked our way across a soft watery plain that slowly grew narrower until imposing rocks closed in around us. Here the path diverged again, and we chose the right fork alongside an old rusting fence that quickly rose up to the point where we were picking our way hand over hand up tree roots, around gullies of weather exposed quartz and rocks standing proud of soft downy grass recovering from its winter under the snow. Higher up, the shadows danced in the light breeze, moss flowed over the rocks and we came upon old trees, wizened, twisted and hung with lichen; stark and sinister among the sparse green pines. We chanced upon a plateau overlooking the Glen where we had only birds for company. We sat in stillness, breathing in the sense of peace in our own secret place among the mountains.

Revived we resolved to head back down and, as is the way of these things, we found ourselves back on the valley floor far quicker than expected and retraced our steps beside the river, at times deep and rapid between narrow rock walls and at others flowing broad and slow over pebbles. We crossed Paddy's Bridge and walked along the road to Lower Fall. Occasionally we spied the bright colours of climbers high up on the cliffs, tiny figures clinging to the rocks, highlighting the immense scale of the mountains and, for all our achievements, just how tiny we are in this landscape.

A delighted squeal from Alison announced the sudden presence of Highland Cattle. There were several long horned and shaggy ginger beasts and a couple of pure black ones in a field and, slightly more worryingly, one on our side of the fence. We dallied a while with a couple from Arizona who like us recognised a bovine photo opportunity when they saw it. Alison chatted amiably to the cows and the Americans for a while. I took pictures and when we were both satisfied we walked back along the river, by now genteel and stately as it drifted through the glen. On we wandered through lush fields where sheep scattered as we passed and eventually found ourselves at the site restaurant where we refreshed ourselves with beer, food and whisky.

Sadly though, we didn't see any more Lesser Spotted Marsh Tit Nibblers.

* * *

Surprisingly refreshed after our exertions we pointed Mavis west and followed a gently undulating road sandwiched between coast and lochs on our left and dark angular hills to our right. The road followed and criss-crossed the Jacobite railway line between Fort William and Mallaig, one of the great railway journeys in the UK, not just because of the amazing scenery but also because it is pulled by a steam engine. What the passengers don't see though are the impressive viaducts that form graceful curves spanning rivers and watery land. It was built for the Mackerel trade when Mallaig was the most important port in the UK for the slippery little fish and was recently voted the world's most scenic railway. It also featured in the Harry Potter films.

Anyway, our destination today was Portnadoran - a hamlet on the scenic coast road a few miles short of Mallaig. We wandered into nearby Arisaig which is settled around a small harbour nestled in a bay strewn with stubby rock islands and fine white sand. It has connections to the 18th century Gaelic poet, Jacobite and lexicographer Alasdair MacDonald and more recently it was one of the bases for the Second World War Special Operations Executive (SOE). It was here at Arisaig that SOE operatives were taught to kill in interesting and stealthy ways. I was particularly gratified to discover one of the prime movers behind the merging of three existing secret departments into the SOE was the splendidly monikered Lord Hankey.

The little information centre that imparted all this and much more was engaging and well thought out, with clear easy to read displays and even a book swap where you could exchange holiday reading. It really is cheering to visit these community run centres. They are invariably free to mooch around in and staffed by cheery and knowledgeable souls. The good folk of Arisaig even clubbed together to save the local public toilets. I love that rather than write badly composed letters to the local newspaper or stern missives to an MP to be filed under 'ignore', the people around these parts actually do something to address whatever irks them.

    We rolled up in Malliag in plenty of time for our ferry to Skye so we took the opportunity to amble around for a while. It's built around a pleasing horseshoe bay with a pier for the ferries, and has the bustle of small harbours everywhere. Workshops buzzed and clanked, small delivery vans parked at acute angles wherever space allowed and determined looking people in heavy oilskins went to and fro on whatever nautical themed errand demanded their attention. Gulls watched intently for any spilt morsels and above everything was the scent of diesel and fish. The rain, which had been threatening all morning, began to come down, sending the visitors scurrying into the plentiful tea shops while the hardy townsfolk carried on their business as usual. We took shelter aboard Mavis and were soon aboard the ferry for the short hop to Skye.

* * *

    We disembarked up the echoing ramp and onto Skye in a convoy of cars, vans and plenty of other motorhomes. We swept around the coast accompanied by the scent of wild garlic, whose little white flowers spread like a blanket over the ground among the trees, and then up across open moorland with mountains looming out of the clouds. The rain brought out a new depth to the landscape and where the sun had previously bleached the detail we now got deep russets and auburn heathers, hills of greens and gold and deep orange, and red cliffs of exposed rock. We went through one gorge of deep sandy red rock on a clear road and half expected Road Runner to whiz past with a cheery *'beep beep'* and wait for Wile E. Coyote to swing by and splat onto the rocks opposite in another ill-judged attempt to snag him. Alison christened it The Acme Pass.

    The road wound on through moors that gave way to passes cut between cone shaped mountains with scree covered peaks. They looked like someone had poured gravel over the top and let it trickle down in rivulets, merging with the hardy dark heathers and grass lower down in long ragged fingers. We cruised on, through the busy capital Portree and out onto the west coast alongside the delightfully named Snizort Bay. The coastline was still rugged, but less wild; lush green fields dotted with sheep, and hamlets with small, neat little houses and refurbished crofts scattered on hillsides. Nearly every property we passed on the west coast looked new with bright white paint, shiny roofs and tidy gardens. Maybe it has seen an explosion of building lately or possibly everyone around here is fastidious in their property maintenance. Or perhaps they just get constantly washed by the rain which was unrelenting on our drive to our stopping point for a couple of nights, the port town of Uig. It sits along a large bay around which the road gently curves down to the harbour. Apart from a hotel and shop the harbour area is the centre of Uig as far as attractions go, with a restaurant, pottery shop, guest houses and, we were very pleased to find, the Skye Brewery.

One of the hazards of life spent roaming from site to site is the risk of piped music in the shower blocks. When we first encountered this it wasn't too intrusive but in Uig it was just horrendous. Goodness knows what station it was tuned to; I didn't wait long enough to find out. My first Skye ablution was to the accompaniment of someone warbling on about how she *'wants a sexy guy...'* I suppose this is reasonable enough when you consider the alternative; no one seems to sing *'I want a sexy guy but I'd settle for a balding fatty with BO who lives with his mum...'*

It reminded me of signs we've seen on our travels for butchers shops advertising *'Quality Meat'* or sandwich shops declaring their wares as *'Fresh'*. Call me Mr. Picky but the least I'd expect if I was eating meat was quality. And frankly if the best you can do is advertise your sandwiches as fresh then I feel that you are concentrating on a point I'd hitherto taken for granted. When purchasing a bread based lunch I look for tasty fillings, a bit of originality or at least value for money. I don't consider that *'fresh'* constitutes a selling point any more than, say, *'Contains Bread'* or *'Now without shards of glass'*. In one small town we encountered a B&B advertising *'Colour TV'*. How desperate do you need to be, how limited are your other attractions, when colour TV is a selling point? Maybe the competitors all have monochrome televisions, or more likely, better accommodation to offer the weary traveller. Once home from our ablutions and gaily singing *'I want a sexy man'* much to Alison's bemusement we spent the morning doing household chores of cleaning and washing with ridiculous pop songs stuck in our heads before our maritime adventure of seal and puffin spotting aboard the SkyeXplorer.

SkyeXplorer is a Mitchell 31 Mk 3 boat. I mention this only because you might be a balding fatty with BO who lives with his mum and will therefore appreciate this information in lieu of not having popular songs written about you. We turned up with our fellow passengers all clad, like us, in several layers of protection against the wind and spray, and stood around making polite small talk waiting for our boat. Standing on the pier a seagull did what they seem to do best and got me from above. An impressive shot but not one I appreciated. I cleaned up with a tissue, a fact I was reminded of later when I inadvertently blew my nose on it!

Eventually we were greeted by a jovial chap called Andi who turned out to be our Captain, or Skipper or whatever. Sadly he didn't have a beard you could hide a penguin in or a wooden leg but in all other respects he seemed well versed in the ways of the ocean and took us on an extended tour over choppy seas to the Ascrib

Islands. We saw, and here we are relying on his knowledge since we've already established my ornithological credentials are severely limited, Razor Bills, Shags, Puffins, an Oyster Catcher and a rare Northern Diver. Plus, Common and Grey Seals which apparently aren't birds at all but furry bags of lard that eat fish. It was all very interesting.

The Islands sit low in the water with the odd steep cliff of layered rock standing proud of the sea and scrub. One particular grassy cliff is home to a nesting Puffin colony. They return here in April every year from about the age of 5 when they are ready to breed, and adopt the same spot each year. Andi informed us the oldest recorded Puffin is over 40 years old. They can only tell their age from when the individuals are trapped and ringed so no one knows how old it was when the ring was applied. Puffins are smaller than we expected and on water look like they should tip forward with their oversized beaks. On land they are as ungainly as any bird and in flight they look like black and white flying bricks with wings beating faster than the eye can see. Only underwater do they truly look sleek and elegant. But most charmingly of all we learnt from Andi that the German for Puffin is Papageientaucher.

The journey back was particularly rough and of the 10 passengers only 4 of us braved the outside of the boat. Well, it was most exhilarating. Alison especially sat there wearing sea spray and a huge grin. In other circumstances we've both been prone to sea sickness but today we had too much fun to notice.

After drying out over a late lunch we took a hike up to the Fairy Glen, an enchanting place a short hike out of Uig. It's a tranquil spot of unusual cone shaped hills, valleys, pools and rock formations, which have been featured in the fantasy film Stardust. It reminded us of something from The Hobbit. Under the sinking May sun it was magical, with long shadows of irregular rocks cast over the vibrant green hills and valleys. Alison climbed to the highest point, but I stopped a little way short on wobbling legs, and from our vantage points we looked out over an alien landscape, a hidden glen in an already remote spot.

The wide Glen Uig in which it sits was a glacier that ran to Uig Bay. The basalt stacks, including the highest point of Castle Ewen that Alison climbed, were created by volcanic activity and exposed by weathering. The odd steps on the cones and hills are the result of the harsh weather in the exposed windy Glen. Even though it was created by geology rather than fairies it was a lovely spot and the views of the sunset over the bay on the journey back were spectacular. Lower down we walked through woodland with a path and facilities thoughtfully provided as a civic amenity by the Uig community and although the pathway was well maintained the woods were left wild as a natural habitat, perfect for an evening stroll.

* * *

We drove out of Skye on a road laid like a ribbon draped across the landscape. It was raining relentlessly which gave a glossy coating to the moors. Sheep grazed seemingly unaffected while their lambs looked cold and huddled for warmth in the ley of rocks or stood forlornly on the sheltered side of their mother. Ghosts of mountains floated on the horizon behind a veil of soft mist, revealing themselves only as we drove close. Echoes of the past litter Skye; standing stones and rings where crude shelters once stood, so numerous many aren't even mentioned on the map, ruins of crofts, low walls covered in grass that are now used by animals seeking refuge from the elements. Here and there skeletons of old machines are left where they died, boats rotting on the foreshore and in a field the shell of a caravan surrounded by bored looking cows. The islanders' life has always been harsh and unforgiving; even now with good heating, good roads and all the trappings of modern life winters are long, dark and bleak.

We were sad to leave Skye, its charms were plentiful and with a smaller vehicle or more time to walk we'd love to have explored all of its nooks and crannies. But for now we were heading inland to Inverness via a deep glen alongside The Five Sisters mountain range. On the lower slopes intensely managed pine forests pressed up against taut wire fences, as if they were being prevented from escaping. Where the woodland stopped, blankets of last year's ginger and rust ferns lay wilted and broken as new shoots reached up, unfurling slowly, one frond at a time, in no great rush now, but soon the whole area would be a lush green carpet waving gently in the mountain air. Higher up, the snow-capped peaks brooded in halos of dark cloud.

Eventually we descended to the shores of Loch Ness. Here the rain had left, and little puffs of steam rose from the pines as warmer air moved in. Loch Ness, a mighty body of water, is only the second largest Scottish loch by surface area, at 22 square miles, but due to its depth it is the largest by volume in the British Isles. Its deepest point is 755 ft. It contains more fresh water than all the lakes in England and Wales combined. It is part of the Great Glen Fault, which runs from Inverness in the north past Fort William in the south and out via the island of Mull and into Ireland. Incidentally that information was from Wikipedia so don't rely on it in a court of law. It may just be an enormous puddle formed by the tears of dying stoats for all I know.

The next day we woke in Inverness, which was handy as that was where we'd parked the previous evening, and met up with old friends of Alison's. In fact it was her old primary school teacher and her husband, parents of a childhood friend from the village where she grew up. Both Scots, they returned to the land of their birth a few years ago and have made Inverness their home. We enjoyed a delightful lunch with them, reminiscing and learning about the local area. They were charming and hospitable company and generous with their time, the very essence in fact of the Scottish people we'd met on our brief sojourn north of the border. They were kind enough to drop us at the visitor centre on the site of the Culloden battlefield. Alison particularly wanted to visit as she's a fan of the Outlander series of books which are set around the time of the Jacobite rebellion. I must confess I wasn't familiar with the details of the battle or events around it, but the visitor centre did an excellent job of telling the tale. As you pass through one side tells the story from the Jacobite perspective while the other tells it from the Hanover's position. It was a fascinating recounting of the story, brought to life by artefacts and a short immersive film that places you in the midst of the battle.

It was at Culloden that the final Jacobite rebellion, hitherto undefeated and having got as far south as Derby, was crushed. Led by 'Bonnie' Prince Charlie Stewart and backed by those pesky French, the Jacobites believed the Bonnie Prince was the rightful heir to the throne, whereas George II had his royal posterior planted firmly on it as the second Hanoverian King. Of course there was a lot more to the build-up than that but on 16 April 1746 the Jacobite cause was all but wiped out by a well prepared and disciplined royalist force under the command of The Duke of Cumberland, whose troops had enjoyed a measure of spirits and some extra cheese in honour of his birthday the evening before the decisive battle. Here was a man who clearly knew how to party. Sadly for Bonnie Prince Charlie the Duke also knew how to fight and the next day with a refreshed and disciplined army smelling faintly of cheese he won a decisive victory for the Hanoverian cause.

It was the aftermath of the battle however that really lives in the memory, especially in the Highlands and Islands. In an effort to wipe out the Jacobite cause once and for all the Duke's men took a bloody revenge on anyone associated with it, women and children included. The effect of this was to punish not only the rebels but also those clans that had been loyal to King George and fought with his army. Many of the lowland clans had prospered under the 1707 Act of Union which brought a common sovereign, currency, parliament and tax system to Scotland and England. The Highlands however suffered under the Union and it was from here that the Jacobite cause had established itself. Today it is still a Gaelic speaking area, road signs are bi-lingual and fading YES stickers from the independence referendum are liberally dotted about. This disparity and the barbarity of the Duke's reprisals sowed the seeds of simmering tension and religious division that still linger today. I suppose most of all I learnt that no one really wins wars. A declaration of war is of itself an act of defeat. By the time the first shot is fired the damage is already done. Irrespective of which side claims victory, when the bodies start to stink no one cares what religion they were or what flag they fought under.

Leaving Culloden in a sombre frame of mind we caught a bus back to Inverness and wandered out along the banks of the fast-flowing river Ness, past the squat cathedral, its soft rose-coloured stone bathed in watery sunlight and into the riverside park and the Ness Islands. These form a picturesque quarter of immense charm. Iron footbridges and tree-lined paths give the area a Victorian feel; we felt we should be promenading arm in arm as we found the canal which led us gracefully back to Mavis. We agreed that we liked Inverness. It seems a city of compact charms with a stately presence reminiscent of a bygone era, like a favourite jumper, warm and comfortable.

Scotland's charms are plentiful. The landscape is amazing, from the green uncluttered lowlands to the rugged exposed highlands, from the city wilderness of Strathclyde Park in Glasgow to the stately parks of Inverness, sparkling lochs, snow crowned mountains and remote hidden glens, we found a surprise around every corner. But most of all it was the Scottish people who won our hearts. They were unfailingly helpful, generous, full of good humour and rightly proud of their country and eager for us to enjoy it. They may not be gregarious and outgoing by nature, but they have an easy-going charm and are quick to smile. We were sad to leave but our journey held one last treat as it took us through the wonderful Cairngorm and Grampian mountains as we bade farewell to Scotland and set Mavis due south.

CHAPTER 9

South Again

We stopped over in Oswaldkirk in Yorkshire on the long haul south from Scotland. (Incidentally can anywhere sound more Yorkshire than Oswaldkirk?) We were overnighting on the edge of the Yorkshire Moors, but first we had to tackle the notorious Sutton Bank, a switch-back climb with a 25% gradient. Mavis made it comfortably, if slowly, under Alison's watchful eye but in the last year 74 HGVs were stranded on it according to the warning signs on the approach and caravans are banned outright. I have fond memories of a family holiday on the Yorkshire Moors, and recall my father's worried grimace as he willed his Mazda up Sutton Bank, leaning forward and gripping the wheel with white knuckles as we chugged up, leading a snaking queue of bewildered and increasingly angry motorists at approximately 3 miles an hour. At the summit he pulled over looking decidedly pleased with himself as a queue of cars whizzed past with puzzled drivers looking for the tractor they assumed had held them up. It wasn't that he lacked confidence as a motorist, he just did things at his own safe, steady and precise pace. If that meant selecting a low gear to crest a speed bump, so be it. It was on this vacation that he took us to wander around the stately remains of Rievaulx Abbey where I resorted to my default game of playing wars by myself. Pretending that there were enemy troops around every corner I moved with stealth so that I wasn't detected by an imaginary foe. I was of course spotted by every visitor. I recall a particularly elegant and over perfumed lady of a certain age who recoiled with a shriek when startled by my red face suddenly popping up over a wall for a split second before withdrawing as quickly as it had appeared. I'm sure in a real war snipers would have spared me out of pity. Oh, and we saw a sheep struck by lightning yards from my bedroom window. It was a most entertaining holiday, although not for the sheep of course.

Oswaldkirk offered few diversions and we were weary from the journey, so we contented ourselves with a pub dinner and early night. In the morning we passed the ruins of Byland Abbey, looking splendid with a pale carpet of mist as the morning sun gently warmed the air. I resisted the urge to perform a spectacular roll from Mavis and run amok among the ruins shooting an invisible foe, but it was a close call. Before long we were back on the motorway network and drifting ever south to Cambridge.

* * *

After an overnight stop in Cambridge to see Alison's parents and raid their fridge, catch up on gossip and do some laundry we arrived in Merstham, just south of London, where we had plans to traipse into the capital to meet my eldest and his girlfriend. The journey was fine except for our satnav choosing a route through Caterham for no other reason other than it's probably sponsored by the Caterham Tourist Board. Looking at Caterham, and we've now seen quite a bit of it, it does appear to need the help. We had a walk to the station from our site which took a winding path through woods. Emerging to cross a road we found ourselves at the tail end of a party of 20 or so ramblers, all looking determined and dressed in walking gear of various vintages. Walking clothes are distinguished from every-day apparel by having a generous pocket to material ratio, too many zips and the occasional carabiner clipped on in a casually alluring way. Quite why people going for a walk inside the M25 need a metal clip designed to fasten you to a mountain is a mystery, but I do sympathise. I have a few and can testify that there is something butch about a carabiner dangling from your trousers. You feel more professional and in your mind that passing stranger takes a glance and thinks, *'gosh, they must scale lofty peaks in gale force winds and hang precariously with one hand from icy Alps, the sexy beast'*, whereby your carabiner gives one final wink in the sunlight and you disappear into the undergrowth leaving the stranger thinking improper thoughts and panting. Meanwhile on the other side of the hedge you continue looking for the number 7 bus to Croydon.

Alison fell into conversation with the group leader, a man whose appearance was so rural you could put him in a smock to sell cloudy cider. His face was rugged, defined by deep laughter lines and a glowing ruddy complexion. He had a shock of white hair that seemed to have a life independent from its owner and a chin strap silver beard that hung from a face that smiled easily. When he talked his face seemed to double in length to accommodate pearly white teeth and a throaty guffaw. He told us the walking club has over 60 members and that they organise walks 3-4 times a week. This one was a 6-mile amble to a pub and everyone present looked to be past retirement and cheerful. He broke off to shepherd the group over the road and bade us farewell with a parting wave and an invitation to join the group if we past that way again.

As we wove our way through them several hikers spoke to us, asking us to join them, warning us not to drink the pub dry if we beat them to it and generally being wonderfully happy in their exercise. It was a sunny morning and they set us up for the push over a hill and down towards the M23 on a path of exposed chalk. We joined the North Downs Way and followed it under the motorway and through a charming meadow of wild flowers and bird song, surprisingly peaceful considering it was sandwiched between the busy M23 and the roaring M25, Britain's busiest road. We found our target, the tiny Merstham station nestled in leafy suburbs.

We rendezvoused in London and went to a Japanese restaurant where you choose a broth and dipping sauce and the rest of the food chugs around on a conveyor belt that passes between the dining areas set around it. The idea is to choose something from the belt as it passes and cook it in a broth that sits bubbling away on a warming plate in front of you. To aid this you're provided with chop sticks, a pair of tweezers and a tea strainer like wire basket on a long handle to fish out your food. Our companions were both adept with the concept and using chopsticks so were soon tucking into hot noodles and an assortment of oriental delicacies. We however were less skilled, and our table space soon became a smear of spilled food and broth. At one point the waiter approached to see if I needed another lemonade because I'd mistakenly dipped Pak Choi in the one that I had. I looked up with a face splattered in bright red sauce and a noodle hanging out of my mouth. It must have looked like I was eating a live baby octopus.

After a while I started stabbing lumps of tofu with my chop sticks in the manner of a spear fisherman and finally resorted to scooping everything out with my little wire net. It was all great fun and I took to experimenting with cooking times, was given more broth because everyone seated near me was wearing my first bowl and ignored everyone in my earnest concentration to snag mushrooms that teased me by rising and falling in the broth. At one point something broke the surface and winked at me, but I may just have been over doing the chilli.

Alison meanwhile took to knitting together her noodles and slurping one long strand of about 2 ft. long, the tail end of which whiplashed onto her forehead leaving a pleasing stain, like a tattoo after surviving a tribal initiation into adulthood. We eventually finished, and my kindly son guided me to the wash room to clean up while the other diners applauded the entertainment and the waiters put hazard tape around my seat and phoned the industrial cleaners.

Walking back Alison told me that I'd have to be on my best behaviour for the rest of the week because we were heading off to the spiritual centre of the middle class.

* * *

Hay-on-Wye sits on the river in a valley overlooked by green hills and irregular hedges. At intervals stood clumps of tightly packed trees and fallow fields of golden buttercups shimmered in the breeze. Behind the hills, dark mountains brooded, their barrenness contrasting with the verdant fields of the valley. Hay itself is centred round the castle, a blend of medieval ruin and Jacobian mansion fused together by myriad reworkings, re-purposing and a couple of fires, the last in the 1970s. Below the castle the town's market square is surrounded by shops and houses lining narrow streets that fall away to the river and farmland beyond. The town is well known for its bookshops. In fact, it is nigh-on impossible to go anywhere in Hay without seeing a few dozen tatty paperbacks for sale. The cafes and, I suspect, the banks and even the chandelier shop all have them. If having a chandelier shop doesn't tell you what sort of town it is then the shops around the market area will. Those that don't specialise in books sell re-purposed, 'vintage' or worse still 'pre-loved' items, mostly in various states of decomposition. Imagine the contents of your gran's garage given a cursory dust and an elaborate price then sold to you by someone who wears a cravat and you'll get the general idea.

Hay really is the epicentre of middle England - in Wales. It is almost the very definition of aspirational middle class. If a meteorite hit Hay during the festival season you'd probably never hear the word postmodern again or meet children named after classical Greek poets. It's where the coriander and Burberry set come to play. It's not hard to see what brings them here though. The town is pretty, the homes well-tended and it's just the right side of twee. The shops are welcoming and mostly independent, the food good quality and plentiful, even if it leans towards the craft beer and organic falafel variety, and the local garage sells unleaded, diesel and gluten free petrol. And of course it is surrounded by pleasing views.

We stayed at a tidy little campsite 10-minutes' walk from the Hay Literary Festival site where we were working for the week. It was compact, clean and rigorously controlled. Most caravans were unhitched at the gate and parked by the owner of the site. We were escorted in, and told that Mavis was to stay put for the duration. Water would be brought to us if we needed it. Several VW campers rolled up after us, at least one hired from a specialist company by people who clearly think it's cool to be seen driving a lump of ill-tempered German engineering at 30 miles an hour and to sleep in a space the size of your average shower cubicle. One family even erected a white picket fence around theirs, possibly to warn unsuspecting passers-by that Jeremy, Philippa and precious little Tristan were in town for the Hay Festival and would love to bore you about how bright 5-year-old Tristan is, that Jeremy does something dull 'in the city' and Philippa's thinking of volunteering at the local Oxfam book shop once little Trist's at university, probably next year the way he's going. I made that bit up by the way - although sadly not the bit about the white picket fence.

CHAPTER 10

Hay Festival

The Hay Festival, and its brash upstart competitor How the Light Gets In attract enormous crowds. But the town appears to embrace them and - ahem - 'makes hay' while the sun shines. The 10-minute walk from town to festival is lined with gazebos and stalls selling wares in front gardens, from wood turning to chutneys, ice creams and charity collections, buskers and crafts, every other house seems to be engaged in a little light commerce. It was actually quite pleasing in a cheery making the most of it way and it certainly beat the junk on sale in parts of the town centre. The first second-hand bookshop in Hay opened in 1962 (some sources say 61) and the town hasn't looked back since. It presently boasts around 30 second-hand bookshops as well as all the cafés and other businesses that cannot seem to resist selling them as a by-line. The first festival took place in 1988 and from an audience of fewer than 1,000 people it now attracts up to 250,000 visitors. Although still firmly anchored in literature the line-up is varied; authors mingle with comedians and singers/bands in an eclectic mix. It's a bit like Radio 4 brought to life. Incidentally, for absolutely no reason other than I found it mildly diverting, the town of Hay is twinned with Timbuktu.

Our Hay Festival experience started closer to home on the impressive festival site, with a steward's induction and tour of the site. It gave us a chance to meet some of our fellow volunteers, a mixture of festival veterans and novices like us. The site was arranged in a grid with a variety of stages, plenty of meeting and milling around areas, a big food court and some traders, not least of which was the very large festival bookshop - which we were delighted (certainly more excited than our bank managers) to find offered a 20% discount for stewards.

The first couple of days were set aside for school children to attend. Thursday's junior school kids were a delight and really got involved. It helped that some authors delivered exciting and energetic talks that kept the young crowd engaged and their teachers seemed enthusiastic. Friday was the turn of the senior school children, who ranged from those who looked younger than the junior school crowd to others who were indistinguishable from their teachers. One of our duties was to take the roving microphones around the audience for people who wanted to ask questions of the authors. We found the children's enquiries incisive, relevant and brief; three terms not always true of the adult audiences. Quite how some authors keep their cool when faced with banal and irrelevant queries from grown-ups is beyond me. Alison witnessed one very well-known author patiently explain that the way to become an author is to start writing, a thought that hitherto hadn't occurred to the questioner, who freely and without apparent embarrassment admitted that they had never actually written anything. Surely the correct response to such inanity is to beat the questioner to a pulp with your latest book?

Our principal duty during our 6-day stint was crowd control at the main stage, a 1700 seat venue with a queuing system of varying success. Generally, the team of stewards managed to hold up to 1700 people outside, clear out the previous house, collect rubbish and then sit the next house in a 30 – 40-minute time-slot. All this while answering queries, directing people, explaining venue changes, collecting lost property, grabbing a crafty coffee and generally being the smiley helpful face of the festival, overseen by the calm and knowledgeable venue heads and their deputies.

We also escorted a farm visit where we learned just how complicated growing apples for cider can be and how important and complex bee-keeping is. The bee-keeping bit particularly fascinated me because I'd fancied keeping a hive or two for a while. It came as a bit of a shock to learn that they don't deliver jars of fresh honey to your breakfast table each morning as payment for letting them park their hives on your lawn but instead you, the bee-keeper, must work blooming hard and dress up in net curtains because the ungrateful little sods want to sting you. It's a wonder we have any bees left though with the array of interesting but deadly viruses, pests, predators and pesticides they are vulnerable to. Hats off to the earnest folk who keep them and have the patience to milk the stripy little buggers every morning so that we can enjoy honey on our toast and polish on our tables I say.

It's not really in the spirit of this book to review the appearances we saw but a special mention must go to Germaine Greer who managed to squeeze two 'fucks' and a 'piss off' into a discussion about Shakespeare's sonnets.

It would be easy to scoff at the Hay festival for being middle class and somewhat up itself, but nearly everyone we encountered was a kind, gentle soul, amiable and there to enjoy the atmosphere and take the opportunity to listen to, and per-chance meet, their favourite author. Step back from the hubbub, ignore the organic asparagus stall, pass by the food court serving lobster, skirt the Daily Telegraph newspaper booth and find the families enjoying each other's company, serious bibliophiles balancing coffee and an open book, older men wearing mustard cord trousers with a twinkle in their eye exchanging views with young women in inadvisable footwear, earnest bespectacled students furiously annotating well-thumbed works with broken spines, women of a certain age and girth gliding down the aisles like galleons under sail and excited children clutching treasured editions signed by their favourite authors. All were alive to the world of imagination, discovery and the simple pleasure of a good book.

If literature gives us the opportunity to grow, to learn, to imagine and to experience the world through others' eyes, then maybe the Hay Festival provides a gateway to a more civilised world. Long may it continue.

CHAPTER 11

Festival Season

Sad though we were to leave Hay we were travelling to a village near Stafford to stay overnight with friends. We followed the broad River Wye for a while, where we admired the oddly ornate Weobley Church, looking as if it was about to take off towards heaven with its Thunderbird 1 style spire. We took a scenic route towards Worcester, passing signs for charmingly named places that read like birth announcements in the Telegraph; To Sir Timothy and Lady *Evesbatch* a son, *Lulsley Alfrick Suckley*; a brother to *Tedstone Bromyard Leominster* and 2nd grandchild for *Sandy* and *Corby Bedfordshire*.

We rolled along through lush green meadows, gently rising and falling with the road, past a ruined castle on a hill watching silently over pastures of golden buttercups, sparse woodlands and carefully tended fields where cows grazed lazily. The Malvern Hills loomed in the background, their shape changing against the Wedgewood blue skyline as we followed the road on its twisting course. We were entranced by the scenery but after unsuccessfully seeking out a suitable parking space for lunch we settled on a spot hard up against a stone wall where we could look at the road or the wall. On a highway with few stopping places we realised that this would have to do and duly tucked in. Setting back off we pulled onto the road, rounded the corner and the view opened out before us, a chocolate box picture of perfect English countryside. Fields divided by neat hedges, willow trees weeping into a river, cows and sheep in meadows of shimmering green, a thatched cottage with a country garden of wild flowers. All next to a bloody great big empty parking and picnicking space. We drove on, grumbling and decided the view was far too twee anyway after Hay. Further on we passed the site of the Battle of Worcester where in 1651 Cromwell's New Model Army fought a decisive victory over Royalist forces in the civil war. If you must fight I suppose it is sensible to do so close to the motorway network and there was even a supermarket just down the road if they fancied stocking up on groceries and to maybe get some flowers for the wife once the hostilities were over.

It was fortunate that Alison was driving because she takes potential hazards like Birmingham's notorious Spaghetti Junction, which we passed through, in her stride. I try to, but a bit of my father's fretfulness occasionally surfaces and I worry about ending up in the wrong lane and having to detour around Dublin to re-join the M6 somewhere further away than where I left it. My early family holidays were usually in Norfolk, a fair drive from Hertfordshire pre-dual carriageway and bypasses. The route took us through the centre of Ipswich where there was a rare (for then) double roundabout which my father considered was built specifically to spite him. He regarded it as a personal duel.

He'd fret about it from the end of our road in Sawbridgeworth and by the time we entered Ipswich he had been through cross, annoyed, blaming the council, telling himself it was fine he'd done it before, threatening to turn around and then asking my mother to find an alternative route, getting hopelessly lost, finding the A12 again by accident but now heading the wrong way, and eventually reaching a plateau of icy calmness. He'd point the family saloon at the roundabout and pull up about a foot from the white line. My mother, forever little miss helpfulness, would be pointing out how easily other cars were navigating it, using a voice guaranteed to raise the tension. I'd hunker down in a nest of comics and sweet wrappers on the back seat where I'd use the opportunity to try and find the stack of paper sheets so I could casually drop them out of the car window while the adults were distracted up front.

With grim fortitude we would edge closer to the junction. The atmosphere inside the car was electric, the noise from outside subdued. Vultures circled overhead, somewhere in the distance a wolf howled. We inched forward. A car on the horizon crested the hill and bore down on us from a mile away. We'd sit and let it pass. Quietly brooding, engine ticking, he would sense his chance as the nearest car was 20 miles away or in the impatient queue behind us, now stretching back to Chelmsford. Easing off the clutch he'd look both ways, admonish my mother for having a head because it was in the way, look both ways again and in a flurry of excitement stall the car and have to start again. Eventually we'd just bolt across with scant regard for other traffic, pedestrians or the juggernaut screaming by millimetres from our rear bumper and then we could all settle down full of cheerful holiday spirit. I'm sure the reason we moved to Suffolk was to avoid that roundabout.

Back to the present and we met up with our friends, spending a most convivial evening with them. They live in and manage a retreat and conference centre. The group that was in residence included people with a learning disability among their number. A gathering in the bar turned into an impromptu sing-a-long. Alison immediately joined in with gusto and by my 2nd pint I was doing the same, reaching hitherto undiscovered notes in my rendition of The Eagles *'Hotel California'*. In fact it may come as a surprise to those present to know that this was what I was singing.

In the late 70's I volunteered at a social club for people who have learning disabilities. I was a spotty teenaged heavy metal fan in triple denim (denim waistcoat included - easy ladies) and here I found a group of people who were gracious and appreciated company regardless of race, creed, colour or religion, who saw you as a person before all else, and you just couldn't help but respond in kind. I also found people who were de-valued, ignored and pushed to the fringes just because they were different and didn't necessarily conform to the narrow boundaries of 'acceptable' society. It was these qualities of non-judgmental acceptance, as well as sometimes being pushed to the fringes, that we had now found in the traveller and festival communities we met up with, and why we had found ourselves so drawn to them. I eventually went on to build a career working alongside and supporting people who have learning disabilities. Tonight was a great boost to us both in the most welcoming of company. To top it all, for the first time since the end of March, we got to sleep in a real bed in a real house.

An added bonus of staying with our friends was the space-age shower they possess; a cylinder shaped white cubicle with glass doors and an array of hoses, water jets and shiny chrome attachments inside. It looked like something Professor Frink from The Simpsons would invent, or perhaps Jeff Goldblum would step out of as half fly, half man. It even had twin seats for the steam setting, maybe so that you can get saucy. If you do I'd advise being wary of leaning against any buttons while in the throes of passion lest you unleash a jet of water somewhere surprising. Perhaps there's a button that makes a mirror ball appear and a cocktail cabinet pop up. I'll leave it to you to experiment. It was all I could do in my hungover state to switch it on and stand under the stream of hot water. I did press a button on the bewildering control panel thinking FM might stand for foot massage, but it turned out to be Radio 4. I exited after a brief tussle with the magnetically sealed doors and to celebrate surviving the shower we fixed a security door handle to Mavis before heading an hour up the road to Uttoxeter for our next festival.

Uttoxeter is a quaint old market town with an imposing soot stained sandstone church and some fine old timbered buildings. Although it's situated in an affluent area much of the town centre is given over to cheap stores and charity shops.

Talking of charity shops is it just me who gets irritated by Barnardos' shop strapline *'Believe in Children'?* Believe in Children my arse, the little buggers are everywhere. It's like being told to believe in bricks or in crisps. There is empirical evidence that they exist, you don't need to believe in them. Some marketing company probably charged a fortune to think up this nonsense.

On the plus side I did buy a walking shirt in one of the charity shops, that I was delighted to discover has a spectacles wipe sewn-in on the inside. I couldn't have been more thrilled with this discovery if I'd found it had a carabiner attached too. I don't know why these little things appeal to me, but they always do.

CHAPTER 12

The Acoustic Festival

The Acoustic Festival is the one that really started me on the road we are now on. As is the way of these things I was following some online links and found the Acoustic Festival website and discovered that they were looking for volunteers, so later that year - 2008 I believe - I found myself on the M6 at 6am nervously heading towards the festival.

I was made extraordinarily welcome, saw lots of great bands, might have been responsible (in a non-litigious way you understand) for accidentally tripping up the mother of one of the headliners, and generally had a great time. I've returned every year since and consider the regular crew and stewards friends. In my second year there I fell into litter picking and generally keeping the site tidy. I'm not sure why but I think it might have been that as an early riser I could be relied upon to get up and clear litter before the punters came onto site. Once I'd got it clean of course I'd want to keep it that way and so discovered the mindless joy of picking up other people's rubbish. Really. I do take great pride in the site and the reviews that mention how clean it is. I should add that the Acoustic Festival crowd is adorably tidy anyway and so long as we regularly empty the bins it is quite painless. It's long hours though and it's about turning your hand to any job that needs doing, from erecting fencing to putting up signs, from car parking duty to selling tickets, and generally helping the public, traders and bands to enjoy their time at the festival.

This year was Alison's third year at the festival and her duties this time were in the box office, where her administrative and customer service skills were welcomed. I turned my hand to doing lots of different things with varying degrees of success, but did put up the flags along the entrance road in such a way that even with a good wind they stayed upright and fluttery. So successful was my flagging that on Monday when I came to take them down I privately swore about each one as I risked life and limb to cut away my expertly applied cable ties.

This year the festival adopted a steampunk theme. If you are not familiar with steampunk it is like science fiction set in the Victorian era. There's a lot of 19th century steam power ascetics and flamboyant costumes; frock coats, embroidered waistcoats, corsets and lacy frills. Goggles on bowler hats seem popular along with copper and brass adornments, pith helmets and a dash of military chic. It's a very stylish look and many people sported lavish outfits in dark colours and more than a few regretted their decision as the sun beat down on them all weekend. Others went for the headgear only, adding copper or brass goggles to their hats. Looking out from the stage the acts must have thought they were performing to a crowd of rusty Minions.

We worked three very long days, grabbing occasional breaks when we could to see a particular performer or to grab some food. I should point out we do the work and hours we do because we love it. We adore this festival and want it to do well. A big part of its success is in ensuring that the paying customers enjoy the experience. If you stand more than one person in a field there will be things that don't go to plan. A festival on this scale is no exception. Imaging having to book the site, all the bands and artists, sell tickets, arrange all the staging, lights, sound, fencing, security, toilets and showers, arrange advertising, attract and manage the traders, food, crew, stewards, waste removal, sewerage, fresh water, tents and marquees and deal with the local authority, fire service, police, health and safety and rely on the weather being favourable and you're not even half way to arranging a successful festival experience for the punters. Things will go wrong and a good festival team knows this and takes responsibility to sort out issues as they arise, before they become serious.

Having said all that this year was the smoothest running Acoustic Festival I've been involved with, thanks in no small part to the experienced team behind it. It also helped that we had four days of glorious weather with the sort of heat where your shadow melts. We saw people in camping chairs guarding their precious place in front of the main stage, glowing lobster red. We could have found them in the dark.

We wrangled some time off to watch a couple of acts, including one that Alison was particularly keen to see. When she was growing up her bedroom wall was plastered with posters of a popular 80's singer who broke onto the music scene by finding a home wherever he put his hat down, so she was excited to find Paul Young, for it was he, playing at the festival with his band. After meeting him before he performed, thanks to the very kind stage managers who know the band, she got to be their 'Tequila Babe' and went on-stage with them to deliver Tequila shots during their set.

The festival finished on the Sunday night so Monday morning was spent dismantling the site. We started nice and early and by mid-morning were at the point where most of the remaining jobs were for the specialist teams; dismantling the marquees, taking staging away and suchlike. So in the spirit of solidarity, with our comrades still working on the site and having to stay under canvas for another night, we buggered off to the Caravan Club site next door and spent an hour each under a hot shower, drunk tea, had another shower, made dinner, had one last shower and finally slept and dreamt of hot showers. Well I did, I think Alison might have been dreaming of a certain 80's pop star.

CHAPTER 13

Pottering About

After the festival we went to Mow Cop, a village that sits on the Staffordshire - Cheshire border and that straddles a steep hill with commanding views and painfully narrow roads. The village was once home to a quarry, the rocks being ideal for making high-quality millstones, known as querns, for use in water mills. Excavations have found querns dating back to the Iron Age. There's a 65ft rock stack called the Old Man O' Mow standing to attention on the north side of the ridge, a remnant of the quarrying days and apparently on the site of an ancient cairn.

Occupying the most prominent position in the village with commanding views of the Welsh hills, Manchester and The Peak District is a folly known as Mow Cop Castle. In the finest tradition of the landed gentry who had more money than they knew what to do with, one Randle Wilbraham built a ruined castle as his summerhouse in 1754. It was on land that formed part of his family estate at Rode Hall two miles away. Old Randle was a lawyer by trade and became a Tory MP. A tribute to him by Chief Justice Wilmot included the grammatically magnificent line *'Randle Wilbraham has not left a better lawyer, or an honester man, behind him'*. I fear precious few present-day MP's obituaries would include reference to their honesty. Sadly, fewer still would use the word 'honester', but I for one would like to see it reintroduced into the English language.

To the west of Mow Cop is a mile long climb up a steep slope that is known among the cycling fraternity as The Killer Mile. Races are run up it by people who look reasonable in Lycra. I mention this because unless you are at least a semi-professional cyclist or under 12 you should be prevented from wearing stretchy fabric in public unless you have a certificate that guarantees you don't look like a bag of angry seals fighting in a neon sack. I don't like to judge, but I silently do.

I shall leave that with you and speak of it no more. Instead, we can cleanse our minds with another noteworthy fact about Mow Cop; it was the birthplace of the

Primitive Methodist movement, when Hugh Bourne and William Clowes began holding open-air prayer meetings here around 1810. Apparently Primitive Methodists saw themselves as practising a purer form of Christianity, so I was intrigued by their practice of Love Feasts and was looking forward to researching some high calorie rumpy pumpy in God's name, but sadly it's just a term used for certain religious meals among early Christians.

By now you are familiar with my struggles to grasp the workings of unfamiliar plumbing and today I found that the sink had a plug of extraordinary complexity. I spent 10 minutes trying to get it to stay closed while I attempted to shave as the water gurgled away. Eventually I leant on it with my full weight and it popped into the hole. I then spent 20 more precious minutes trying to empty the sink until I levered the plug out to the sound of a loud and probably expensive snap. It was a classic case of over-engineering. If ever a sanitary fitting was fit for purpose, from pre-historic times onward, it is the humble plug. Here's a definition I found online: *'Typically plugs are made from a soft material, such as rubber, or have a soft outer rim, so that they can be fitted to holes slightly smaller than their diameter; this ensures a tight seal.'* See, it's not difficult is it? All I want is for the water to remain in situ until I've finished with it, then drain away when I'm done. Why do they have to be made to pop up, pivot, lever, spring and otherwise bugger about? If you are a Master Pluggist, or whatever the noun is for one whose job is to design plugs, give up, retrain as a ballet dancer or design a better moustache trimmer. There really is no need to tinker with something that already works without your continued bloody interference.

Back at Mavis Alison greeted my face, half of which was smooth and shiny and half raw stubble, with the special look of pity and resignation that she reserves for my frequent grapples with domestic life. She guided me gently to the bathroom, mopped off the suds, water and last night's BBQ sauce, calmly suggested my underpants might be better suited inside my trousers and left me changing while she went back to the toilet block to mop up after me, collecting the items I'd dropped along the way and leaving a little note of apology for the owners.

After attending a gig by Martyn Joseph in nearby Biddulph we tried to get away sharpish from the venue as we had an overnight drive to Cambridge ahead. Annoyingly some daft and selfish sod had squeezed their car into a space behind Mavis, presumably sideways so tight was the fit. We were just preparing to barge into the pub and demand that the prick of an owner move their infernal blooming car forthwith when it beeped to signal it was unlocked and Martyn appeared holding the keys. Well, we complimented him on his parking, what a clever idea it was to take up that space, no it's really no trouble at all, we've all the time in the world thank you and so forth. Needless to say he was every bit the gentleman, moved it immediately and then changed his shirt in the car park, causing Alison to remark that maybe we shouldn't be too hasty leaving.

* * *

In Cambridge for family matters and a bit of a post festival recharge I chanced upon some notes I'd written a couple of years previously when we undertook a bit of a compressed tour of the UK, starting in England, hitting Scotland, then Wales, all in a week. We imposed ourselves upon Alison's friends in each location and they were all saintly and generous with their time. Although I had met them all before it had only been briefly at functions and I was a little rusty on matching faces to names. Alison's promised set of revision flash cards had never materialised, so I was left cheerfully greeting lovely warm people and subtly interrogating them to find their place in Alison's extended family of colleagues, ex-colleagues, folks she knows from church and people she met once in Tesco and is now a Godparent to their children.

In Edinburgh I was armed with the names of our hosts and a mental picture of their faces. We were greeted at the door of a charming house by a wonderful gentleman who bade us welcome, made tea, served us biscuits and showed us around. As Alison seemed relaxed and he was most amiable, I assumed we were in the correct house and set to work assembling clues to their relationship to one another. His wife returned from work, hugs and felicitations were exchanged and we sat down to a fine meal and cosy chat around the fire. We eventually retired and lay in bed reading when I had to admit defeat:

Alison: *'What a lovely evening'*
Me: *'Delightful, charming people...Alison darling?'*
Alison: *'Yes dear?'*
Me: *'Err, who exactly are these delightful charming people?'*

Once explained, mental pictures rearranged accordingly, and secretly hoping I was never tested on the finer details, we had a wonderful time with them. It turned out to be much more illuminating and moving for me than I'd ever have anticipated. What follows is what I've written up from notes I made at the time and had just rediscovered.

Chatting around an Edinburgh fireplace one evening the subject turned to the traits we have in common with our children. I casually mentioned the poor handwriting, spelling and unusual writing stance I share with my two sons, making light of it as I always do. After some gentle questioning I was referred to a website about Dysgraphia. It's an interesting and sobering read but one that makes sense of experiences from my childhood. Here is a handy definition:

'Dysgraphia is a neurological disorder, characterised by the inability to write properly. Dysgraphia in fact refers specifically to the inability to perform operations in handwriting. It could be described as an extreme difficulty with fine-motor skills...It is very important to recognise dysgraphia as soon as possible, before it impacts on a child's self-esteem.'[ii]

I'm not making a self-diagnosis; I have no idea if I or my children have it. It seems pointless, except maybe out of academic interest, to find out now. I've always tried to park my school days as something I had to endure, a kind of extended initiation into adulthood that I'll thankfully never have to repeat. My education was typified by under-achievement and by the time I got to secondary school I'd found I could fade into the background and drift around largely undisturbed by the powers that be. In spite of that, since leaving formal education I've done okay. I found that you could work for a living and learn what you needed to know for the job, and not, for example, about ox-bow lakes. My children did well at school but had the constant spectre of the handwriting and spelling police looming over them too. We have all become experts at coping. Stoicism could be our middle name – if we could ever be relied upon to spell it correctly that is. But some experiences do linger and lying awake in the dim light of an early Edinburgh morning I reflected on what I'd read and upon my own battles with low self-esteem and depression.

- Having speech therapy at primary school because, in the words of my delightfully politically incorrect mother *'Raymond spoke like a little chinky Chinaman'*
- Being told by the headmaster at junior school he had a *'bone to pick with me'* because I clearly wasn't bothering to learn and was *'letting down my family.'*
- Spending a term toiling from worksheets sitting outside his office in the dining hall as some sort of remedial therapy.
- Being admonished for not knowing the sounds letters made and giving my first smart ass answer, *'because I can't hear them Sir...'* It wasn't a wise move and bought me more dining hall time.
- My mother coming home from a parents evening in my last year at junior school and angrily declaring to my father that I should be in a special school.
- This becoming a recurring, faintly sinister theme during my youth with her lobbying my father for me to be sent away to school.
- Being moved from the A stream to the B stream in middle school. That slow walk back from the headmaster's office fighting the tears with his *'we're trying to help you Raymond, it's our fault for putting you with the brighter children'* speech echoing around my head.
- My first (of many) truancies the next day.
- The endless frustration that even when I tried, my head and hands seemed like they were controlled by different people.
- Being ridiculed by my English teacher for my handwriting in my first year of High School after I had put considerable effort into a piece of

descriptive writing that interested me. Never again would I make that mistake at school.
- Watching my grades and expectations dwindle – every school report said I didn't try. Gradually this became true.
- Shutting the world of education out. It was a world that existed between 9 am and 3 pm, during which time I'd mostly reside inside my head.
- Leaving 12 years of formal schooling with one Grade 1 CSE, although I did end up doing an extra year and gained 3 Grade C O' Levels. I'm not sure how.

But if all this seems like the promotional text for a bleak autobiography then it really isn't. Coping is a family trait and in spite of, or maybe because of, these experiences I seem to have done okay. I even held down a job in corporate communications for a while. The biggest benefit for me, and I guess for my children too, is the computer. Having no need to write longhand has been a revelation. I've moved from avoiding writing to actually enjoying it. Maybe some of my grammatical quirks persist and I make more use of the spell checker than most. In fact for me it is close to the greatest invention ever. Just behind the record player and ahead of chocolate. (It's close but don't despair chocolate, we're still friends).

I also want to pause here to pay tribute to Alison who proof reads and improves everything I write, except for this paragraph because if I let her see it she would remove it out of modesty. And I do mean everything I write; I've found shopping lists that have been gently corrected. She has also found it within her considerable resources to provide me with more nurturing and encouragement in just a few years than formal education ever did, and it was supposed to be their job. I'm not blaming teachers. Education is characterised by political interference and the dictates of fashions and trends that they have to conform to. I do though wish some teachers had remembered why they were in the profession and taken a few minutes to think about children as people rather than damp sacks of hormones squeezed into a nylon uniform.

I'm not sure I'd have wanted a different path to the one I chose though. What I would have changed is the attitude of my teachers and parents, the humiliations and the stress of not understanding why I couldn't do what was required and, assuming, indeed being told, that the fault was mine.

Dysgraphia is just one of many conditions that can go unrecognised and children and students with them often don't stand much chance of getting the support they require. This needs to change but I fear it won't in our education factories where conformity, obedience and exam success are prized over individuality, imagination and personality. Again, that's not generally the teachers fault and I could name one primary school teacher who did more for my two offspring than she'd ever get credit for by the politicians and authorities who measure success by grades and not by genuine learning and growth.

* * *

And on that slightly glum note we'll get back to writing about our travels, Alison's ability to make friends in the unlikeliest of places and my struggles with the skills needed for basic survival, starting when we hit London for a concert at The Royal Festival Hall.

First though we needed to get a new railcard. This should have been simple but for reasons best known to themselves Cambridge Station have elected to site their photo-booth on the platform, causing me to struggle with the conundrum of getting a photo for the railcard to enable me to get the ticket that would allow me to get onto the platform to get to the photo booth to enable me to get the photo I needed to get the railcard to get the ticket to get onto the platform.... Fortunately, Alison chatted amiably to the Transport Policeman, explained that we needed new photos for a replacement rail card because her name had changed and anyway the ones we had make us look like a Police photo fit. Mine looked like I was featured on America's Most Wanted. Happily, he let us through and I look a little less like a serial killer in the new one.

Once in the city we made our way to The Royal Festival Hall, which appears to have been renamed The South Bank Centre, along with all the other theatres and recital rooms that make up this concrete jungle on the banks of the Thames. I think. It was all a little unclear to me. It was built in 1951 for the Festival of Britain and according to their website it's the largest single run arts centre in the world. I'm not completely sure whether this is an achievement to be proud of or not. It reminds me of cricket commentators who proclaim meaningless statistics like *'That's only the 3rd time a left handed medium paced bowler has delivered an off spinner on a Wednesday at Trent Bridge from the sewage works end against the wind since Bertie Fudge-Trollop in 1431. That reminds me, Mrs Verity Panty has sent us a chocolate cake, and very fine it is too.'* And so on and so forth.

It took us a while to find our way in, since the ground floor is given over to a variety of brash chain restaurants, but eventually we followed some grim stairs up a dank passageway between neon eateries and found the entrance. This was only a temporary victory as inside its vast lobby things got seriously confusing. It may be my age (I'm excusing Alison who is tender in years you understand), but why is it so difficult to navigate a concert hall whose one function is to usher you seamlessly to your seats? We eventually found the booth to pick up our tickets and were directed to a lift that was full with only three people in it, in a venue that can seat 2500 people you understand. We opted to walk up to level 6, and found ourselves on the yellow side - according to our tickets we should have been on the blue side. This appeared to be their one concession to navigation as it divides the auditorium down the middle so you enter via the colour that matches the side your seats are in. Well, we did, but most people seemed as confused as us. Once we'd finally settled we enjoyed a fabulous evening in the company of the Manchester based band I Am Kloot, made all the better by the warm glow we felt in having thwarted the South Bank Centre's attempts to confuddle us.

After arriving back late we were up and away in the morning in good time, excited to be spending a couple of nights in The Peak District. We hold a special place in our hearts for this beautiful part of Britain. It's where I took refuge when I needed a break from other pressures in an earlier lifetime, we've visited since meeting for weekends away and it is where we honeymooned.

* * *

The Peak District was founded in 1951 as the first of Britain's 15 national parks. It covers an area of 555 sq. miles and sits plumb in the middle of England. 20 million people live within a one-hour journey of the park, and its resident population of around 38,000 people is swollen by an additional 10 million visitors a year. It is an area of great diversity; dark moorland, dramatic limestone edges, lush farmland, forests, reservoirs and hills. They are not really peaks; that term probably comes from Pecsaetan, an Anglo-Saxon tribe who settled the area. The highest point is Kinder Scout, a relatively modest 2086 ft. Walkers and cyclists are a common sight but a significant number of the visitors don't venture more than a few yards from their car or coach, preferring to take a few quick snaps to bore the grandchildren with then retire to a tea room to complain about the price of the cream tea they've just purchased and to catch up on gossip.

But before we could get there we had to negotiate Alison's home town, so it was inevitable we'd bump into her old friends and acquaintances. Being experienced at this now we'd allowed ourselves plenty of time and exchanged pleasantries with a host of good folk. I try not to be too petulant in these situations but I just get lost after an introduction of: *'How's the weather/car/wife/husband/children/cat/lumbago?'* When Alison has you ensnared in her conversational spell it's like witchcraft. All manner of information is traded, from the trivial to the dramatic without me ever really working out what's actually happening. One minute its hugs and squeals as she meets some acquaintance from school and then 30 minutes have gone and plans are in diaries for a 'proper' meet up and I'm coming round from a vacant stupor and worrying that I've missed some vital nugget that I'll be tested upon later. After a short intermission while I said goodbye to people I had no recollection of meeting 15 minutes previously we bundled into Mavis and sped off northwards. Our hearts lightened as we hit the southern end of The Peaks and the rolling hills became studded with the dramatic outcrops that form The Roaches, a gritstone escarpment made up from the Lower and Upper Roaches, Hen Cloud and Ramshaw Rocks.

The Roaches are a haven for walkers and climbers so late the next morning we set out from our site to climb them. Well, climb is a bit of an exaggeration, we followed the footpath up where only thousands have been before, but the incline was steep and rugged and our attire was of the sort favoured by serious hikers and had lots of pockets; I may even have attached a small carabiner. We started walking in steady rain, of the sort that quickly penetrates everything. Turning off the main road we took to open access land and up the first ascent of the day, Hen Cloud. Halfway up the steep path we met notices alerting walkers to keep to the path and not venture off because of nesting Peregrine Falcons. Intrigued, we elected to head back down and investigate the shed where Staffordshire Wildlife Trust volunteers stood vigil over the nest, per chance to discover more.

While Alison was viewing the falcon through their powerful scope I was being talked at about map reading. I love maps so at first I thought I had met a kindred spirit as we discussed the merits of OS mapping, but his devotion led him to regale me with tales of him finding lost people, guiding parties to safety from certain doom, or at least from being mildly inconvenienced, and how he'd print out his maps and laminate them...at least I think that's correct. Frankly I tuned out and let him carry on while I fantasised about chopping him up and feeding him to the falcons.

Alison eventually tired of bird spotting and roused me from my semi-comatose state and we went on our way. I chanced a look back and my erstwhile OS superhero was gesticulating to thin air, probably pointing out where he had saved a party of nuns from plunging into a disused mine shaft because they were using the wrong scale OS or some-such inflated nonsense. I'm not sure he realised I'd left and was now cheerfully half a mile away, making good headway up the path towards the lower tier of The Roaches.

The path ran below the jagged edge of the rocks, beloved of climbers, and weaved along the top of a delightfully dappled area heavily populated with pines. The feeling of being able to reach out and touch the top of a mighty pine tree was uncanny as we walked on, closer now to the edge as the path narrowed. The rain had abated and everything was fresh and green as we rounded an outcrop and met the rock steps leading to the upper tier. From the top of the steps we could see Tittesworth reservoir, grey and murky at first then bright and silver among the greenery as the sun came out in the valley. Above the reservoir the hills were half illuminated by sunlight struggling through low grey cloud, the patchwork of irregular fields split by deep green hedges in contrast to the dry-stone walls around us.

We discovered a rough seat hewn into a rock, poised precariously above a sheer drop and above it a plaque commemorating the visit to this very spot of the Prince and Princess of Teck on Aug 23rd 1872. We had no idea who the heck the Prince and Princess of Teck were, but subsequent research revealed that the Prince was a minor German aristocrat and the Princess was Mary Adelaide, cousin of Queen Victoria, who was still unmarried at the ripe old age of 30. Reports mention her lack of income and, rather uncharitably, *'lack of attractiveness'* as contributing factors. Being the way of things then, a match was sought with someone of suitable royal blood, and somehow they unearthed Prince Francis, Prince of Teck in Württemberg. Pictures from the time show the Prince and Princess surrounded by a jolly party crowded onto the rocks to take in the views. Today though we appeared to have them to ourselves as we took the ridge path along the top and made our way along sandy trails, scrambled over rocks worn smooth and shiny by countless walking boots, past the lonely dark waters of the tiny Doxy Pool, through dark peaty mud and on to the trig point that marked the summit of our walk, at 505 somethings. Metres I believe.

I had the strange experience of attending primary school when the country adopted decimalisation, along with selective bits of the metric system. In theory this should make me adept at understanding both imperial and metric measurements but in fact I understand neither. Alison kindly translates things like weather forecasts for me since having once told me the temperature would be around 30 I presented myself in woolly hat and thermals to be met by a familiar look of resignation and was gently escorted upstairs to put on clothing more suitable for 30 Celsius, t-shirt and shorts etc, rather than the 30 Fahrenheit I'd prepared for.

Anyway, from our lofty position at 505 gallons above sea level or something, we could survey the panorama around us. The broad valleys, low green hills creeping up to purple and golden moors, verdant wooded slopes out towards Flash, England's highest village, to our north, the arrow straight Roman road of the A53 cutting between the open farmland and moors to the east and more rugged terrain crested by the Roaches that we were standing on. Below us were the Ramshaw Rocks, looking as if they had been swept upwards in the manner of sand as the tide recedes, left to dry as exposed and windswept monuments to the seismic events that formed them. Picking up the pace we descended rapidly to stony outcrops and an alien landscape of peculiar weather-sculpted rocks. Away from the wind we stripped off layers as the air became still and muggy and we joined a minor road to set off back under the cliff face of Roach End, beneath the rocks and then dropped down a steep side road to Roche Grange. We were going to cut through on footpaths to the village of Meerbrook but they were mostly overgrown and uninviting, especially since the sun was now out, making the still air buzz with insects that stuck to our skin. We eventually found a suitable path and struck off through fields of open meadows resplendent under vivid yellow buttercups and flanked by willows, hawthorn hedges and lone trees. About to enter one such field a frisky foal spied us, whinnied and darted over on spindly legs. It seemed delighted to have human company and bounced about like a dog eager for a game. Its mother looked up and with slight shrug returned to grazing, I suspect secretly pleased to have him off her hands for a while.

Lovely though it was to be greeted so enthusiastically he worried us with his playfulness and we'd made progress across the field when he galloped up from behind, touched my shoulder and turned away with a flick of hooves and a deep resonant fart. A nearby cow gave us a 'kids, what can you do?' look and resumed chomping her way through the long grass. We hurried on and he lost interest as we climbed a stile and crossed a stream to join a way-marked route which led us through another field of horses, thankfully much more placid then the foal, and into the village of Meerbrook and the snug pub where we took liquid refreshment and reflected on a fine day's walking in a part of the world that keeps calling us back.

CHAPTER 14

Sonic Rock Solstice Festival

We left the tranquillity of the Peaks with the mix of excitement and trepidation that always marks the start of another festival; new people, new surroundings and new jobs to do. The journey wasn't that long and we soon pulled into the car park at what appeared to be a village hall sandwiched between a canal, a road and fields. The hall's sports field was littered with tents and vans of the ramshackle variety favoured by a certain type of festival goer, and a burger van sat in the car park, so we had a good idea this was the right place for the Sonic Rock Solstice Festival.

We made ourselves known to a group sitting around a gazebo at the entrance to the field and were directed to our contact who bade us welcome, introduced us formally to the good folk at the gazebo and then promptly departed on an errand. Feeling slightly uncomfortable and at a loose end we got to know our companions for the weekend who hailed from all around the North West and Midlands and together make up a motorcycle club. If we'd been told in advance that we'd be with a motorcycle club hired to provide security we might have felt nervous, but parachuted blind into their company as we were, we didn't have time for worries and they couldn't have been more welcoming and hospitable. The first afternoon was odd because we really felt we should be doing something other than sitting around so we found a few odd tasks and generally made ourselves useful but by evening we succumbed to the charms of food and beer and watched a couple of bands before a relatively early night.

Saturday morning found me cleaning toilets (someone had to, and it was small payment for the free entry and seemingly endless supply of beer) and Alison helped on the gate. We took a walk to the village shop and then generally bummed about watching bands, doing odd jobs and generally feeling like we should be busy. Come the evening though we felt really settled and spent a raucous time around the camp fire with the bikers and a few others. I'm not quite sure how but at one point we had a 5-piece kazoo orchestra going, three bikers, Alison and me. Frankly I'm surprised and a little hurt that we weren't booked for a stage slot on the Sunday, but such is life. Sunday was much the same. The headliners on the Sunday night were veteran punk band The Vibrators. As they were late arriving and Alison needed to get them checked in we had the added enjoyment of her asking passers-by if they had seen a car load of Vibrators.

During that last evening we looked around a packed hall and saw a young man who had come over from Russia especially for the festival, hippies in rainbow tunics dancing, a couple embracing and twirling each other around, bikers and punks head banging together down the front, a young man in tracksuit trousers and vest jigging along beside a bowler-hatted steampunk. We saw smiles, hugs and people enjoying themselves; music, as ever, was a great leveller. We loved it.

Monday morning brought with it a healthy dose of reality. The rain had been non-stop overnight, the field boggy and half empty. We trudged around occupying ourselves with small tasks but really it was all done. Around us people with heavy eyes and drooping shoulders were packing away wet tents and preparing to return to normality. The entrance to the camping field oozed with thick mud squelching through the remains of the straw we'd put down. We bade a few last goodbyes and settled in Mavis for the journey, tired, aching and happy. Before we pulled away we had one final farewell to perform, so while the engine idled Alison popped out to say goodbye to Hope, the world's worst guide dog. She'd been merrily leading her master around the site all weekend, although not necessarily at his behest. This morning, while leading her owner to his taxi she caught a whiff of the burger van and led him off at a brisk pace towards it, licking her lips in anticipation. A quick intervention by a bystander set her back on course where she promptly made another 45 degree turn to greet Alison like a long lost friend. Our last view of her was sitting on her owner's lap and licking the taxi drivers' face as he tried drive away.

CHAPTER 15

Friends and Family

After the festival and a brief stop-over in Cheltenham we returned to Colchester to attend a concert that happened to fall on 21st June, a date that marked an anniversary for us as two years previously, outside the Sacre Cour in Paris, Alison had rashly agreed to be my wife. It was peculiar though, that for all Colchester's familiarity I felt no sense of coming home. I first arrived there as a shy and awkward student nurse, squeezed into a room in the nurses' home. I spent three years there training, more years working as a qualified nurse, took my driving test, was a school governor, a union official, worked in the town centre, bought my first house, got married, raised a family, got divorced, attended many functions, events and concerts, arranged gigs, used our living room as a concert venue, made many lasting friends and generally worked, slept and played in the town for 30 odd years. Alison moved in for the last two and from that point life took a different direction.

The town itself seemed featureless and slightly moribund when approaching it as a visitor. What I did miss, apart from friends, was the thriving DIY music and arts scene, the bustling little side streets and the odd little glimpses of its history that poke out from years of thoughtless town planning; fragments of the Roman town walls embedded in the basement of a new shopping precinct, the Siege House restaurant with its bullet holes from the Civil War, the fine Norman castle keep that appears from around an unpromising corner at the ragged end of the High Street, and the hidden ruins of St Botoph's priory, hiding its grandeur behind a busy street of kebab shops and cheap supermarkets.

We were staying with friends who'd rather foolishly agreed that we could park Mavis on their drive and then went the extra mile and invited us to stay in a proper bed, treated us to a delicious homemade curry and generally spoilt us. We went to the concert together that evening and thoroughly enjoyed it as the artist was a local singer/songwriter, and friend, Adrian Nation. Adrian played at one of our house gigs when we still lived in Colchester, played at our wedding and has generally brightened our lives with his music, as well as being a charming and erudite bloke who makes a mean cheesecake.

We enjoyed another fine meal the following day when we called in to visit my youngest son, before wrecking his flat by trying out his new micro drone with varying degrees of success. He and Alison soon got the hang of it, but my attempts ranged from useless to very useless. I've never been the most coordinated of people and this rather underlined it. I played soccer for a youth club many years ago; I suspect it was to make up the numbers. Somehow football combined both my lack of coordination and my inability to do more than one thing at a time. On one notable occasion I made a fabulous run from my team's 18yd box, effortlessly swerving past startled opposition players and found myself tantalisingly close to their goal. I raised my right foot to shoot, only then realising that the ball wasn't there. In fact, I'd left it just outside our 18yd box and it had since enjoyed life in the company of the opposition and was now nestled safely in the net at the back of our goal.

After a while I progressed from being awful at football to adequate, generally the level that guaranteed a starting place in Saxmundham Youth Club B team. While my feet could normally be relied upon to work together or at least chop down a forward (this being in the days when anything short of a firearm was considered okay for a defender to deploy) I never got the hang of heading. In the unlikely event that my head made contact with the ball I'd stumble about in a state of mild concussion admiring the pretty lights. A football that bounced off my team mates' heads like a helium balloon would strike me like a bowling ball fired from a cannon. Some primal survival instinct forced my eyes to close at the crucial moment, so the ball could strike my back, an arm or a startled opponent. Our goal keeper got so used to my ineptitude in the air that when we conceded a corner he'd tackle me first.

Back in the flat I tried getting the drone to hover at eye level, and thus sent it under the sofa from where it reappeared in a spray of dust and loose change to ricochet off the wall, a plant and finally to rest in Alison's hair. Twenty minutes later, having solemnly sworn never to touch it again we extracted the last rota blade from her head and left him to pick up broken crockery, wash bits of cactus off the walls and clean chocolate cake up from where I'd been sitting.

While in the area we took the chance to vote in the Brexit referendum to decide once and for all whether we muck up the country ourselves or let someone else help us. The result was a shock; we spent a while over breakfast contemplating what it would mean. With the benefit of hindsight it seems like the result caught everyone by surprise, including those who campaigned for it.

DOWNWARDLY MOBILE

* * *

In a thoughtful frame of mind, we joined others for a friend's annual camping trip at Hinton in Suffolk. It was through this mutual friend that we'd met 6 years ago. Truth is we didn't really meet until 5 years ago as that first year I'd been off playing football and frisbee most of the time, and when I wasn't I was quaffing whisky. The following year though, a beautiful vision wafted towards me through the smoke of the BBQ as I was stabbing a sausage, and introduced herself as Alison. Following that weekend we exchanged many emails and arranged our first proper date, so we share a lot of affection for this annual trip. The party was a mixed affair of those who were fervently pro Brexit, staunchly anti-Brexit and those who were indifferent, but we all knuckled down to have fun, play games, moan about the football and generally enjoy each other's company. Irrespective of our differences, our similarities and shared hopes were far stronger than our differing opinions on the referendum.

Over the years we have stayed on many different campsites around this area of East Anglia. One year we tried a site where, on a rainy afternoon, one of our party discovered that the reason his electric hook up had shorted out was because it was delivered via two domestic extension cables, joined by plug and socket and wrapped in a supermarket carrier bag in a futile attempt to keep the rain off. The covered pool we'd been promised was essentially a paddling pool with a tarpaulin stretched over it and the only place to avoid the particularly fierce insect life was in a radius of about 20 feet around the septic tank, where the smell made your earwax melt and caused dogs to whimper. On the plus side we were pretty much left to our own devices and so we'd cook over an old cattle trough where the heat became so intense you could cook a burger by throwing it frisbee style to a companion on the other side of the flames. Proper cooking over it was impossible. Meat would start to singe before you could place it on the grill, and once there you'd have a window of about 30 seconds before you'd stagger from the smoke with a soot stained face, streaming red raw eyes and no eyebrows, holding a smouldering ember on a pair of metal tongs that were so hot they were beginning to droop.

Saturday morning found us up and about in various stages of alertness, from ridiculously perky to 'sod off and leave me alone'. The morning was hot and sticky and after a communal breakfast we settled into daytime activities; walks to the local shop, dog walking, games and general lounging around in the sunshine. The weather started to turn though, and the afternoon and evening grew steadily wetter, although we did manage to get the BBQ's going in a light drizzle in typically stoic English fashion.

Ray Canham

* * *

The weekend over and people dispersed we moved on to a nearby site that I've visited many times in the past with my children as they grew up. It sits in Rendlesham Forest, now recognised as a haven for birdlife, including the elusive kingfisher and is a special protection area for the nightjar and woodlark, whatever they are.

Sitting outside in the evening with the dying sun poking through the trees house martins kept us amused by dive bombing insects and flitting over the open spaces. A lone fieldfare stalked around under a tree, eyeing us watchfully, taking to the air with only the slightest movement. There were plenty of woodland creatures too, a gaunt fox skulking around the bins, squirrels bounding skittishly around and rabbits, hundreds of them, from old grey ones to tiny babies, perfect replicas of their older kin. Their gait appeared awkward, half hop, half lunge forward. When they sensed we were approaching they'd sit up, ears turned towards us and inscrutable soft brown eyes unmoving but always watchful. If we got too close, they would casually hop away, white tails flicking defiantly, but when startled or if we were between them and the safety of the hedge they'd break into a run, sleek to the ground, darting and changing course by acute 45-degree angles to escape predators. The baby ones seem tamer and would nonchalantly hop off as we approached but seldom seemed to startle. Occasionally one would take flight, stop for a moment to graze then continue its flight.

Apart from seeming to house 50% of the world's rabbit population Rendlesham Forest is also well known as the site of supposed UFO sightings in 1980. There is even a UFO trail you can follow to see…well, to see trees; it's not like the interplanetary visitors left anything behind. Maybe the credence given to the story, in some quarters at least, comes from the witnesses being serving USAF personnel who reported strange lights in the sky and took above average radiation level readings. Whatever it was there does appear to have been something odd, but not necessarily extra-terrestrial; remember all this took place during the cold war, when service personnel were on high alert. Some reports talk of a downed Russian Cosmos satellite, which was covered up for security reasons, and in 2003 an ex-security policeman alleged that he and a colleague made the whole thing up using car headlights and a loudspeaker, which seems the most plausible explanation to me.

Back in Mavis our night's sleep was disturbed by low flying aircraft and what sounded like engines running on the nearby runway. Annoying though it was, it reminded me of growing up around here and watching the American planes overhead; the loud Phantom with its odd down-turned rear wings, the mighty Hercules dragged up through the sky by four whining propellers, the stubby silver

A-10 Tankbuster with its cannon poking through the nose, the Jolly Green Giant twin rotor helicopter and my favourite, the sleek F-16 Falcon. I loved planes of all sorts so to catch a glimpse of them in flight, as well as the occasional spy plane carrying huge satellite dishes on its back, was a treat.

Our choice of transport today was decidedly less sexy than a sleek fighter jet. We saddled up and headed off to nearby Orford by bike. We both love Orford and have made a few visits to it with friends, and I came here often as a child on school trips or just cycling over with friends because the castle was free then and there was a pub nearby with a particularly relaxed attitude to licensing laws. Our first stop was Orford Quay, from where you can see, and nowadays visit, Orford Ness. The Ness is a spit of pebbly beach that separates the river from the sea until it finally reaches Shingle Street. I was going to name the river, but this being Suffolk at some point The Alde becomes The Ore and it's not worth upsetting the locals by getting the dividing point wrong. The spit of Orford Ness is created by longshaw drift (see, occasionally I did pay attention at school) and was a place of great mystery and intrigue when I was a youngster as it was most definitely out of bounds to civilians. The most notable feature then was an enormous shell shaped array of radio masts and the oddly shaped bunkers on the island. More about those anon, today we were going to Orford Castle.

Only the polygonal shaped keep is left standing, prominent amongst earthworks marking former walls. It is a fine example of a keep, with well-preserved rooms built into the walls where you can feel the history surround you. The castle itself was built between 1165 and 1173 by Henry II for the sum of £1,413. It's a prominent landmark on the low-lying Suffolk coast, looming over the town of Orford whose pattern of streets are little changed since the castle was built. The castle is embedded in the local scenery in other ways too, as most of the outer walls have been spirited away to be reused in local buildings. The castle sports some interesting graffiti, carvings of names and dates into the stone, the oldest I found dated from 1628 and included an intricate geometric carving.

Inside, Alison opted for the recorded guide but I just wandered, partly in awe of the castle-makers skills and partly re-living past visits; the place where Simon G sprayed everyone with Coke because he'd just cycled 7 bone-shaking miles with it; the spot where Chris K used the 'pee hole' in the castle Chamberlain's former quarters; the steps we'd sit on around the Great Hall making up stories about girls and discussing what we'd do if we'd lived in medieval times, which as far as I recall largely consisted of sex and torture; the balsa wood glider we tried to launch from the roof, which nose-dived into bushes, never to be seen again and from that same roof trying to see into the mysterious Orford Ness and wondering what went on behind its closed doors. Probably sex and torture we concluded.

The one big difference from my school day visits is that English Heritage have converted the area immediately inside the entrance, over an oubliette as I recollect, into the ticket office and gift shop. I can understand selling postcards and toy swords but why does every heritage centre, stately home, castle and museum insist on becoming an expensive delicatessen too? I've never wandered around a castle, peered closely at paintings, enjoyed the displays of torture implements, read the stories about castle life and thought, *'I know, what I require to polish off this visit to the 12th Century is an overpriced jar of raspberry conserve and box of fudge with a faded postcard glued to it.'*

Our route back included a little off-road jaunt, which we enjoyed from the waist up. Everything below, legs, buttocks etcetera bumped along protesting with new and interesting types of pain and promised much sufferance later... and did not disappoint. This made it all the more surprising when the following day we decided to try cycling again, this time to visit nearby Woodbridge. We set off gingerly; slowly lowering numb posteriors onto saddles made of solid concrete and trundled along roads that were familiar to me from living in the area for many years, although somehow I didn't recall them having the Alpine like gradients that we seemed to encounter now. As we trudged ever on, our distinct cycling styles became apparent. Alison had something of the Victorian lady in her approach, sitting erect upon the saddle, elegantly deported and maintaining a steady pace. I attacked the hills, legs spinning like the Roadrunner cartoon character while travelling at the speed of a caterpillar towing a steamroller, until, cresting the hill I'd collapse wheezing onto the handlebars. Meanwhile Alison glided up at the same stately pace, summited, and gracefully slowed to a halt. Time stood still until gravity took back control and she gently toppled sideways against a wall.

My progress was further hampered by the bike's unfamiliar 18 speed gears. Most of them seemed to be made for sweaty folk in stretchy shorts to cruise up and down the Pyrenees. To keep me on my toes the colour coding for up and down gear changes was reversed on each handlebar, thus I'd often change from a steady cruising gear to a much harder one just as I reached the foot of a hill. Frantically pushing levers, I'd hit every gear between 2nd and 17th in one angry grinding crunch until finally something appropriate for the terrain eventually clunked into place. By this time I'd have careered off the road and over the pavement, scattering startled pedestrians, burst through a hedge and out the other side pursued by an angry squirrel, to re-join the road with a birds nest on the handlebars and corn poking from the wheels, searching frantically for Alison lest I'd joined a different road altogether, and eventually find her chatting amiably to a stranger two miles further on, to whom she'd patiently explain that, *'it's okay, my husband's experimenting with bicycle camouflage'* before promising to exchange Christmas cards, thanking them for the invite to their daughter's wedding and with a cheerful *'Hup'* heading off leaving me bright red and slumped across the frame.

Woodbridge is a charming town on the River Deben, boasting a High Street heavy on quaint tea shops and designer outfitters, a working tide mill and an old-world cinema of the single screen type now to be found only in such places where they are lovingly preserved. We shopped a bit, had lunch and returned via a different route to take in some fun off road tracks, which were fine downhill but less fun heading upwards on sandy paths. Our bodies again promised retribution and thus our evening was spent creaking and groaning every time we moved.

※ ※ ※

In order to rest our complaining joints we took Mavis to Southwold. It's a town of contrasts. Once it was a thriving fishing harbour that was home to salty seagoing types who worked ridiculously long and gruelling hours in one of the most dangerous jobs in the world. Nowadays most of the tiny terraced fishermen's cottages are deluxe holiday homes for the sort of people who buy 4X4's to drop their children at school and whose closest affinity to the sea is to wear expensive nautical themed clothes and wellingtons with dolphin patterns on. It competes with Aldeburgh to be the east coast's most middle-class resort. It's famous for its pier, lighthouse and Adnams brewery. Speaking as one who remembers Adnams being delivered on horse drawn drays, their designer shop, full of cheese making kits, oils, unction's and expensive knick-knacks is slightly depressing. That said they're a successful company and if that means marketing your beer to people who think they need an Adnams drip mat and a copper fondue set then so be it. Actually, I think I have an Adnams drip mat somewhere but I'm pretty sure that I stole it from a pub.

The town itself has some wonderful nooks and crannies, stunning views and charming shops, and joy-upon-joy had a record fair where Alison deposited me in the company of the surly proprietor while she joined her friend for some serious shopping. Having spent my pocket money I wandered a bit and sat on the breezy sea front listening to a family on the adjacent bench munch and moan their way through fish and chips. The youngest girl, I'll call her Chomper, would alternate between taking a bite and wiping the grease down her trousers. Father chastised her for this between every bite, with no apparent effect until his wife intervened and handed her a moist towelette, prompting the other daughter, who I christened Fangs, to demand one too, spraying the pavement with half-digested fish. Clearly Fangs thought this was favouritism towards Chomper and such behaviour must be challenged immediately without recourse to chewing and swallowing. I wanted to ask them if they always have to eat outside because they dine like this but I remembered Alison's lecture on not upsetting people, so I sauntered off to find some grass to wipe the half-digested fish I'd stepped in off my shoe. I found Alison with her friend in the Swan Hotel where we ate shortbread biscuits and drank tea. It was very civilised, and we masticated quietly and wiped the corners of our mouths with starched white napkins as one should in Southwold. News and gossip exchanged we walked back to our parking spot in Walberswick, which sits on the other side of the river across from Southwold harbour and until comparatively recently was Southwold's poorer cousin. It seems quite gentrified now and with easy access to Southwold via the ferry or old railway bridge is well suited for a quiet holiday.

I stayed here once as a child with my parents and an aunt, uncle and cousin, but my only recollection is of sliding down the banister and hurting my knee. I was a bored near-teenager at the time and much as I try that's all I can recall of the house. I know we walked over the railway bridge to Southwold and the smell of gorse still transports me back to those days. I played on the cannons on Gun Hill and we took brisk walks along the front, brisk walks being a form of free family entertainment favoured by my father, although his definition of entertainment was close to the opposite end of the scale to mine. We'd wander onto the pier, my aunt wrapped up in about 17 layers against the chill easterly wind, so much colder here than her native Pinner. If the wind caught her unexpectedly her windcheater coat would inflate like a balloon and she'd squeal through polished ruby lips in mock horror, arms flapping down her sides as she sought to restrain it before she was borne aloft on the breeze and set down in the North Sea, or worse still, Belgium.

In some ways it's sad that I recall so little. For all I tease him now he's gone my father worked hard to provide family holidays. Thanks to his careful budgeting and willingness to brave out of season east coast weather we got a couple of holidays in each year. I was fortunate in so many ways but, as is often the way of teenagers, monumentally ungrateful for what I now treasure.

With the tang of nostalgia in the air we called in to see my mother who lives close by. Our visit coincided with the centenary of the start of the battle of the Somme and she was watching the commemoration service on TV when we arrived. It sparked some conversation during which we discovered that my great grandfather was wounded at The Somme and walked with a limp ever after. Evidently this wasn't enough to stop him fighting and he was eventually invalided out of the army after being gassed. Entranced, we listened to many stories from my mother about her relatives, stories that she hadn't had any inclination to share before and if I am honest I had no interest in hearing as a young and moody teen. We learnt that her maternal grandmother was *'a bit of a girl'* who had seven children in total and many dalliances, including allegedly with her own step sons. She married the person my mother knew as her grandfather complete with three children already in tow, one of whom was *my* maternal grandmother. Her new husband also happened to be the brother of her ex. My mother recalls going off to stay with *'Uncle Harry'* then after a rueful silence added...*'there were so many Uncle Harry's...'*.

Her paternal grandparents were from Old Harlow; she was a hardworking woman and he had the greatest job title ever...Peacock Feather Curler. Apparently curling feathers for hats was an occupation that suited him as he was prone to epileptic seizures. We heard about a female relative called *'Old Dollops'* who had *'great big hands, with knuckles like walnuts'* but was awfully kind. There were stories about people with names that place them in times gone by, of Albert, George, Hilda, Grace, Elsie and of Alice who took my mum out shopping, always calling afterwards into a Lyons Corner House for tea and cake. A morning of cheerful reminiscing done we wound our way back to Rendlesham in good time to greet friends from Colchester who, with their young daughters, were unwise enough to agree to camp next door to us for the weekend.

After a thoroughly pleasant evening with our new neighbours we awoke to a cloudy but dry day and opted for a return visit to Orford. They drove, and we chose to cycle and rendezvous with them at the castle, before a slightly hurried lunch to enable us to catch the ferry to Orford Ness Island. Incidentally it's not an island; it's a spit of land but is known locally as The Island. The spit starts at Slaughden, which sits to the south of Aldeburgh. It's not much more than home to a Martello Tower and the yacht club now but was once a thriving shipbuilding port before falling victim to the coastal erosion that the east coast is known for. To the north of Aldeburgh was the city of Dunwich, which was the size of medieval London and is now little more than a single street, testament to the power of the North Sea.

Orford Ness has been variously a test centre for very early aircraft, home to a lighthouse, a weapons and armaments research and testing station, was instrumental in the development of radar, housed the experimental Cobra Mist radar station - the vast shell shaped array of aerials that so bewitched us as children - and umpteen other functions, many clandestine and secretive. It now houses a radio transmitter for the BBC World Service and is a National Nature Reserve, home to rare plants and rarer still vegetated shingle ridges, migrating birds, saltmarshes and provides grazing land for rare breed sheep. As I said before, the island was a place of great mystery to me growing up and although I have visited once before with my then young children, I was eager to see it again and armed myself with the excellent book *'Most Secret, The Hidden History of Orford Ness'* by Paddy Heazell. Our trip this time was extra special because we took an escorted trailer ride around the island on a tour that the driver/guide was at pains to point out absolutely was not a guided tour, despite the fact that he provided us with an astonishing amount of fascinating information about the site in exactly the manner of a guided tour.

The flat landscape provided the perfect big sky experience, with only the red and white candy-striped lighthouse standing stark against a restless bronze sea and powder blue sky with foamy white clouds. Inland, Orford castle and church flanked the town, most of which was hidden by trees except along the quayside with the black fishermen's huts on shallow stilts and small boats bobbing about at anchor on the river. Leaden clouds gradually moved in from left to right, rain like a fine net draped across the horizon while we stood watching in sunshine.

The wind was up and the scenes over the mainland weren't encouraging but we made it back across on the small ferry in comfort, and parted with our friends for our separate journeys back to the campsite. Cycling out of Orford the wind became fresher and buffeted us from all directions. Nevertheless we made good progress until around halfway back a few heavy spots of rain warned us of trouble to come. Within seconds of the first few spots the deluge started, small hailstones ricocheted off our helmets, rain fell so hard it bounced up to have a second go and the road became shiny and slick with running water. Alison was leading and forged ahead gallantly while I kept my eyes firmly fixed on her rear wheel. As swiftly as the rain started it stopped. The road steamed where the sun hit it, the water that coursed along the gutters slowed to a trickle and we saw a rainbow, a bright arc against the dull watery sky.

We stopped to wring ourselves out and then panted up the hill out of the village of Butley, through puddles and onto roads where it seemed that no rain had fallen at all, and down to the site where the advance party had kindly prepared tea in anticipation of our arrival. They were perplexed by our sogginess as they'd had no rain at all and to this day I'm not sure that they believe that we were caught in a sudden storm. Cleaned up and dried off we had a barbeque and an evening of chatting and generally putting the world to rights. For all our travelling and meeting new and interesting people, for all the sights, sounds and smells of our adventures, for every new place visited, for every festival worked, sometimes the simplest pleasures are a pot of tea and old friends for company.

After lunch the following day we exchanged fond farewells and left to our own devices we decided to try the 6 mile off-road way-marked course through the woods on our bikes. It was a glorious ride out. It took a while to acclimatise to bumpy tracks; Alison started singing...'*you shake my nerves and you rattle my brain...*' and I joined in with a heartfelt and appropriate '*Great balls of fire...*'

Our confidence grew as the bikes were shaken up. Neither of them have suspension so when I started taking sections seriously and finding the small jumps and hillocks that make downhill on a mountain bike so much fun Alison reminded me that the bikes were not only borrowed, but in fact borrowed from a vicar so if damaged, thunderbolts may be forthcoming. We passed through shaded glades and woodlands of sweet smelling pine, through deep sand traps and boggy puddles, along hard packed mud tracks cut into the grass, down steep drops, up winding paths, picking our way around tree roots and along pebbly tracks. We passed families with tiny children on tiny bikes, were overtaken by serious mountain bikers on a mission and slalomed around dogs off their lead. We were whipped by ferns, briars caught on our sleeves, low branches pinged off our helmets and mud splashed our legs. We paused at 5 miles to check the route and in the act of dismounting my pedal slammed into my knee. Alison remarked that only I could ride furiously for 5 miles off road and injure myself while stationary and reading a signpost. Nevertheless, we enjoyed every second.

* * *

Fresh from our exertions and the mundanities of packing up complete we called in to a relative of Alison's who is an inspiration to everyone fortunate enough to meet her. Comfortably past her 90th year she was still driving, entirely self-sufficient in a delightful flat and has the sort of twinkle in her eye that betrays a wicked sense of humour. Her life story should be a book in its own right. Marrying an ex German prisoner of war just after the end of hostilities was the only the start of an engaging biography that has been marked by a stoic and cheerful outlook on life.

Duly invigorated by our visit we set off for Peterborough. I'm always a little suspicious about big sites that claim to be intimate and close to nature, but this was a splendid place, in part because we appeared to be by far the youngest people on it, and that includes some of the pet dogs being dragged around like dusty carpets. In the evening we went for a stroll around the park. It was the tail end of a warm day and we were joined by dog walkers, joggers, cyclists and fellow walkers in the ample parkland and woods set around three lakes. Couples wandered aimlessly, fisherman sat staring intently at the waters, families trailed pushchairs loaded with the detritus of picnics, over-tired toddlers and older siblings on scooters wished the slopes only went down, a couple of young boys played football and provided their own simultaneous commentary, hearing the roar of the stadium as they delivered the perfect arching shot past the keeper, and then were brought back to real life by having to retrieve the ball from nettles, and a large group of mixed race, gender and age playing an energetic game of dodgeball just for the fun of it. It was all quite becoming, and we wandered back to Mavis in a quiet but contented mood.

We wanted some time to visit Peterborough Cathedral so took the walkway/cycleway that runs from the park and is sandwiched between the Nene Valley Railway and the river Nene. It provided a pleasant, peaceful path, mostly through countryside and then into the city centre. Only for the last half mile or so did it become more urbanised, as the path joined the River Nene to pass under an assortment of iron railway bridges. Crossing the river, we came first to the rather dull and uninspiring Rivergate shopping centre. Based around a supermarket it's one of those brick monuments to consumerism that seems to host all the slightly embarrassing shops that a town wants to hide away; pound shops, gift shops selling the type of cards you get as a child from an aged aunt showing racing cars or kittens playing with a ball of wool, and huge badges that declare you are 21, or 40 or whatever and that you would be embarrassed to wear even in the most drunken of states. We wanted to pop into the café for a revitalising cuppa but the old boy sitting outside looked like he'd moved on to a better life – presumably one that didn't involve The Rivergate Centre, and his fellow customers weren't much less cadaverous, so we decided to try elsewhere; clearly the correct choice as once we'd crossed a busy road the rest of the town centre was a delight.

At street level was the usual array of brash glass shop fronts you find in any town but look up and you see that the upper stories around the wide central square have been carefully preserved. There's a large medieval market square with the gateway to the cathedral at one end and the church at the other, between them modern fountains spurt directly out of the paving, hazardous to the unwary adult but a source of great delight to young children. The far end boasts a splendid market hall built of soft golden stone resting on pillars. It's a fine centrepiece but was decked out in patriotic bunting and a big picture of the Queen to mark her 90th birthday which disguised its imposing stature somewhat.

The cathedral is, of course, a magnificent building. An imposing 13th Century Gothic style with 3 central arches sandwiched between two ornate towers. The architect clearly liked arches. There isn't an inch of stonework that isn't carved or moulded into an archway, whether it's a window or for decoration. Only at the top of each of the three central archways have they placed a round window, probably inserted there to piss off the architect after he went home early one evening.

We were greeted outside by an attendant who told us there was a children's service taking place inside, but we were welcome to have a wander round. He sold us a photo permit and guide book for a total of £6. There was no admission fee, no hard sell and a pleasing lack of commercial space, just a modest gift shop tucked away in a corner. The no frills attitude continued with a modest but interesting series of display boards explaining the cathedral's history, and tucked out of the way in plain wooden display cases were a small collection of the interesting and quirky, such as ornate gold chalices and the remains of an incendiary bomb dropped on the cathedral in WW2.

The choir stalls had the comfortable aroma of polish and candles and the shiny patina of regular use. To the front of the stalls, in the nave, a golden figure of Jesus hung from a blood red 'rood' cross, sinister empty eye sockets looking down over an emaciated body, across the spacious nave and towards the 13th century marble font. It's a potent symbol and is visible from almost the entire cathedral. It is also relatively contemporary, completed and hung in the 1970s. But for all its ornate carving it looked curiously out of place, dwarfed against the 4 story high walls. It hangs below a wonderful painted ceiling, which retains the original 1250 design. In fact, the ceilings throughout are impressive; a luscious blue with gold above the Presbytery and in 'The New Building' (new in this case being 1509) each of the carved pillars fans out onto the ceiling in a series of intricately carved, yes you guessed it, arches.

The cathedral has its own music school for choristers, and we joined them for Evensong. I tried to mumble along until somewhere into the second hymn Alison pointed out that they were singing in Latin, which explained my worse than usual vocal performance. Instead I sat back and let the crystal-clear voices waft over me; strange harmonies in an alien language, beautiful and moving, drifting upwards in the vast space above and far better without my accompaniment. After the service we walked back the way we'd come and settled in for the night, unaware of the drama that was about to befall us. From first light the site was alive with rumour, gossip and huddled chatter about the dramatic events of last night. Angry letters were being composed on carefully preserved Basildon Bond stationery and sent post haste to the president of The Caravan Club. Grandchildren would soon be sitting in rapt awe as they were regaled with stories of *'the night that the site in Peterborough had a power cut'*. I expect special commemorative tea towels were being ordered. In years to come we will be able to say to naive young caravaners barely out of their 50's that *'You weren't there man...'* when they scoff at us. If I was the cynical type, I'd suggest that for many people here this was the most exciting thing that had happened to them for quite some time. As it happens I am the cynical type and I'm fairly certain that for quite a lot this *was* the most exciting thing to happen to them for some time, certainly after dark. One chap approached me and asked if the power was out for us too. I affirmed that indeed this was the case and he informed me he thought he'd caused it operating his electric pump. I smiled and went about my business wondering why he'd need a pump in his caravan. Probably to inflate his girlfriend I concluded.

* * *

We left the site to the repairman, who was being harangued at every opportunity by the powerless and therefore prevented from restoring the very power they craved. It was a long haul to Northumberland but Mavis took it in her stride and we trundled up to our campsite in good time. It was a peculiar place on a farm, set back from an arrow straight road leading to Hadrian's Wall a mile to the north. The site had all the usual facilities and the owners were clearly trying hard to run a large arable farm as well as the caravan site. Many of the caravans appeared to be permanently stationed with elaborate picket fences, dim solar lights and awnings turning green from accumulated debris and damp. What we think were probably turkeys but may have been a form of mutant chicken created by the site's owners during those long dark Northumbrian winter nights wandered around scratching in the dirt. It was all a little forlorn.

The maintenance seemed to be done by their elderly father, who pottered around in a golf cart and clearly lacked company. Alison of course soon fell into conversation with him, so seizing my chance I snuck into the shower while he was diverted. They were still chatting when I re-emerged in a haze of shower gel, citrus and wasp or something equally butch. Whatever it was it kept the insects away and once Alison had extracted herself from conversation about goodness knows what, and we were both refreshed, we went for a walk to Hadrian's Wall...which was missing. It runs for over 80 miles and we chose the one spot where someone has stolen it. Undeterred we took a stroll along the path where Alison somehow managed to find the only stone of the wall left in these parts and promptly tripped over it. Back at the van we discovered that if we'd turned left instead of right for our walk we would have found it soon enough. Goodness knows what damage she'd have done if we had.

The reason we were in Northumberland was The Corbridge Festival. When we started planning our summer in Mavis we put a note on social media asking if anyone wanted help at festivals over the summer. A friend of a friend suggested we might like to help at Corbridge and sold it to us on the strength of the line-up and beauty of the area. We arrived nice and early so that we could spend a little time exploring the town. Set around the church and market square it's a quaint and picturesque place in a stunning location. It boasts lots of independent shops, including a butchers, greengrocers and bookshop. The children's outfitters had a sale of organic clothes in the window which probably gives you an insight into the nature of the town's inhabitants. If that doesn't then the eye watering prices in the estate agents will. Nevertheless, its charms were plentiful although its present status as a peaceful and upmarket town has been built upon centuries of turmoil. It's been burnt down three times, the price of being in contested border country; there's still a fortified vicarage in the town centre.

It sits uphill from the broad rust coloured River Tyne and the wide valley is lined with meadows and fields studded with bright poppies sweeping upwards to wooded hillsides with the occasional big house peeking out from the trees. On the south side farms and cottages lay amongst green and gold fields and dark woods on the steeper slopes. The majestic 17th century Corbridge Bridge still spans the river, today a busy single carriageway road. Incidentally it was the only bridge to survive the Tyne flood of 1771. The valley still floods in spite of modern defensive levees, the last time being in December 2015 when Storm Desmond struck. The Rugby Club where the festival was held was under at least 6ft of water after the storm, and work to repair the damage to the club house was due to begin on the day after the festival. All the houses nearby were being repaired as we drove in, although sensibly we noted the builders had made sure the pub and Indian restaurant were finished first.

CHAPTER 16

Corbridge Festival

Corbridge Festival is a few years old now and is attracting some big names. Although it's really a one day event the campsite opens and a couple of bands play in the beer tent stage on the Friday evening.

The site opened officially at noon on Friday so after a morning helping set up around the site and a break to get provisions from the town we commenced car parking duties. We've done this at a couple of festivals and the majority of customers are lovely folk who just come to have a good time and appreciate your help. The odd ones however find something to grumble at you about. At Corbridge we had a few who objected to having to park their car and walk to the campsite. This wasn't some Glastonbury style multi field event, they were parked in the same field they would be camping in. Some asked for special dispensation on a variety of spurious grounds which translated meant they couldn't be arsed to carry their boxes of beer 20 yards. When you are in a windy field, being rained upon and you've been on your feet for 6 hours, being polite to Mr and Mrs Audi driver is sometimes tricky. To tell them, *'no, you can't just park over there to set up the tent and return later, and maybe you could hurry up and park because there's a queue of nice folk in sensible cars who've travelled miles with fractious children in the back and are now stuck behind you while you try and negotiate special treatment because you drive a fucking Audi and have a boot full of Waitrose organic craft beer in recycled gluten free bottles and poor Gemma cannot possibly walk 20 yards as she might be allergic to ants...'* in a polite way is a skill.

But don't get the wrong impression about Corbridge, you get these folks everywhere and most of the time it's just because they've had a long journey and people don't see the logistics from the point of view of the organisers, who have to jump through numerous hoops to satisfy the local authority. Without doing so there would be no festival. The majority of the people who came to Corbridge were unfailingly polite and understanding. What also helped was the attitude of the organisers, who checked on us regularly, provided water and sun cream when necessary, gave us breaks, and reminded us that they appreciated our assistance.

By early evening we got away from car parking duty and wandered into the site for some food. Festival food has really improved in the last few years; the days of a choice between a slice of pig or a lump of grated cow in a bun are long gone. Not that I worry too much as I was brought up on my mother's cooking so a greasy burger in a stale bun with limp chips was a feast when I started going to gigs. I'm not saying my mother couldn't cook, but she really didn't have the patience or inclination to do so. To her the cooker had two settings, 0 and 6. As far as she was concerned numbers 1-5 were just to fill up the space on the knobs. Vegetables were served either as a soggy lump or raw. Often, for reasons I've never understood, she'd just fry them. I may be one of the only people to have experienced peas and whole carrots fried together in butter and served up as soon as the peas started to bubble. The peas were at best lukewarm and the carrots were raw. There's a good reason why this hasn't caught on. Guests not experienced in the eccentricities of her culinary feats have bent the tines of their forks trying to stab a lump of carrot. Come to think about it we didn't get many dinner guests...word soon gets around a small town.

She also seemed to believe the oven was sentient and would know when she expected whatever she'd put in it to be ready. My father and I would cheerfully eat the thin layer of moist fluffy baked potato sandwiched between the charred crispy outside and the solid centre. I was about 15 when I realised that potatoes didn't have a stone in the middle like an avocado. It didn't help that she was always busy and would forget that she had started to prepare dinner, blissfully unaware that she'd put something in the oven earlier. On more than one occasion she'd open the oven to put something in and to her surprise find a whole plated meal that she'd prepared the day before. She'd shrug and say, *'Oh Raymond, that's handy, you can have this'* handing me a red-hot plate of shrivelled fish fingers and beans.

My father accepted all this with charm and grace, although I suspect the only reason we had a dog is that it acted as a repository for all the crunchy bits we couldn't manage. In fact the dog always enjoyed the best food. We had a fishmonger call by twice a week with the morning catch still twitching in the back. My mother would purchase the freshest, whitest cod fillets and cook them until tender and juicy with crispy skin and perfect fluffy succulent flesh. My father and I would sit down, gently salivating and find charred fish fingers and instant mashed potato with fried carrots shoved in front of us while the dog got perfectly cooked cod. Not only that, she sprinkled herbs on the dog's dinner. So, festival food holds no fears for me.

After a late evening of litter picking the dawn arrived too soon, heralding the day of the main festival. The day went past in a bit of a blur, car parking, trundling big wheelie bins about the site, running errands, checking up on the campers and, when not otherwise engaged, litter picking.

During the afternoon Too Many T's, rappers with an energetic old school rapid fire hip hop style entertained everyone and worked the crowd well, especially since a largely middle class and middle age Northumbrian crowd were probably not their key demographic. They were whippet thin young men with bags of energy and skill, and they were also authentic South Londoners immersed in the scene. None of which applied to the fat, balding white men who thought it 'cool' to grin stupidly and 'throw shapes' and gang culture hand signs when they came on. One of them even put his hat on backwards. It's the same mentality that causes otherwise sedentary people to head-bang for 30 seconds when a heavy metal band comes on or pogo if it's a punk act. Maybe too much Pimms and Waitrose strawberries makes them lose the power of speech. Instead of leaning into their beloved and whispering – *'I think these chaps maybe a Hip and/or Hop outfit dear'* they had to communicate by interpretive dance. Twonks!

There's not a lot to say about the day after the festival. It was mostly litter picking and the innumerable other jobs that are needed to turn a festival and camping site back into a spotless rugby club. It was hard physical work but the team at the festival was great to work with and everyone was friendly, helpful and worked hard. Any festival of any scale stands or falls on so many variables, the line-up, the crowd, the weather for example, but overall what makes them, what actually delivers the atmosphere and energy, what brings punters back year after year, retains volunteers and crew, are the people at the helm. Corbridge was no exception. The organisers and crew were without fail charming, helpful and appreciative, all the more impressive when you consider the stress they endure during the build-up and during the festival itself. It's one of the main reasons we are working small to medium festivals, the ones that retain the personal touch and where we can make a difference in return for experiencing some delightful parts of the country and seeing some great acts.

CHAPTER 17

Romans, Rest and Recuperation

Northumberland, at least the part we saw around the Tyne valley and Hadrian's Wall, is simply stunning. We started exploring at Corbridge Roman Town, an excavated street and former Roman garrison which offers a fascinating glimpse into military and domestic life. The street drains, grain store with its ventilated floor and the foundations and floor plans of many buildings are all still there to see. What sets it apart though was the finding of The Corbridge Hoard, a wooden trunk filled with armour, tools, weapons and personal items. Most appeared to be broken so one theory is that it was set aside for repair or recycling. Whatever the reason it has provided a fascinating insight into Roman life here at one of the Empire's furthest outposts. The other artefact of particular note is The Corbrige Lion, a stone effigy of a lion standing over its kill. It seems that the experts can't agree on whether the victim is a stag or goat. Personally, I'm not sure that I'd call myself an expert if I couldn't tell a stag from a goat.

We wandered around transfixed by the fascinating little museum and were equally enchanted by the lady manning the gift shop, who insisted on giving us an itinerary of must-see places to do in a day. She loaded us up with bundles of maps and leaflets and seemed genuinely happy to be of assistance. She wasn't alone in this, the Northumberland people we encountered were almost without exception pleasant, interesting and keen to show off their county in a modest kind of way, almost as if it's a surprise to them that people want to come here and visit. Even the lady selling coffee at a desolate and remote carpark high on the hills above Hexham braced herself against gale force winds and told me about the area and the nearby Temple of Mithras. She bade me return if I should require a refill, more hot water and any amount of milk, sugar or a second cup if I fancied one. As I climbed into the welcome embrace of a heated Mavis she returned to her station to huddle up in the rain, warming herself around the espresso machine and pulled out a tatty paperback with pages flapping around in the wind.

Duly charmed and inspired to go further afield we took the rest of the day to drive along the former military road that runs parallel to the wall. The scenery was a delight, innumerable shades of green on smooth rolling hills with tufts of trees, remote stone cottages and almost empty roads. We stopped to enjoy a good scramble through the ruins of Housesteads fort. The views were to die for now the rain had abated and the sun was peeking through the clouds. One could imagine though just how bleak it was to be stationed up here through a Northumberland winter with raiders from the north waiting to surprise you with something sharp or clubby. On the plus side they had an onsite brothel and rather splendid communal latrines that have been well preserved and appear to exert an endless fascination to all who see them, especially young children. We didn't linger too long though as we had yet to secure accommodation for the night - which taught us a lesson.

* * *

We called ahead to what, according to the guide given out at the tourist information office, was a promising site. Our suspicions were raised though when we had to pass under an uninviting railway bridge and through an industrial estate. The lady who greeted us was amiable and talkative; she runs the site with her sister while they share caring for their 80 something year old mother. I thought it impolite to take notes while she was talking so I cannot recall their exact circumstances, but we got a whole family history spanning several generations of, from what little I remember, breeding and dying, punctuated by mundanity.

Our pitch was set among static holiday homes and was perfectly adequate but for the price we paid we expected at least serviceable facilities. The toilet block had clearly seen better days, some of them probably during the Roman occupation. The gents had one shower, which you accessed through improvised saloon doors made from an old kitchen worktop. The tray was dirty and cracked, the shower hose oddly lumpy and the shower head corroded. I've no idea how it functioned because to add to the sense of fun they expected you to pay 40 pence for the privilege of using it. Over the whole building there hung a curious aroma; hints of damp and mould with an undercurrent of effluent and high notes of dead animal. To help create the right atmosphere they'd thoughtfully put in brown tiles of a pattern that's never been in fashion and whitewashed the walls directly over the peeling plaster before lighting it with a yellowing 40-watt bulkhead light. Still, we survived the night and after a peaceful sleep we dodged whatever dire afflictions await anyone foolhardy enough to use the showers and decided to head south to a Caravan Club site in Cromwell, just north of Newark, where we'd be sure of cleanliness and bright lights.

* * *

Which is exactly what we got. After a short stroll to look at the quaint local church we retired and were lulled to sleep by the man 3 vans away who seemed to have no volume control. Accompanied by the occasional *'ummm'* and *'yes dear'* from his wife, he held court on all manner of things in loud staccato outbursts; *'My father would turn in his grave if he saw that…'* *'Want some bread with your butter?'* *'How does this work without a battery?'* and so on into the night. The last thing I recall hearing sounded like *'ducks, pa! I've seen more zebras playing golf….'*

After an eventually peaceful night our route took us in an arc from Grantham to Kings Lynn and then down to Thetford. The Lincolnshire Fens really are rather special; dull, monotonous and endlessly flat in a strangely hypnotic way. Broad, smooth fields of pale greens and yellows swept away from the road with arrow straight hedges little more than markers between the crops. Settlements of box like red brick houses sat alongside the roads at intervals, a legacy of the manpower once required to cope with the demands of the 4,000 plus farms of the greater fenland area, 70% of which is arable land growing cereal crops, ornamental flowers and plants, vegetables and fruit, alongside some livestock. The area we passed through was busy with articulated lorries constantly ferrying the yield and all manner of supplies back and forth as we made our way through the fens and into Norfolk.

Thetford Forest Centre is a tranquil place, secluded but benefiting from a café, cycle and walking way-marked routes, ample picnicking areas and a high wire adventure attraction. It was this that brought us here, not to take part but by kind invitation from friends to join them for a post adrenaline picnic. We enjoyed a wonderful afternoon, ate well and played games. At one point I had to hum a tune as a forfeit in a game and even the most musically accomplished failed to spot The Beatles 'Yesterday'. Then again, it's not that much of a surprise to me; at primary school I had a singing part in the nativity play until I opened my mouth. The Virgin Mary fainted, paint peeled, insects fell stunned from the rafters and there were suspicious puddles forming around small plimsolls. I was gently moved from a solo part as a wise man to the choir of shepherds and then less gently to a non-singing part as a tree.

The only drawback of the Forest Centre was the outrageous cost of parking. Oddly Alison and I have often disagreed on what constitutes a reasonable parking fee. As a Cambridge-ite she has been brought up to accept anything under three figures for a day as reasonable whereas I was raised by a father who would park in the next county if their car parks were 10p cheaper. Today however we agreed that the prices were extortionate. I know the money goes to a good cause, helping to maintain the forest, but we've paid less for overnight pitches with showers and electricity included than we did for 5 hours parking at Thetford forest.

* * *

Goodbyes said we took Mavis up to Hemsby on the Norfolk coast. Approaching it from Norwich we started going through holiday towns that rely upon tourists for their income. One such place was Filby which declared itself *'A lovely place to be'* on its elaborate village sign. *'A lovely place to be what?'* I wondered; a Smurf, dead, drunk maybe? Despite the inanity of the strapline it did indeed seem most becoming. The townsfolk obviously know how to grow flowers; every lamppost had hanging baskets suspended from them and most of the gardens and civic amenities were enlivened by elaborate arrangements of colourful blooms. I think they should seriously consider amending their strapline to *'A lovely place to be - if you don't have hay fever'*. Everywhere was very neat and tidy, almost sinisterly so. Alison felt it was the sort of place you'd soon get a visit from *'the committee'* if your lawn wasn't trimmed to the requisite length. We wondered if at the end of the season the hanging baskets were replaced by the heads of villagers who failed to maintain their grounds to a suitable standard.

I passed the time by inventing suitable inane straplines for other places around here where I'd stayed with my parents when this area of Norfolk was our regular holiday destination:

- Caister-on-Sea: 'Not quite a shithole'
- California: 'The name is where the similarity ends'
- Scratby: 'Shithole'
- Newport: 'The Sellafield of the south'

And so we rolled into Hemsby – strapline, *'At least it's not Scratby.'* We chose it because its home to a good site, close to a couple of places we wanted to visit and it had the added bonus of being gloriously tawdry. If Southwold is the Waitrose of holiday resorts then Hemsby is the Happy Shopper, bold, cheap and unpretentious.

The village is split in two by the Yarmouth Road. To the west lays the village proper; clustered around a school, modest shops and a social club are houses and bungalows of no great distinction. East of the road lay a few cul-de-sacs of neat retirement properties, the sort where the lawn gets cut twice a week because there's nothing else to do, and a fat little dog waddles up and barks half-heartedly when you walk by. The road then gently falls away towards the sea and is lined with holiday villages. The old Pontins was shut up and derelict but at least three more camps are still going. A couple of them looked like they'd seen better times, with peeling paint, hastily mowed lawns and weedy carparks. One did seem to be making a good go of it, with colourful flowers, tidy lawns and retro chalets that looked well kept. It felt like walking past a bit of a time warp. The clubhouses to these camps boasted of dubious delights, *'Stan Sings the Hits'*, *'Gary Page – hits of the 50's to 70's'* and whom amongst us could resist *'Rita's Red Hot Karaoke'*?

Further down the road Hemsby becomes a pulsating neon glare, vulgar, noisy and smelling of burnt sugar and fried food. Along this strip portly men wander, squeezed into football jerseys designed for trim athletic bodies, lads in vests that fall short of their sagging jeans follow them and women with taught determined faces herd sticky children and overexcited toddlers fighting sleep so they can have one more go on the mini dodgems. Older women with weathered faces play joyless bingo while their lobster red husbands sit outside reading the tabloids, their concession to being on holiday a pair of cheeky sandals to show off their crisp white socks.

The shops sell the usual array of cheap beachwear, confectionary in worryingly luminous colours and a new addition to the seaside (to us anyway) vaping supplies. There is a bewildering selection of accompaniments to choose from, including filters, batteries, various flavours and coils. I'm supposing this last one is a necessary part of vaping paraphernalia rather than holiday contraception. One shop that caught our eye had *New York-London-Paris-Rome-Hemsby* painted under its name. I find it hard to picture a supplier of beach toys and vulgar postcards having branches in the major cultural capitals of the world, I imagine the main culture in Hemsby requires antibiotics and a stern lecture from someone in a white coat rather than the hosting of internationally renowned arts and fashion outlets.

One thing Hemsby doesn't seem to do is decent food, particularly of the vegetarian variety. The Dolphin pub, based on the site where we were staying, had nothing, absolutely zero, on its evening menu that would pass as a meat free dinner unless you count a plain baked potato as a meal. A pub on the seafront boasted of a selection of veggie options with a proud green V next to each of them. One such dish was the Carrot and Courgette Spaghetti, served with sundried tomatoes and chicken breast. Now, I'm prepared to accept that some foodstuff can confuse, cheese for example may have animal rennet in it, but what sort of brain dead nincompoop believes that chicken is a variety of vegetable?

We noticed that the pubs, shops and the campsite we were staying on had racks of glossy leaflets on display whose sole aim seems to be to convince you that everywhere else is more exciting than Hemsby. Which may very well be the case, but we resisted the lure of boat trips, wildlife parks and model villages. This last one has always puzzled me; I've never quite understood the allure of a model village. My ever-resourceful father used to take us to a hill overlooking a real town for exactly the same effect and all for free; a win-win as far as he was concerned.

Meanwhile we had an evening appointment to watch the stock cars and banger racing at the nearby Great Yarmouth Stadium. We've both got histories of attending these events, Alison with her mother's parents and me with my father. We used to go to a grass track in Suffolk, cheerfully devoid of all but the most basic safety precautions. Dodging a flaming tyre was all part of the fun. Latterly I took my children to a small shingle circuit until a bypass was built over it. Occasionally we'd really splash out and go to a proper concrete arena. These were high octane affairs with plenty of spills, which, let's face it is the main attraction of motorsport. It's all very well watching a parade of F1 cars whizz round a track, but the real excitement happens when a car gets airborne or catches alight, ideally both, and if you have to duck to avoid a stray limb spiralling past so much the better. Back in Yarmouth we found ourselves a spot on the grass bank and watched cars crashing into each other. The racing seemed to be taken particularly seriously by the pit crews who got extraordinarily animated over supposed breeches of the rules. Quite how they could tell in the maelstrom of screeching tyres, crunching metal, roaring engines and noxious oily smoke was beyond us. It was terrific fun and one of us squealed and leapt about at every minor prang or nifty bit of overtaking and expressed genuine sorrow for the people who had to retire mid race.

On the way home, in one of those moments that even with the benefit of hindsight I simply cannot explain, I fell off my bike. To be entirely accurate, I was walking it across a busy road at the time. One minute I was sauntering out into a gap in the traffic and the next I'm laying underneath my bicycle looking up at a car coming my way. I bounced up before my limbs had a chance to protest, Alison waved the car down until I'd shuffled onto the pavement where she joined me. It was over in a flash and I was enjoying a jolly good swear when Alison, a look of affectionate pity on her face, took me gently in her arms, planted a kiss on my forehead and gently whispered in my ear *'only you could fall off a bike you weren't riding dear'*. Presently, with little more than a bruised ego and a sore knee to show for it we cycled back to Mavis.

* * *

Up the coast from Hemsby is the village of Winterton, where we walked the following day. It was a pleasing little community, sedate and tidy in an olde-worlde way. It had a variety of old cottages, many in the local flint, and a couple of shops, one of which seemed to have changed little since the 1950's except, maybe, some of the stock. It was in here that we stood with ice creams gently melting while the proprietor served the people ahead of us, engaging in meandering conversations and moving at the pace of a man who only gets a few customers a day and is determined to eke out every single one. We eventually got served, I dragged Alison out before the proprietor had the chance to strike up conversation and we left a trail of dripping ice cream as we set off towards Martham Broad.

The Norfolk Broads were mainly formed from the flooded remnants of medieval peat digging, lagoons joined by rivers snaking through low lying marshes and fields, and they now have National Park status. Some areas are protected and are off limits to casual users as they are nature reserves of national and international significance. They cover an area of around 117 sq. miles and attract around 8 million visitors a year, swamping the resident population which is only around 6,300. Mind you the visitors are estimated to contribute over £568 million a year to the local economy so I don't suppose many of the locals are that upset. The Broads are also one of the UK's driest places in terms of rainfall, as well as one of the flattest. The highest point is the mighty Strumpshaw Hill at approximately 38m above sea level. It might be of interest to the residents of Stumpshaw that if they climbed the hill 233 times they'll have exceeded the height of Everest. Then again it may not.

After walking in shade around the Broad we took an overgrown path beside the river bank in the full glare of the afternoon sun. The river was hidden behind an impenetrable border of reeds so afforded us no chance to cool off on its banks. Tantalisingly, faint breezes rippled the reeds and silvery willows but faded as quickly as they appeared. The grasses, reeds and thistles over the path scraped at our bare legs, which now stung with sweat. The air shimmered over the broad flat fields and a few cows lay around their water trough, tails lazily swooshing away the flies. Unseen insects buzzed and chirruped in the undergrowth and shimmering dragonflies zig zagged across our path as we passed a ruined red brick wind pump.

In the 1800's there were around 240 such pumps busily whirring away, most of them used for draining the marshes and pumping the water into the rivers and watercourses, but a few of them were more traditional windmills used for grinding corn. Today around 70 survive in various states of repair. To help me write this I started to look them up and found myself falling ever deeper into the precise orderly world of the wind pump enthusiast. I feared though, that in that direction lay tedious men with fussy moustaches and ruler straight partings, under which tidy minds buzz with specifics about fantail designs and faces contort with a sense of pity that the enthusiast reserves for people who don't take an active interest in their chosen specialty.

Gradually the path became more defined and we entered an area obviously used by anglers and dog walkers, which brought us to some welcome shade and the drag up a paved road to Martham. It's a pleasant settlement, set around two greens with a duck pond and a few traditional shops. Alison visited Martham with her former work colleagues on a regular basis, and along with Winterton beach it holds many happy memories for her, as well as reminding her of the good friends from back then who she is still in touch with and who enter our lives from time to time. We walked back along a busy road, through the long grass and litter on the verges, hopping drainage channels like 5-year olds until we could veer off to skirt the edges of fields of tall corn.

The following day was the hottest one of the year so far. The air was still and a haze hung over the countryside. Midday was eerily quiet; children were inside or sat at tables by their tents occupied by activities that didn't require energy. Slippery toddlers slathered in sun cream were frequently herded back to the shade by anxious parents and it seemed most people just slept or read in the shade of their caravans. Down on the beach the air was fresher and smelled of ozone and the sweet tang of drying seaweed. I stripped off to only my shorts, waded in and enjoyed a cheerful swim in the cool waters, diving under the rich camouflage green saltwater and bobbed up to find I was surrounded by jelly fish. Now, I've swum in the sea plenty of times and don't mind the odd one, but these were big buggers and taking evasive action only increased the chances of brushing into another one, so like the brave little soldier I am I flapped for the shore and emerged like a silent film of Oliver Hardy running into the sea played backwards. I scuttled up to Alison who was emerging from a cocoon of towels under which she had changed into something skimpy. I advised her of the jelly fish situation, so she just enjoyed a paddle and happily for me spotted a few jelly fish to verify my tales of heroic struggles on the Hemsby foreshore with these beasts of the sea and my eventual cunning escape to dry land for tea and medals.

The only task now awaiting me was to change out of my sopping shorts and into dry ones. Other people don't seem to have trouble with this. They wrap a towel around their midriff and 30 seconds later whip it aside to reveal a pair of pristine swimming shorts with everything tucked in, cord tied and the clothes they've removed neatly folded on the floor in front of them. I wrapped the towel around me, managing to do it up in such a way that the split down the side revealed my entire right flank up to my armpit. With a bit of jiggling I secured it more modestly and set about removing my wet shorts. This was of course entirely impossible. After much cursing and cheeky glimpses of white flesh to anyone unwise enough to be watching, I found I'd hopped and staggered a quarter of a mile up the beach. Now bent double and with one leg out and one inside my shorts and with my free hand clutching the towel I found most of the beach was stuck to my legs, making every movement feel like I was being caressed with wet sand paper. In an effort to secure the towel I reached in and grabbed what I thought was one end of the bit I'd knotted, realised that it wasn't and that I now had a firm grip on a part of my anatomy that a gentleman shouldn't grasp on a public beach. Letting go I made a grab for the towel, stepped free of the shorts and stood upright and set off on my long journey back to

Alison who I found was explaining to a passing stranger that I was affected by the tide.

At this point I'd like to apologise to the nice family whose lingering memory of their fortnight in Hemsby may well be the sight of my pale bottom waddling away because the knot in the towel had twisted round to the back, framing my buttocks like curtains in a theatre. Alison kindly pointed out that I was lucky no one was on the beach looking for a place to park their bike.

It was our last evening in Hemsby so we took a final stroll around the village and down to the sea front in the cooling evening air. For all its brashness, and even though it may be fuelled in part by calories and vulgarity, Hemsby is fighting a rear-guard action against foreign all-inclusive holidays and boutique resorts with all the pretentions they have on offer. Down the coast Southwold and Aldeburgh may have fancy beach huts, expensive restaurants, craft beers and shingle but Hemsby has chips, lager, fun and miles of fine golden sand with sheltered dunes and a shallow inviting sea. Everyone seemed to be making the most of their time to relax and enjoy themselves. It's all very working-class England in a way that's slowly vanishing, but while it remains it's a source of cheap, cheerful pleasure and long may it continue.

* * *

In the morning we said goodbye to Hemsby and Norfolk, crossed the border into Suffolk and stopped at a 1950's style diner for lunch. It was one of many independent restaurants we'd seen on our travels trying to bring life back to former Little Chef premises. It was spotlessly clean, the staff cheerful and attentive, although with only a few customers the ratio of staff to clientele was about 1:1. The food was good, if on the pricy side.

It happens that I experienced possibly the worst meal I've ever had that wasn't prepared by my mother in a Little Chef, so I applaud anyone that is trying to usurp them. On the occasion in question I knew as soon as my arms stuck to the table that I should have left immediately. The waitress tossed a menu on my table, a duplicate of the one I was reading so quite why I never discovered. Maybe in case I vomited on my copy. The whole place was dirty and unkempt, spiders had colonised the rafters and insects feasted on the debris around the skirting. I considered curious white marks on the carpet and concluded that they must have been from the staff trying to scuff out the chalk outline the forensic team left around a previous customer.

The food was so late I asked for it in a take away box as I needed to be elsewhere. Thus, the waitress, who I christened Adolf on account of her moustache and clear hatred of humanity, dumped what may have once been a vegetable-burger in front of me. In its short journey from the kitchen it had come completely apart in a box far too big for it, and now sat forlornly in an ooze of mayonnaise and limp lettuce. It brought to mind the stage in an operation when the surgeon turns to the nurse and informs her that there's nothing further they can do for this one except make him comfortable so stitch him up and get him back to the ward. It also arrived without the promised chips so I interrupted Adolf on her way to fetch more botulism and enquired after their whereabouts. 10 minutes later she delivered them on a plate. Not wanting to disturb her again in case I too became a chalk outline I went to the lady on the till and pointed out the idiosyncrasy of a takeaway in which half is served on a china plate and half in a box. Her face appeared to melt with concentration as she struggled with this delicate conundrum. It was like I had asked her to explain quantum theory in return for a tip. Eventually she offered to put them into the box with the burger but when I opened it for her she actually recoiled at the sight. After some negotiation I was given a separate box for my chips, and asked to pay for everything. Short of time and patience and frankly rather scared of Adolf lurking in the background I paid up and ceremoniously dumped the box containing the burger into the bin beside the till. The chips were awful too.

Back on our travels we were heading for Wincanton. After an overnight stop enroute we had to negotiate the A303 that skirts Stonehenge in all its underwhelming glory. The main feature today was the crawling traffic, not helped by people gawping at the stones while they were driving. A lot of people place great importance on Stonehenge, as an historical monument and as a spiritual centre, but for me the part of the journey I was most looking forward to was driving along the A303. This is because a song I rate as one of the best and most important of the 20th Century mentions it. *The Battle of the Beanfield* by The Levellers chronicles the violent clash between 'New Age' travellers and the Wiltshire Police on 1st June 1985.

The police were preventing a convoy of several hundred travellers, the so-called Peace Convoy, from setting up the 1985 Stonehenge Free Festival. After an initial skirmish at a roadblock 600 or so travellers took refuge in an adjacent bean field. After some further scuffles the police, numbering around 1300, attacked them in a brutal display of state endorsed violence. Pregnant women were clubbed, coaches and vans (people's homes) were smashed and children injured. 16 travellers and 8 police were hospitalised and eventually 537 travellers were arrested. Reports of the travellers having petrol bombs were falsely spread in the wake, but no evidence has ever come to light that supports any justification for the heavy-handed tactics. The Earl of Cardigan, on whose land the convoy had previously camped, witnessed the events and subsequently refused the police access to his land to *'finish unfinished business...I did not want a repeat of the grotesque events that I'd seen the day before'* he said.

Only one officer was found guilty of actual bodily harm in 1987, and in 1991 a civil court action awarded 21 travellers £24,000 in damages for false imprisonment, but as the judge didn't even award them legal costs it barely covered their legal bill. Whatever the rights and wrongs of denying access to the monument, whatever the tactics of some convoy members, and many were no angels, the response from the police was characteristic of a country in transformation; a country where tolerance and respect for alternative ways of life was challenging to the conservative mainstream and was being openly and sometimes violently repressed; a country where traditional industry was closing, where miner's jobs were being fought for, where whole communities were being decimated and there was an overriding sense that a bleak and threatening regime was struggling to retain order. The genius of The Levellers Battle of the Beanfield is that it captured the sense of threat, of violence and injustice and channelled it into a 3-minute song.

'Down the 303 at the end of the road
Flashing lights - exclusion zones
And it made me think it's not just the stones
That they're guarding' [iii]

I should point out that for the most part the Peace Convoy and others living on the fringes of society were handled if not compassionately then at least sensitively. As is ever the case, the police and authorities who handle anything controversial mostly do so with diplomacy and skill and therefore receive no attention in the press. The vast majority did a fine job in 1985 and still do, unrecognised and unheralded. To my eyes it's a sad state of affairs that good work seldom receives attention while bad and sensational news dominates the headlines. Unhappily, selling newspapers is more important than reporting the news and as a result we get a dismal view of the world that is distorted through the prism of editors eager to satisfy their shareholders.

I was still ranting on about the state of the world when we pulled into the Wincanton site and retired for an early night; fortuitously so since we had no idea of what lay in wait for us the next week. We had an appointment with God.

CHAPTER 18

New Wine Festival

New Wine is a Christian festival of talks, seminars, children's activities, worship and music spread over two weeks, with most delegates attending for one week or the other. New Wine itself is an international umbrella organisation for what I think of as charismatic 'happy-clappy' churches, although I'm sure that's not how they'd tag themselves on social media.

We awoke in good time to drive to the site a few miles away and after a leisurely breakfast checked the details and discovered that we should have been there the previous afternoon for a full stewards' briefing. As it happened the horrendous traffic of the day before would have prevented us getting there on time but nevertheless we rather felt we'd started on the wrong foot. Our fears though were unfounded as the crew, stewards and staff were unfailingly polite, helpful and gently dismissive of our apologies. The warmth we felt continued as we parked up at our little encampment over-looking the site, where we were joining friends who were there as delegates for the week. We started work that afternoon and settled in to meet our fellow stewards under the amiable guidance of our team leader.

New Wine is well organised, as befits the largest festival we've worked at, perhaps with the exception of Hay but that wasn't residential. Stewards were divided into teams and worked on a rota system. We found it tough at first, the hours were long and the shifts were often split so we'd get a few of hours off between morning and evening duties to eat and rest.

One duty was site patrols, where we'd wander around in our purple stewards' tee shirts with a high visibility jacket and a radio. Apart from the occasional misplaced child this was mostly a customer service job and on patrol we soon developed the plod, a slow walk where you swing each foot in turn, letting the downward momentum carry your boot on the upswing like a pendulum and thus one would proceed in an orderly fashion, slow and steady, alert for miscreants or anything amiss, like emptied fire buckets being used as goal posts or barbeques raging out of control.

The delegates got a day off from all the seminars, workshops and meetings on the Tuesday so many made haste for the supermarkets or for the local delights of Cheddar Gorge or Wookey Hole, which I thought was a pornographic Star Wars spin off but apparently is a cave system. Most decided to leave via the main gate en-mass. The organisers had a plan to cope with so many cars moving on site and our part in this was to be marshals directing traffic. I ended up as a kind of human roundabout at a major intersection in front of the main gate and Alison was doing a similar job on the opposite side of the site. About 99% of the drivers were patient and cheerful despite the volume of cars and Somerset Council's decision to deploy rolling roadworks on the main road outside the site on the same day that 10,000 people wanted to look at a valley of cheese or a Wookey's hole.

The mathematicians among you will of course realise that 1% are unaccounted for. These are the people who either drive Audi's or should go out and buy one so that the rest of us have fair warning. These were the folk who drove against the direction of traffic and insisted that they were correct despite all available evidence, like signs every 10 meters, gesticulating marshals at every junction and there clearly being no space on the road for two lanes anyway. One woman shouted at me for standing in her way to stop her careering into a family crossing the road and Alison had a similarly fractious altercation with someone who couldn't leave the site exactly when he wanted to because of a missing child alert. Credit where it is due though he sought her out later and apologised.

One duty I had was stewarding at a marquee during an afternoon showing of The Peanuts Movie. If a room full of sticky pre-teens wasn't grim enough the film was diabolically bad, although I guess a 50+ year old bloke in a neon vest wasn't the filmmaker's core demographic. Scanning the audience I could see that most children looked attentive but their parents less so. Generally fathers were asleep, stooping forward on their chairs, occasionally their head nodding violently so that they'd snort and jerk upright with wide eyes, trying to recall where they were. A faint glimmer would cross their face, relief that little Peter and Jane were still beside them watching the film, and then the realisation that it was The Peanuts Movie so they'd gently drift off again. Others went for the full legs out head back approach to napping, propped across the chair like a warped plank, arms flaccid by their sides and head dangling over the back of their seat. Sometimes a bulb of dribble would hang from the side of their mouth and the nearest children would stare at them rather than the film in gruesome fascination as a puddle formed.

The women present were more resilient in the ways of childcare; I guess they've sat through many films of dubious quality and seemed to use the time more effectively by chatting, knitting, rearranging changing bags, eating and some actually watched the film. I wondered if these were just veteran nappers, wise women who could catnap and recharge while appearing to be awake and alert. This is a formidable skill and means their offspring are always wary and on their best behaviour whereas most could have used their fathers as trampolines without fear of waking them.

The week got easier as we went along, the hours less demanding, and slowly we became familiar with the duties. All in all it was a worthwhile and enjoyable festival to work, the crew was fun, you always felt like your contribution was appreciated and like most festivals we've worked at we came away with new friends, which is a positive bonus of our lifestyle. We were though astonishingly tired. The days were unnecessarily long because of compulsory stewards' briefings at 07:30 every morning, even if you'd finished late the night before, and the shift pattern really didn't suit us. I'd hoped that I could spend a little time exploring faith by taking advantage of the seminars and teachings but found that we needed the break between a morning and evening shift to recuperate and catch up on food, sleep or just to chill with our friends. At most festivals the quid pro quo is that in return for your service you get time to enjoy the attractions of the event. Sadly this wasn't the case for us at New Wine.

What follows are my personal reflections of the event from a more spiritual dimension. I wrote them after a busy week filled with hard work and emotional moments. They are my views and mine alone and I'm sure that they will resonate with people in different ways.

*   *   *

'God didn't build himself that throne;
God doesn't live in Israel or Rome'[iv]

I've never really got the whole faith business. I've been to church, sang the hymns, day dreamed during the sermons and can recite The Lord's Prayer. Beyond that nothing's really touched me. I've never felt any stirring of my soul, whatever that is. I have an enquiring mind; I like to question and find answers. In short, I have never really believed that God exists.

But when I met Alison I started to question that. Her faith shone, radiant and immovable in the face of my cynicism. Even my youngest son, a man who was rapidly acquiring grand master sceptic level by the time he left primary school, confided that he found her faith charismatic and that *'she lived it.'* When conversation flagged I'd interrogate her. I'm sure you know the type of questions, those oh so clever ones atheists reserve for people of faith that are supposed to catch them out.

And she took it all in good spirit. Every time I thought I'd served an ace she returned a compassionate lob or loving volley. I came to realise that I wasn't trying to change her mind but to have mine changed.

Most of my adult exposure to religion was as a sneering outsider. I'd pick up on the contradictions, on the schisms, on the tanned TV evangelists living in mansions, on the ridiculous God Hates Fags type memes on social media and the neo-fascist Britain First, hiding their hate fuelled agenda under the cloak of Christianity. But living with Alison was a revelation. She lives compassion, tolerance and love, and not only on Sunday mornings so that she can feel righteous for the rest of the week. She doesn't seek confession to cleanse herself in order to make way for new and exciting ways to sin next time; which is a shame as I have an interesting list for her to try. She just lives as a normal human being; a selfless, charming and flawed human being. Yes, flawed, as we all are. We all make mistakes, and we all wish we'd made different decisions sometimes.

And so, on my quest to cement my atheism as a part of my identity I started questioning my views. Maybe there was something in faith. Maybe, just maybe, I was wrong. With almost no objection I agreed to marry Alison in church with the whole Christian marriage service. The two ministers who led the service and preached understood my values and feelings, and my doubts too. In a sunlit church on a September afternoon I felt as close to God as I ever had; an inexplicable feeling of warmth, of stillness, of peace and of oneness.

Since then I've been to a few services, although in the spirit of a full and frank confession one of those was to gain free entry into Canterbury Cathedral. As it happened it wasn't free. The price was further doubts, further discussions with Alison's wise counsel, and further soul searching. I readily agreed to accompany her to New Wine.

In the course of our time at New Wine I witnessed some interesting things that have helped my journey, although not necessarily in the way that they were intended to. It's hard to reduce the complexity of faith into handy bite size paragraphs, so for simplicity's sake I have picked up on four topics that piqued my curiosity during the week. These are: worship, healing, prayer and testimony (personal stories of God in action or sometimes, in the faintly ridiculous idiom of some 'God-incidence', not 'co-incidence'). I'll consider each one in a little detail below.

Worship: In the spirit of enquiry I attended the full-on communal worship one evening, and I struggled with it. Every song was about how wonderful God is and every talk about his magnificent love, his grace and his mercy. So I sat there and asked myself, what sort of insecure deity requires constant affirmation? How low is his self-esteem? I got the feeling that here God is viewed as some loving but insecure father figure, a dysfunctional family patriarch who will fly into a rage with the slightest provocation and has to be appeased with constant approval and attention. Where were the pleas to God or to the congregation to stand up and fight for peace and justice?

The previous evening I had been on duty at a gig by Andy Flannagan, a singer songwriter who happens to be a Christian. He sings songs about injustice and about hope. I connected with him immediately. Here perhaps was the gentler meditative approach I felt comfortable with, delivering real lessons and inspiration, a direct line to my conscience. It was a quote from his song 'The Reason' that gave us the title for this book. What a shame that only a handful heard his message while the main arena was standing room only the following night to tell God how great He is.

The worship was certainly done well. After some testimonies of 'miraculous' interventions we listened to a short speech from a senior figure before we were launched into five songs from an upbeat rock band. They were good. Very good actually but as they delivered songs of praise, with words on the big screens so we could all sing along, I saw a performance, a slick well-presented and well delivered performance. By chance I sat next to another introverted person who was a committed Christian. We shared our stories and watched as most of the room was whipped up into fervour. The devout here sometimes receive the holy spirit in extreme (to our eyes anyway) ways. There are people whose whole body will shake, some fall dramatically backwards, others are frantic head nodders and some spoke in tongues. I know at least five sensible, down to earth people who have experienced these phenomena and testify to their authenticity. I've heard and discussed their personal stories about it. I cannot explain any of this. The atmosphere was charged, and mass hysteria may be an explanation. God may be another.

The whole New Wine worship and seminar experience does give practicing Christians a chance to reflect and recharge their faith amongst likeminded people. To do so is clearly important and to see people actually enjoying their devotion was inspiring. Plenty of the seminars and speakers are a challenge to the faithful too, proof that you can preach to the converted and still make them think.

Healing: There was plenty of this going on, with prayer for recovery or relief. A lot of people gave witness to God's intervention and for God healing their bad back or whatever. I suspect they have found respite and that's great. It may be the placebo effect; it could be divine intervention, although I wonder why it always seems to be successful for things you cannot really evidence in a scrupulous and scientific way. To my knowledge no one has had a limb grow back after it has been blown off by a land mine and He's never healed cerebral palsy.

There is video footage on-line of a lady at a previous New Wine meeting born with one leg shorter than the other who was receiving healing. Her shorter leg 'grew' by one and half inches. Miraculously so did the leg of her jeans. But where is the supporting data? Where is the follow up testimony, medical evidence of the before and after? A miracle occurred that might convert hundreds, thousands, millions maybe and it's not on national TV? My father used to do a 'trick' where he'd appear to have one arm shorter than the other and then it wasn't. (It was a laugh a minute growing up with him let me tell you). I think the video shows a similar illusion – albeit probably done sincerely and without fraudulent intent.

Prayer: I can find prayer quite enlightening and positive. What I didn't connect with was the type of prayer we were supposed to join in with at the stewards' briefings requesting from God that everyone follow correct procedure. It's wasn't so much a prayer as a reminder of the stewards' manual. During one medical emergency I assisted at most people were concerned but understood the patient was in good hands and so moved on, but a couple of passers-by actually interrupted the medical team while they were working to ask if anyone had prayed for the lady involved. I shooed them along but why ask? If you believe in the power of prayer just get on with it somewhere convenient and leave the medics alone to do their job.

I can understand prayer as a form of meditation. We all require 'me' space, time to be alone with our thoughts. I use music, some walk the dog, some pray. What I discovered at New Wine is that people pray openly and 'actively'. Towards the end of the week I consented to being prayed for twice. In the past I'd have politely declined; actually, probably not that politely. Here I thought, meh, what's to lose. On one occasion it was with Alison in the crew room where our fellow team stewards gathered around and prayed for us. I don't know if God was involved but the feeling of warmth, of love and concern from fellow humans with whom we've no more than a passing acquaintance was genuinely moving.

On the very last day I popped into the *'Just Looking'* seminar. This ran every day for people like me who are curious but not convinced. One woman managed the unusual feat of being more cynical than me. She was challenging and direct in her questions and dismissive of woolly answers. At the end of the session the minister leading the discussions offered to pray for us in turn on a subject of our choosing. She agreed, but with the caveat that he listen to God first and provide the subject or message God wanted. Which he did, and his response connected to her in a deeply personal way and reduced her to tears. I don't believe it was cold reading or a trick. I don't think she was a 'plant'. It could have been luck but it was certainly uncanny and I witnessed something I cannot explain.

Testimony: We heard testimonies about finding lost keys, operations at exactly the right time, bad shoulders improving and similar examples of God's apparent intervention. I'm not in any position to claim that they were or weren't the work of God. I did though find myself thinking that a lot were uniquely first world problems. At approximately the same time that I was listening to the story of a car being miraculously refilled with oil an elderly priest was being murdered by two knife wielding assailants in the French city of Rouen, and Syria was ripping itself apart in a bloody civil war, all in the name of religion. I think they were much more deserving of divine intervention than a minor automobile inconvenience, but who am I to judge?

I came to New Wine as a non-believer with an open mind. I met people from all walks of life, including a tattooed and pierced sound engineer, policemen, angry teenagers looking for a cause to rebel against, gentle pensioners, a young man with Down Syndrome and couples in matching Hunter wellies with Waitrose shopping bags. I encountered many lovely people; the delegates were almost without fail charming, gracious and friendly. These are not traits unique to people of faith; I could say the same about most festival crowds. What I found was tribalism hidden under a veil of religion. The New Wine tribe is of course one of many spin offs from the greater Christian tribe, which in turn is one of three Abrahamic tribes. Like tribes everywhere, like the biker club we camped with at the Sonic Rock festival for example, they have badges (the crucifix and the fish) they have mottos, (Not Ashamed, WWJD), they have initiation ceremonies (baptism) and they indoctrinate their young. And like all humans there is a tendency to be selfish, flawed and self-absorbed. Praying to find your lost keys is all very well but people are being slaughtered around the world, people are starving, living in poverty, sick, struggling with their mental health and suffering in countless ways and you're praying to the almighty, miraculous all-seeing God full of love, grace and mercy for your fucking keys?

I feel angry and frustrated by this. Supposing the 22,800 people on site over the fortnight started something momentous? Imagine if the great work being done in the name of faith for refugees, for Syria, for starving people in Africa, for the homeless were coordinated and harnessed, freed from bureaucracy and ego, from church and faith factions. During my week at New Wine I was reminded of sheep standing around in flocks being minded by the sheep dogs. Suppose a shepherd led them? What a wonderful, powerful army that would be, how simple it would it be to overthrow the wolves. Jesus didn't ask the money changers in the temple if they'd maybe consider moving along please, if it's okay by them, when they get a chance, no rush. He was angry at corruption and injustice and He showed it.

Change can come with directed righteous anger, without the party politics, without the endless bloody church meetings to decide what colour bunting to buy this year, without the administration and hierarchies, without egos and tribes, without schisms, without the bullshit and without the evangelism; uniting people of faith and of no faith. People are of course already trying, working hard, selflessly giving of themselves to bring change, saving lives as I sit in comfort sipping coffee whilst typing this. As Alison wisely pointed out, thousands are striving for political and social justice under the banner of faith, attempting to build a better world from the rubble of our fractured, selfish planet. The Trussell Trust, for example, is a

Christian organisation that set up and runs the nationwide network of food banks that are doing so much to keep people fed as austerity bites.

Visualise a world where all the people of faith are a blazing comet sweeping millions along in its tail. Genuine change would drive people to follow. No need to evangelise because the power, the true spirit of human kindness, the genuine love people have for their fellow humans would do that for them. Supposing our prayer is in the action we take, that genuine worldwide equality is our worship, that we deliver the means to help people heal and then maybe, just maybe, everyone will proclaim that as testimony.

Am I closer to finding God after New Wine?

I've witnessed things I don't understand, I've felt 'different', and I have a much more open mind, but I cannot shake the over-riding feeling that the path to God would be a whole lot simpler if he didn't put human beings in the way.

'God will remind us what we already know,
that the human race is about to reap what it's sown,
it's forgotten the message and worships the creeds...'[v]

CHAPTER 19

Reflections and Fried Chicken

We left New Wine late on the Saturday morning, anonymous in a stream of family saloons packed to overflowing and neat caravans, all returning to the real world; a hot shower and a proper bed. Around the site tents were being dismantled, caravans packed, and patches of bright green dotted the hills where tents had already been safely stowed away. We departed with conflicting emotions; happy to be heading to a nearby site to relax, relief that we'd finished working, sad that we were saying goodbye to friends old and new, and spiritually concussed from the week's events.

After parking up in the grounds of a charming pub a couple of miles outside Shepton Mallet we both fell asleep sitting in Mavis waiting for the bar to open for dinner. Feeling refreshed the following morning we took a walk into Shepton Mallet, which seemed sad and underwhelming late on a Sunday morning. The town was drab, shops looked uncared for and the detritus of whatever passes for Saturday night merriment in these parts littered the streets; mostly fast food and Costa coffee as far as we could tell by the wrappers and paper cups in shop doorways and spilling out of the bins.

Even more sadly a gleaming glass and steel shopping netherworld on the edge of town was doing thriving business. Anchored around a Tesco's it also housed a Costa and those strange stores that always seem to be busy but where no one appears to actually buy anything. There was a bedding shop that also sold toys, presumably so that little Todd or Betty can pester mum or dad to buy them a model bus while they mull over which of the 25 or so slightly different pillows to buy. Next door was an Edinburgh Woollen Mill shop. For anyone not familiar with this chain of stores they are a bit like Ann Summers shops for people of a certain age who favour man-made fabrics and want to furtively stock up on pastel trousers, nylon blouses and cardigans with lacy cuffs, while pretending that they only popped in to buy shortbread. Maybe they get a thrill out of the static charge as they scurry home. As nowhere else seemed to be open in the town we settled in for an afternoon of doing as little as possible…and I am happy to report that we almost succeeded; the only interruption to our inertia was to make plans to visit Glastonbury the next day.

* * *

Glastonbury is one of those places you feel you have to visit because it's so well known, mostly for the festival at nearby Pilton. It's a small town huddled under an impressive tor; a tor being either an outcrop that rises abruptly from its surroundings or one of Mother Nature's bosoms if you're the kind of person who feels Glastonbury is the spiritual centre of your tie-died world. We passed a sheltered housing complex on our way into the town centre and wondered if it was a bit like The Chelsea Pensioners Home but for fading hippies; instead of a parade in the morning they have a communal chant and then shuffle off to polish their chakras until the nurse comes round dispensing the tabs and tokes. Come to think of it, that sounds like a good retirement plan to me.

Maybe it was the damp weather or having to circuit the town twice to find somewhere to park but I couldn't warm to the place. The Abbey looked impressive, but we contented ourselves with a browse in the gift shop rather than pay to wander around the ruins in the rain. As Alison kindly pointed out, if she wanted to see a wet old ruin, she always had me. The shops were nearly all rubbish. And I mean that in a kindly constructive way. Apart from a tiny jewellers who fitted a new watch strap for me and the odd bookshop, they were either selling arcane nonsense like crystals and healing bath salts for extortionate prices or tee shirts with transfers of wolves howling at the moon on. One shop had rows of dark shelves populated with mysterious looking concoctions in quasi medical bottles marketed as *'healing potions'*. Now, far be it from me to dispute their effectiveness but to paraphrase Billy Connolly, if you are laying in the road after being struck by a car you don't want to hear someone shouting, *'let me through, I'm an aromatherapist.'*

We soon grew weary of the shallow spiritual sustenance on offer and took refuge in a quaint café that catered for vegetarians with variety and ingenuity, one of the plus points of Glastonbury, I guess. I never expected what followed. Well, I expected the Mediterranean couscous and halloumi since I'd ordered it not 15 minutes beforehand and I was heartily tucking into it when, in response to a simple question from Alison, years of suppressed feelings about my father's death 30 years before bubbled up from goodness knows where and flooded out. I've written about him in here, I hope with a sense of affection among all my foolishness and teasing, but today was different.

Ray Canham

We lost him to lung cancer on 23rd September 1986, after a year of chronic and at times bitter illness. We lost the man born to accountancy like a duck is to water. Staid, conservative and stolid but who also possessed an anarchic sense of humour, revelling in The Goon Show and The Navy Lark. These shows were birthed from the Forces entertainment troupes whose off the wall humour melded with the pre-war musical variety shows and became a coping mechanism and release valve from the horrors of war. My father served as a Bevin Boy for a brief spell until he was called up to the Navy. He didn't see much active service but visited the devastated ruins of Nagasaki among other Far East adventures. As is so often the case he didn't talk about it, but I have his photo albums and postcards from his service days. They show a slight, blond Petty Officer, fit (he was a dab hand at the pummel horse), often smiling in a kindly knowing way, a man who seemed to be more comfortable observing than participating.

The night he passed away I had just returned from the theatre. I remember the phone call, the sense of helplessness because I didn't drive and had to wait to catch the train the next day, the guilt at not being there, the hurt, anger, loss, betrayal and, dominating everything, a sense of numbness; not being able to comfort my mother properly, not knowing what to do, to say or where to turn; being a man, strong, stolid and organised, betraying no feelings. And the numbness, always the numbness.

30 years later in a small town café on a wet Monday was the first time I cried for him, the first tears I was able to spill over the man who gave me life, nurtured me and guided me, who never judged me despite me giving him plenty of opportunity. Here were my feelings of guilt at not being there during his illness anything like as much as I should have been, at my countless thoughtless indiscretions and imprudence, my errors and lack of emotional literacy, my fragile ego being more important than his suffering. At not being the son he deserved.

And something lifted. I certainly haven't atoned for my sins, for my selfishness all those years ago but some of the numbness that's lived with me lightened. Alison again gave wise council, ever my safe harbour in the storm. We sat watching the rain, quiet and still, not at peace exactly but aware that something was different, then we walked back to Mavis in silence except for the sound of our footsteps on the rain slick streets.

* * *

Under a veil of murky early morning fog we set off for Cambridge, gently rolling through the lifting mist, wispy tendrils rising from the trees and hedges as the morning sun broke through. We passed an ancient hill fort like an enormous turtle covered in grass, paler than the surrounding fields with the shadows of ancient earth fortifications scarring its summit, then pulled over for coffee. We use services for the same reasons as everyone else, toilets and coffee, in that order. Today we fancied a change and gave into our dark sides. Now, I know we try to avoid eating meat and have successfully eschewed red meat for some time but now and then we have chicken and today we both confessed to a yearning for fast fried greasy food of no nutritional value served in a cardboard box.

I have a long-standing suspicion of fast food. I know welfare standards aren't high and I'm sure they aren't model employers, but I think my antipathy mainly comes from many years ago when, in a rare treat that involved spending money, my father bought a family box of fried chicken. Well, this was like Christmas for me, with the added excitement that it didn't involve anything cooked by my mother. Locked in the back of the family car with the sweet smell of fried chicken the whole way home I salivated while plotting how I'd attack the awaiting feast. Coleslaw first obviously, after all it's just wet salad. Beans second, tasty but really just a tub of orange farts, and then fries or chicken? And how much chicken would there be? Would I get a leg and breast? We unloaded the shopping, a task in which I was for once an eager participant, laid the table (we did have standards – my dad ate crisps with a knife and fork) and I sat with cutlery poised to dive in, my plan having been refined to a ratio of 3 chips to every bite of chicken. My father ceremoniously placed the steaming bucket in the centre of the table. Whipping away the lid in the manner of a magician to reveal the delights inside his expression went from pride to curiosity and then to dismay. Subsequent enquiry led to the revelation that in order to buy time to unpack the car and put the shopping away the entire bucket had been placed in the Aga to keep warm. Hence my first ever fast food was piping hot coleslaw, beans mixed with stringy molten plastic and chicken shrivelled onto the bone with the coating disintegrated into fine burnt crumbs. At least the fries tasted the same as they always do; awful.

Happily, todays experience was much better, the chicken succulent with crispy coating but the fries as dire as ever. We agreed that the guilt was worth every finger licking bite. And on that note we prepared for the next 5 days at The Cambridge Rock Festival.

CHAPTER 20

Cambridge Rock Festival

The Cambridge Rock Festival (CRF) is now in its 12th year and is spread over 5 days, the Wednesday being a single stage charity event for Addenbrooke's hospital, before the full-on 3 stage festival kicked off on Thursday lunchtime. Our role in all of this was as back stage crew for the main stage, and we soon settled into a rhythm that was to characterise the next few days; bursts of intense work followed by milling around until a van reversed up and we'd all swarm around like a plague of ants grabbing gear and occasionally spare tyres, the drummer's lunch and anything else foolishly left within our reach. Once the act had finished we took everything off stage and loaded on the next act.

Among the local arts and crafts stalls I was gratified to see a large Radio Caroline stall. I grew up listening to Caroline and some of the other pirate stations of the era, a small act of rebellion at a time when they were frowned upon by the grim suits at the BBC and in government. My fondness for music blossomed under these stations. Caroline DJs played all sorts of music, album tracks and whatever else tickled their fancy, a policy I adored. Apart from the people and music the other joy for us at CRF was being paid in beer tokens, a useful currency since the real ale bar stocked 70 or so beers and ciders over the weekend. We limited ourselves though as most artists wouldn't welcome slurring uncoordinated fools slinging their $5,000 Fender into the loading bay from 20 feet away.

One evening Alison borrowed an illuminated cape from a friend, a sheer translucent material with coloured lights in the arms, giving her the appearance of a luminescent jelly fish. Having wafted about back stage to the pulsating rhythms from the stage she was heard to mutter *'I'm really quite shy you know'* before leading the crew out into the arena to dance about among the audience, a floodlit pied piper cavorting around to the melody and briefly stealing the show from a Pink Floyd tribute act, before whirling out into the open air, startling the timid, alarming the children and making some serious drinkers look deep into the glass in front of them and wonder just how strong their pint of *'Speckled Old Cobblers'* really was.

Later in the weekend, and admittedly rather irritable through lack of sleep and unaccustomed heavy lifting, I had to endure the long rambling tunes and unnecessary changes of time signature that characterise Progressive Rock. Prog rock to those who enjoy this kind of thing, has choruses heavy on the 'la la far de la's' and in the worst cases four or more keyboards littering the stage and the band's set list will inevitably contain the word suite. If you are really unlucky the singer will whip out a flute or dress up as a daffodil.

There's really no excuse for this nonsense, prog was the reason that punk was necessary. Having said that though, some exponents can convey more political nous than the cartoon anarchy of many of punk's pioneers, and some of the space-rock we've come to enjoy isn't that far removed from prog. All in all though, it's an area of music I generally find hard to warm to so to escape an afternoon of meandering, noodling and self-indulgence we took ourselves off for a brief nap.

CRF was the most coordinated multi-day music festival we've worked at, although of course we've only seen it from the perspective of working in one place but it's definitely one we'd return to. The crew was an absolute pleasure to work with, nearly all of the bands were refreshingly ego free and grateful for our help, the committee and organisers of the festival were appreciative, and the punters laid back, friendly and polite. We were sad when the last extended chord from Dutch band Focus signalled the end of the festival.

Well, almost the end. When we'd finished loading the van their roadie entertained us with some card tricks, having first explained that 6 pints of lager *'...or maybe 7, I'm not so good at counting...'* improved his skills. Amazingly he appeared to be correct as he wowed us with some close-up card manipulation. Their van packed, the band pulled away, stopped at the gates in a squeal of smoking rubber and reversed at speed back to the stage door. Apparently they had just realised they were missing their guitarist. The main singer/keyboardist is a man of considerable talent but was unencumbered by wisdom on this particular evening. He leapt out of the van and started wandering around the bar shouting *'Hello'* and asking if anyone had maybe seen a guitar player? His searching rapidly turned into mass appreciation by inebriated punters. Eventually someone dragged him away from his admiring public and back to the van where Alison was barricading the door to prevent the errant guitarist, now reunited with the van having walked from the gates where he had been waiting for it, from searching for his singer and getting lost again. We waved them all goodbye a second time and as their van puttered up the access road and out onto the waiting motorway we felt our energy drain, but not enough to prevent us from joining the rest of the crew for one last beer.

Some people don't understand why we do what we do for no financial reward but after a few days at CRF we'd learnt new skills, heard some great music and made new friends. There was talk of a reunion later in the year for the crew and offers of accommodation, driveways for Mavis and help finding paid work. We slunk into bed after our Focus related shenanigans and reflected that this would be our last music festival of the season and we agreed that we went out on a high.

CHAPTER 21

On The Road Again

We left Cambridge Rock around midday and felt ourselves slowly wilting as the afternoon wore on; physical work on limited sleep was beginning to take its toll. It got to the stage where every time we stood up we would accompany ourselves with oohs and aarghs, joints would crack or pop and we'd hold our backs or stiff legs dramatically. After a festival we found it best to do as little as possible so we took refuge at a Caravan Club site near Royston in Hertfordshire. Caravan Club (CC) sites are all very similar, a bit *'Stepford wives'* as Alison puts it. We tend to favour them when we know we want a good shower, which for me means one where there is an even chance of being able to operate it without outside assistance, a laundry and peace and quiet.

I suppose two out of three isn't bad. Freshly showered and laundry on, we sat with tea in hand resting our aching limbs, listening to a large party of caravaners guffawing and cackling away as they told each other dull tales. As if listening to *'the day that Roger broke the kettle'* and *'that time Margery forgot the napkins'* accompanied by their raucous laughter at such thrilling comedy gold wasn't enough, a yappy dog joined in, the icing on our aural cake. It was their good fortune that we were too tired to bother beating them with a rolled up copy of the CC magazine, an action sure to attract a stern rebuke from the Warden. In time they drifted back to their own vans satisfied with the evening's merriment, the dog went mysteriously quiet and we finally fell asleep.

In contrast to the uniformity of the CC site our next stop in Burford, Oxfordshire was idiosyncratic and charming. The owners were hospitable and kept it immaculate but not too fussy, the pitches were generous and screened by hedges and the facilities clean and well thought out. It had personal bathrooms that each contained a shower, toilet and wash basin all in one private room. The only slight drawback to the site was the effort needed to extract Mavis from her position wedged into a rectangle of neat hedges, so instead we decided to use public transport.

Buses are wonderful. They are essential for transporting commuters through busy city's or across rural landscapes, a lifeline for the elderly and a greener option for the socially conscious. I mention this because I've been reacquainting myself with the positive side of bus travel after a hair rising journey from Burford to Woodstock.

It started with our driver pulling up 5 minutes late, but really that was nothing when you saw the traffic he had to contend with in Burford. Once aboard we lurched off and dashed up and down the by-ways of rural Oxfordshire like a bus out of hell. We slid around on the seats as the driver took corners without brakes and we reflected that at least roller coasters have harnesses to keep you in place, whereas we just had each other. Alison gripped the seat in front with knuckles white against the vivid swirly patterned seat, while I seriously considered getting off at any stop within sight of civilisation and calling a cab to complete the journey. Somewhere around Brize Norton we slowed to a mere gallop and started taking on more passengers. At every stop the bus shuddered alarmingly, a ball of barely harnessed energy eager for our driver to unleash it. And he did, a purr as it went into gear, a modest crawl out into the road and then we'd be forced back in our seats as it bolted forward in a cloud of gravel to hurtle through sedate villages and picturesque market towns. Well, I assume they were pretty; it was hard to tell at the speed we were travelling. Mostly we saw a smear of colourful landscape.

Eventually we arrived at Woodstock, the pretty town that sits on the edge of the Blenheim estate which we'd visited earlier in our travels. Now, I know that on occasion I may be prone to exaggerate slightly for comic effect, but honestly our first stop was the pharmacy for travel sickness pills to accompany our return journey. Second was the Co-Op to get something light for a picnic. I choose only ingredients that would taste as good coming up as going down, just in case the pills didn't work. On this visit to Blenheim Palace we took advantage of a free guided tour of the state rooms which helped fill in some of the detail we'd missed on our previous visit. Afterwards, suitably sedated for the journey we caught the bus back. This time it was busy with commuters and if not exactly sedate it was certainly more comfortable and in no time at all we were crawling through Burford with what seemed like the rest of Oxfordshire.

During the day Burford appears little more than pleasant background scenery for its constant parade of coachloads of tourists and lorries transporting expensive fripperies to nearby Chipping Norton. Thus beautiful Burford, ranked sixth in Forbes magazine's list of Europe's Most Idyllic Places to Live in 2009, is choked by traffic, and its fine citizenry spend their days poised grimacing over the steering wheels of their 4X4's as they try and ease out of quaint side streets between the caravans and coaches.

Away from the busy High Street, St. John the Baptist church is a wonderfully erratic affair, much altered, added to, subtracted from, and generally mucked about with over successive generations. Today it's like an architectural historian's wet dream. I was particularly interested to find that it was once used as a prison to hold The Banbury mutineers. These were around 400 members of Cromwell's New Model Army who became sympathetic towards the Levellers political movement during the English Civil War. The Levellers believed in popular sovereignty[vi], extended suffrage, equality before the law and religious tolerance. They spread their message by successful use of leafleting and pamphlets – the social media of the day. Inside the church you can see where one of the prisoners carved their name in the lead lining of the font. Apparently the graffiti artist survived but three of the leaders were executed on 17 May 1649 in Burford. A plaque on the wall of the church commemorates these men and Burford celebrates Levellers Day in May each year.

* * *

Our next stop was back to our friends' retreat and conference centre in a small village near Stafford, close to Izaak Walton's cottage. Walton was an author whose best-known work *The Complete Angler* was first published in 1653. He was born in nearby Stafford and as an adult lived and worked as an ironmonger in London until 1664 when he 'retired' to rural Staffordshire in a move prompted by the Royalist defeat in the Civil War, a time when many Royalist English gentlemen sought retreat in the less volatile countryside. He thereafter spent his time wandering around the country, mostly it seems in a quest to impose himself upon eminent people of the day, like clergyman and gentlemen who liked angling, and presumably taking copious notes over the brandy as he wrote well received biographies for them, collectively known as Walton's Lives.

On arrival at our friends' place we were promptly whisked off to the local pub for lunch with barely any resistance and in the evening we all retired to the lounge for a game of shuffleboard. This was new to us but shuffleboard is apparently a pastime much favoured by the Dutch, somewhere just behind competitive tulip racing and growing windmills and narrowly ahead of recreational pharmaceuticals. It was great fun until I started losing. Fortunately, shuffleboard isn't encumbered by random drugs testing so we were able to imbibe the red wine with careless abandon.

We awoke mid-morning with the sun peeking through silvery clouds scurrying overhead, and restless trees swaying in the wind. Also swaying and windy was young Alison on her way to the bathroom, a vision of green tinged loveliness.

'Morning my precious, how's the head?' I cheerily enquired. I'm not sure about her reply from behind the slamming lavatory door, something about the duck being off I think.

Later, in full ruddy health courtesy of Mavis's extensive on-board pharmacy, we went over to Ilam near Dovedale where we met up with friends of our hosts and accompanied them on a walk to Dovedale stepping stones and then up the lofty pinnacle of Thorpe Cloud. Well, as lofty as 287 metres high is. Not a long walk but steep and the views over the surrounding countryside were magnificent.

From our elevated position we could see back to Ilam Hall, a brooding lump of dark gothic sandstone standing proud of shadowy woodland in a broad curve of the River Manifold. To its left were parched fields of pale green and gold bounded by stone walls that tumbled into the valley below. Where the terrain made arable farming impossible sheep grazed on grassy hillsides cropped short by their constant attention. In the sun burnished fields on the broad valley floor cows lay or wandered sluggishly, picking at the grass here and there and lazily watching walkers pass by. We could also see where a significant amount of the flat ground had been colonised by visitors, farmers' fields repurposed as campsites or car parks, windscreens twinkling in the sunlight, reminders that it is a tourist heavy area. In many ways Dovedale represents the best of the Peaks in one handy place; tranquil meadows, gurgling river, picturesque stepping stones, broad deep valleys, rock formations to scramble up, caves to explore and the light toil up Thorpe Cloud or nearby Bunster Hill for the more energetic.

Driving back we went through a cloud of dust from the harvest in a neighbouring field. It reminded us that when we started our adventures in April the crops we walked or drove past were just poking through and now harvest time was upon us. Our days on the road have been mostly spent outside, as close to the rhythms of nature as we've ever been, responsive to the temperature, clouds, wind, sun and our environment in a way we never really experienced in our former lives flitting between home, car, office and supermarket. It was also a reminder that our summer tour was drawing towards a conclusion. We'd given thought to how and where we would winter but hadn't reached any conclusions beyond wanting to continue our adventure. It was the very lack of planning too far ahead that had been so stimulating for us, but by the same token we realised that winter in Mavis would be impractical and the pragmatist within was beginning to rise up and exert some control over our inner bohemian. Staying with our friends gave us time to reflect and although we didn't know it then it was also to provide us with a solution to our quandary later in the year.

Sunday was once observed as the day of rest, but on this particular Sunday we had agreed to help in the gardens instead. Fortunately for me this meant real manly gardening – uprooting ancient pampas grass, lopping trees and generally doing butch stuff with absolutely no finesse required. Alison on the other hand dived into path clearance in the style of a painter of fine portraits, diligently removing every last blade of grass, spot of moss and decaying leaf with delicate precision. The results were a stiff back for Alison and lacerated arms for me; all in all a fine day's work we felt. Jobs done we left late in the afternoon after fond goodbyes to friends old and new and made our way to one of our favourite spots in the whole of the UK.

* * *

We honeymooned in a stone cottage in the Staffordshire village of Flash. It was the place where we realised that being able to relax and enjoy our life together was more important than the trappings of the rat race. Originally part of a large estate the cottage was sold as a *'cottage with Post Office'* at auction in 1922 when the estate was broken up. It then commanded a rent of £7 a year. Since it was built in 1904 it has been the village post office, a parish lending library and reading room, and was subsequently converted into a family home. By 2008 though it was little more than a ruin until renovation work started to turn it into the home we were able to enjoy. The cottage sits a little way out of the main village of Flash, which clings to the hillside clustered around the church and pub. It acts as a centre for the many isolated farms and tiny hamlets scattered around the area. Most of the land is given over to sheep farming nowadays. The village also has the distinction of being the highest in England at 1514 feet above sea level, and in winter is frequently snow-bound. A local saying is that Flash has 9 months of winter followed by 3 months of bad weather.

The area was once known as a rough place, attracting hawkers and villains who would squat in the desolate moors. Illegal activities such as prize fighting apparently took place nearby and local legend has it that counterfeit 'flash' money was pressed here. Undoubtedly the village's proximity to the borders of Cheshire, Derbyshire and Staffordshire at nearby Three Shires Head made escape easy for local miscreants, effortlessly crossing into neighbouring counties where the local authorities were unlikely to follow. Local Tory politician and landowner Sir George Harpur Crewe visited Flash around 1820 and is on record as saying that Flash village was *'dirty, and bore marks principally of Poverty, Sloth, and Ignorance'*. George was a considerable philanthropist, driven by strong Christian principles and was considered *'too conscientious for a Member of Parliament'* according to The Gentleman's Magazine in 1844. It was his descendant, the strangely aloof and tyrannical Sir Vauncey Harpur Crewe, the 10th Baronet, who broke up and sold part of the estate in 1922.

We were spending a few days holed up here in return for continuing with our newly acquired gardening addiction, having promised to clear the weeds from the driveway and ragwort and other intruders from the verges. Like the battle hardened horticultural troopers we are we unpacked Mavis and promptly put the kettle on. After a cheery cuppa we immediately put the kettle back on and settled into an evening of watching lithe Olympic athletes on TV while we sprawled on the sofa shovelling carbohydrates into our faces.

Feeling slightly ashamed at waking up after 9am we pottered about on the driveway and gradually got into our stride, clearing everything not anchored to the bedrock and as our momentum slowly built we found ourselves ferrying bags of weeds and debris up the hill to their final resting place. Mid-afternoon we stood back and admired our handy work, before jumping into Mavis for an essential supply run into nearby Buxton. Here we provisioned ourselves with goods of the type that require an oven. As we don't have one in Mavis we have learnt to 'top cook' on the gas rings. Having a range oven at our disposal was a novelty and so we set in motion our plan to survive on a baked and roast diet for our time in Flash.

Next morning we were greeted by a friend armed with a smile, a strimmer and an exciting weed killer spray with a back pack like an astronaut's. Therefore the morning past for Alison in a blur of whirring vegetation while I pranced about liberally spraying everything that was vaguely green and pretending at various times to be a space man, a deep sea diver and a Ghostbuster. Talking of Ghostbusters reminded me that at times my mother had an uncanny resemblance to them. She kept a special vacuum cleaner of the old cylinder type whose solitary purpose was to suck up spiders. Her phobia of the harmless arachnids went far beyond mere fear to a place of special loathing, as if they'd evolved over millions of years for the express purpose of giving her a bit of a fright. I'd often call in to an apparently empty home to find her on the landing wearing my late father's beige mackintosh for protection, towing the hoover with its specially engineered extra-long hose. She would place a finger to her lips and whisper *'shush Raymond, I think there's one under the chair'* and turning on the mutant appliance she would attack the poor beast with all 1300 Watts, sucking up anything in the vicinity, tissues, sheets of wallpaper and the dog for example. To be fair we did get some large spiders. Occasionally you could hear their footsteps on the kitchen floor. Even the dog avoided them. If the infestation was severe, more than two sightings in a month as far as my mother was concerned, she would employ some sort of chemical smoke bomb. Goodness knows where these came from, probably via some black-market army surplus store. They were certainly effective. The house would rattle to the sound of bugs falling from the beams while she took the dog out so that it didn't inhale any of the toxic vapour now wafting around. Returning to the house she would crunch over twitching creatures of all varieties, a few birds, the odd bat and me, as I was still in my bedroom with the record player turned up to 11, coughing away through the cloud of noxious fumes and admiring the dancing unicorns coming out of the wallpaper.

Happily I survived all manner of such attacks long enough to be able to play in the garden at Flash until, with a sad face I realised the weed killer had run out and Alison took me for a walk before I got over excited. The first hurdle was a small stile into a field. A local man was busy painting the footpath sign and advised us to take a short diversion as the cows in the field were particularly aggressive and stealthy. Apparently this meant that they crept up behind you to deliver a nasty shove. I had visions of them sneaking up on tip-hoof, tapping us on the shoulder and then disappearing behind the nearest rock, sniggering as we looked about for the mystery shoulder tapper. Or maybe I had just inhaled too much weed killer.

Forewarned we walked on, picked up the path and found some comely rocks to perch on overlooking Knotbury, the hamlet that lies in the valley behind Flash. It was a lovely day, sunny with a cooling breeze, the moors vivid purple with heather and the fields green and gold. There were no signs of life in the valley save for a few sheep grazing lazily on the hillside below. Apart from occasionally checking over our shoulders for cows creeping up it was a perfect moment. The path led us through a gap in a hedge, over Axe Edge and onto a faint footpath, cutting off at right angles to the track at the point where the River Dane springs from the gap between Axe Edge and Featherbed Moors. Our route took us through moorland wrapped in heather, the scent wafting over the heavy peat and rich earthy aromas from the watery ground on either side of the path. Deep black trenches appeared underfoot, overhung with heather and green moss, bright against the murky soil lower down. In some the water trickled away to join the many streams that feed The River Dane while others held pools of dark stagnant water, fingers of pale green algae spreading across the surface of shadowy mirrors.

We crossed over a boggy area where the path had petered out and like previous walkers before us we picked our way across by whatever route promised the driest crossing. At one point we 'rafted' over, hopping across floating beds of moss, springing onto the next before we had a chance to sink into the ooze, until we made firmer ground where we could pause, watching the bog burble and bubble back into shape after our rude traverse. The recent dry weather made our passage a lot more comfortable than we could otherwise have hoped for and soon we picked up the path and rested at a rocky outcrop for water and a check on the map before descending via an old drovers road to cross the busy A537 and onwards through old coal mining country, now almost clear of the scars of heavy industry save for warning signs around abandoned shafts.

By way of more footpaths and pavements we found ourselves in Buxton's busy formal civic park, several acres of manicured lawns and recreation with the river passing through, splashing over rocks and around the toes of paddling children. It was a bright sunny afternoon and the folk of Buxton were out in force enjoying the weather. Elderly visitors wrapped in cardigans sat within sight of their coach, watching children play while they supped milky tea, lovers wandered arms linked as if their very life depended upon each other's touch, mums awkwardly kicked footballs for toddlers to chase, children piloted pushchairs with baby siblings in, sticky with sugary confections, and couples sat silently together wondering what to say to each other while their children amused themselves in the playground. It was a wonderful summer scene, sunshine and shade accompanied by the constant soundtrack of shrill laughter, screams of delight, chattering and the murmurs of diverse accents and languages fading in and out, fragments of conversations, glimpses into others' lives as they strolled by, dialogue heard and instantly forgotten in the joyful hubbub.

We sought refuge from the sun in the cool oasis of the tea rooms, where genteel folk were finishing an afternoon beverage before being whisked home on their coaches. We supped as politely as two parched and sweaty walkers are able to, a pretence that we dropped as soon as the chocolate mint cheesecake arrived and we dived in with gusto. Pausing only to apologise to the cake flecked diners around us we ventured out into Buxton just as it was closing. Signboards were being dragged in, shutters closed, and open signs turned to face in. Without any real plans we got a cab back and made arrangements to move on.

We were sad to leave and we packed up slowly. After a final goodbye to the oven we pulled away as the morning fog was lifting and the sun was warming the fields. On our journey southward we reflected on how much we like Buxton. It has a good range of shops, many of which are still independent, a railway line into Manchester, good walking into the Peaks, fine civic amenities, cheap housing, a charming park and even an opera house; food for thought.

CHAPTER 22

Beaches, Ponies and Poo

The fields were burnished pale orange as we trundled down the motorway heading south through bustling rush hour traffic; cars buzzed in and out of lanes, eager to get to work in time or just to escape whatever chirpy drivel was belching from their car radio. From this chaos we eventually emerged at the Caravan Club site in Littlehampton in time for lunch, our first return to a site since taking to the road. We were happy to come back to Littlehampton, and I suspect that there are not many people who have had cause to say that.

Happily lunched we took to our bikes and made the station 30 minutes early for our train. In view of the heat we decided to grab some water from the nearest shop, a Polish supermarket. I still cannot fathom how the cheapest bottled water, at 50p was imported from Poland while the Buxton or Malvern varieties on offer were over 20p a bottle more. Just how do the economics of this work? And while I am on the subject, of all the things to import, all the little things that remind you of home, that bring you a taste of nostalgia, a comforting flavour or favourite delicacy, why water? As far as I could tell it tasted of water, no better and no worse than any other clear flavourless beverage. I suppose the fact that you can import it from Poland and still undercut the local suppliers is quite a good reason. Anyway, the shop was very nice, the service warm and we were able to enjoy our journey adequately hydrated to arrive cheerful and open to the delicious mayhem that is Brighton.

We pottered and shopped for a bit before meeting up with family for a chat over a beer on the beach. In contrast to our convivial little group enjoying the evening sunshine responsibly, a large proportion of the beach goers who'd visited earlier had left their rubbish liberally scattered over the beach for the gulls to fight over, as if by some magic the detritus of their pebbly banquet would disappear as soon as they fucked off home. Alison was particularly apoplectic at people's thoughtlessness. She expressed it in her journal better than I can so here is an extract:

'As we have travelled this summer I have found that there are some people who are either stupid or selfish, maybe both, and who disregard the rules that are put in place for the safety or comfort of others. Take for example the people who enjoyed a lovely day on Brighton beach on Wednesday and then left their bottles, cans, plastic wrappers etc. behind. They obviously don't care about the child who will cut their foot on the broken grass or the sea bird that gets tangled in the wrapper, or indeed for the hero of a man who went behind them in the evening with a litter picker and a bin bag just trying to make a dent in the piles of rubbish to make the beach clear for the very same people who will be back the next day to do it all again...'

We took her to the pub to calm down. Fortunately, The King George pub in Brighton produces rather excellent food and drink. The atmosphere was cosy with snug nooks and crannies, a wide range of good beers, charming staff and a menu that is completely vegetarian. We all tucked in with enthusiasm, the batter on our halloumi shattered and liberally sprinkled our plates, salty fries crunched, and mushy peas were scooped up with fresh homemade tartar sauce and washed down with good local ales that, I was pleased to see, had no-nonsense names like Best Bitter and Pale Ale. There was none of this Wrinkled Bishops Bogie or Speckled Goblins Knob craft beer nonsense that men who seem to be built like barrels with a beard appear to favour.

The train journey home was full of tired revellers and late commuters rattling along together, slumped across their seats, nodding off with the rhythm of the train. I listened in to a group of teenage girls swapping increasing improbable tales about their school. For all their gaiety the laughter seemed false, as if the appearance of enjoyment was more important than actual levity, a smokescreen for insecurities and anxieties that couldn't be acknowledged in public. If you want to understand the worries and lack of confidence that lies within the tender shell of apparently confident, strident young women then I recommend reading Viv Albertines's autobiography Clothes Clothes Clothes, Music Music Music, Boys Boys Boys. I'd just finished reading it which is why I was more curious and understanding about them than I might otherwise have been. Viv was the guitarist with seminal punk band The Slits and writes with refreshing and brutal honesty.

Taking full advantage of the sunshine in Littlehampton we sat outside the following day with a cup of tea and our books. I had my bare feet on our little camping table and absentmindedly excavated my ear with a satisfying squeak that I thought only I could detect. Alison snorted her tea out over her book, giggling at my uncouthness. In contrast our neighbours were sitting primly at their camping table, travel condiment set positioned between them like a little Tupperware barricade, napkins folded neatly and cutlery polished as they tucked into a carefully constructed salad. He complained to her about the untidy state of the trees on the site, various ailments that afflicted his family and then the infidelities of his work colleagues. Such was his all-consuming dullness he couldn't even make extra marital rumpy-pumpy sound interesting. She barely said a word. I rather formed the impression she had heard it all before and was possibly longing for some rumpy-pumpy, marital or otherwise, to enliven her time confined in a caravan with Mr. Tedious.

We weren't surprised to see him don an apron over his pastel shorts to wash up and to our delight noticed that he was wearing long white socks with sandals. He was also pale, as in not at all tanned, despite the unrelenting sunshine. This isn't necessarily a bad thing given the risks involved but quite how you keep your face as pallid as your legs in this climate is a mystery. But credit to him, he clearly knows and understands the risks. Around the site were many examples of men who quite clearly believed they were immune to radiation. There were lean, crisp skinned men who looked like they'd been hewn from teak, wobbly blokes whose ample flesh had been seared by the sun to the point of blistering, sweaty pale men with a glossy sheen upon whose skin the sun's powers seemed wasted and the portly retired sun worshippers who glowed with a carroty veneer. These are the full-time outdoors caravan enthusiasts. They probably winter in Spain and have been harbouring ambitions to learn the language for the last 5 years since giving up the day job and buying themselves a 4 berth Concorde-Raid-Laser-Starfighter-Xtreme11 caravan with their redundancy settlement. Their wives or girlfriends seem to come in two types, erect and willowy, with neat hair and a *'can do'* attitude or plump and glittery with a *'do this'* attitude.

Of course I'm making ridiculous and unfair generalisations. After all some motorhomers eat fish finger sandwiches outside, ooze tomato sauce down their open shirt front, drink beer from the bottle and belch loudly. All of which I'm proud to say I did before bidding our startled neighbours a ketchupy adieu and retiring into Mavis to plan our itinerary for the next few days.

* * *

With the August bank holiday closing in fast we found sites booked up or asking obscene amounts for touring pitches, unless we went to a site without ablution facilities and relied on our on-board shower and toilet for the next four nights. We opted for the latter and so ended up in the New Forest.

Whatever the drawbacks of being so self-sufficient, and frankly there weren't very many once we'd overcome our British reserve at using the lavatory in such close proximity, the positive was the most picturesque site we could have wished for. We parked up in sun flecked woodland within the New Forest National Park. Ponies clomped by or stood tugging at the grass outside as we pitched up. We sank low in our chairs and drank in the peace while the rich scents of the forest enfolded us, earthy and fresh from the gorse and sweetened by the heather. The sun warmed our bodies and the bird song lulled us into that warm, fuzzy dozing state that comes from truly switching off, where you're not quite awake or asleep and you drift through consciousness with your mind wandering down peculiar paths, a safe dream-like state where you have limited control and you're free to explore thoughts and see where they lead you.

We were rudely woken from our cosy slumbers by vicious barking. The pitch next to us was occupied by an enormous American style RV which was home to 3 bear-like dogs, each possessing a surly and fiercely territorial manner. If they were cars they'd be Audi's. Over the weekend we noticed that their owners seemed to spend most of their waking hours barbecuing. It would be fired up for breakfast and reheated in time for dinner every day, the man standing over it turning and prodding whatever unfortunate beast he was blackening for consumption. At least in the evenings the smoky haze gave a dash of panache to the light as the sun set in long orange fingers through the trees.

The first time I visited The New Forest was as a child in the company of a friend and his well-meaning family on a long day out. I recall standing in the middle of sandy heathland looking at the nearest tree somewhere on the distant horizon. I was bitterly disappointed that we weren't in the middle of a dark tangled forest, the sort of foreboding place that Tolkien would think twice about making hobbits walk through. I expected deep shadows, winding paths, murky glades, insects that bit and sucked and buzzed and stung, weird noises and warnings from locals not to stray from the path. Instead I got open spaces, heather, sandy paths, horse poo and drizzle. It was awful. The woods, such as they were, were dull, green and leafy. The locals fed the adults tea and biscuits and warned us not to get wet in the rain, which they presumably felt should be taken as sage advice from folk rich in years and wisdom. We walked around for a bit, got wet in the rain, looked at horse poo in various states of decay, ate a picnic in the rain, walked around a bit more and squeezed back into their car for the long journey home, smelling of damp and horse poo.

It took a long time after that for me to visit again. Eventually I took my boys to a site near Brockenhurst for a week's camping because I thought it was time they came to appreciate the joys of horse poo and rain for themselves. We arrived in sunshine and I cleverly pitched the tent in a slight hollow to give us a smooth floor upon which to sleep. Somewhere in the early hours a gale blew through Hampshire from the south, picking up most of the English Channel on the way and dumping it on us. At around 2am it occurred to me that another term for slight hollow is deep puddle. One son wisely pitched the spare pop up tent and sought refuge therein. The other elected to sleep in the car while I took to the tent porch, which was on slightly higher ground, and horse poo. The gale intensified and ripped the zip from the door; and consequently my night went by wrapped in a moist sleeping bag with one foot out to hold the tent flap down. In the morning we discovered the car battery was flat, everything in the tent was becoming fusty in the morning heat, my clothes were soggy and fresh horse poo had been deposited outside the tent. To cheer ourselves up we watched a herd of New Forest ponies dismantle a nearby caravan awning. Incidentally, in case you were wondering what the difference between horses and ponies is, let me explain; horses are big wild-eyed lumps of bitey malevolent evil and ponies are slightly smaller wild-eyed lumps of bitey malevolent evil.

I'm happy to say though that this visit in Mavis was turning out to be rather splendid and made up for my previous experiences. There's still a lot of heathland and horse poo but it's also full of charm, stunning views and lots of interesting wildlife, including the rare Smooth Snake.

We visited nearby Lyndhurst by bike, taking the off-road track so that I could skid, slip and slide all over the stony paths and generally act like a 12-year-old who has swallowed all the sherbet and fizzy pop. Alison glided on sedately, bobbing along over the bumps and dips until she reached the brow of a steep hill, whereupon she plummeted forward, let out a blood curdling shriek and went ricocheting through sandy hollows and over heathery paths. Freewheeling out of control she overtook me, rebounded off a bush, wobbled from side to side like a see-saw, bade a breathless good morning to an astonished couple coming the other way and eventually ground to a sandy halt halfway up the other side of the hill. 'Right' she declared as I caught up, *'let us never speak of this again'* and after a brief pause... *'and don't you dare mention this in the blog...'*. As we pulled away at a more sedate pace she added... *'and by the way, we are taking the road way back'* which, after an afternoon looking around Lyndhurst and admiring its church, is exactly what we did.

But not before we'd popped into the New Forest Visitors Centre where we learnt that the New Forest was declared a royal forest around 1097 by that loveable French scamp William the Conqueror, whose son Rufus was accidently killed in a hunting mishap in the forest. It's been a playground for royalty and tourists ever since William's day, becoming a National Park in 2005. I know I've skipped over about 908 years of history there. It's not that I didn't pay attention but I found the centre all rather lifeless and lacklustre. The bit about the role of the forest in WW2 was mildly diverting but a re-creation of a local parlour was about as exciting as you'd expect a stove and some plastic vegetables to be and the wildlife section was a collection of sad dioramas that had seen better days. I have nothing against the place but I just found I couldn't raise any enthusiasm for learning any more than I already knew.

* * *

Later we visited Lymington. It's well known as a sailing resort, the sort of place where the shops sell pricey nautical trinkets to people who'd never dream of placing their expensive loafers on the deck of anything smaller than a luxury cruise liner. We took a walk along the sea walls and past a lido, full of children shivering their way over an inflatable obstacle course. Sometimes a mother would accompany the ones too young yet to be embarrassed by a hovering parent or too slow to escape their attentions. There were some fathers around too but they tended to be less concerned with nurturing their offspring and more interested in showing how undignified 16 stone of quivering blubber looks when it's scrambling over rubber ladders and scattering children into the pool.

Apart from sailing and the lido the other attraction of Lymington seems to be watching traffic, an attraction it shares with Lyndhurst and probably most of the villages and towns in these parts. The New Forest is a wide open space at the foot of the heavily populated south east and so an easy destination for a day trip. Traffic increases by over a third in summer. Even though the forest boasts 4 railway stations most people choose to visit by car, swelling the resident population with around 13.5 million extra bodies each. Some come to use the 320 or so miles of public footpaths, bridleways and cycle routes. Most it seems, to me at least, come to drive around, park at random to take a picture of a pony doing a poo and then retire exhausted to a pub or tea shop for a nice sit down.

The following morning was bright and warm. It was also a Bank Holiday so almost every car in south east England decided to converge on Lyndhurst, where they spewed out sticky fractious children, perpetually bored teenagers and argumentative couples secretly wondering how old the children need to be before they can file for divorce. Well, that may be a tad cynical, but we were watching the chaos from the comfort of a restaurant which served excellent breakfasts but where I was losing a battle with the seasoning. I wrestled with a combined salt and pepper mill, liberally seasoning the floor, nearby diners and Alison's lap in the process. It was another armament in the unholy battle to over-engineer the perfectly simple by the application of complicated fuckwittery. Adding seasoning isn't improved by expensively designed codswallop when you're not even sure which end of the infernal machine will dispense what. All because some twonk with half a degree in making pointless things out of shiny chrome couldn't be arsed to finish his design because he left early to wax his beard in time for Countdown.

Happily the ride back to Mavis was enlivened by Alison's turn to have a rant, this time at the expense of gormless day trippers. I quote from her journal:

'... *Or the idiots who pulled over on the side of the road today so that their children could stroke the New Forest ponies; ponies that are not tame and who will no doubt bite or kick your little precious and cause her parents to complain to the local council. I hope that the local council point out the hundreds of signs that tell people not to approach the ponies for that very reason. They didn't even seem to care that their car was causing other road users to have to pass onto the other side of the road on the brow of a hill, potentially causing an accident. As long as your precious little darling can see the cute pony...*'

Thoughts of their precious little darlings being casually booted into the next field by an irked pony cheered us no end and by the time we were back we were grinning like Cheshire cats and listening out for the screams.

* * *

Leaving the site we headed north over the South Downs. In contrast to the sandy heaths and ancient woods of Hampshire the Downs undulate with patches of exposed chalk, vivid open wounds on the cropped green hills, interlaced with winding sheep tracks. As the Downs levelled out golden bales of hay were stacked neatly in the corner of fields marked with ruler straight lines. Their uniformity pleased Alison immensely; she is a lady who likes order and precision. That may be why some mischievous little sprite occasionally off sets pictures by a fraction, un-pairs shoes or casually leaves a fork in the knife drawer. It keeps her on her toes.

Eventually we chugged into the small Hertfordshire village of Braughing, our home for a fortnight to house sit, look after Maddie the chocolate Labrador and to plan our future.

CHAPTER 23

Pause for Thought

We were in Braughing in Hertfordshire to house sit for good friends of ours and to look after their chocolate Labrador Maddie while they went on holiday. It was a rare spell of conventional domesticity for us. One of our aims while there was to pause and think ahead about the coming winter and where we could settle to wait out the inclement weather. Mavis wouldn't be suitable for the full force of winter as she's designed to jettison the on-board water if the temperature drops too low in order to save the pipes from freezing and splitting, which would be a slight embuggerance in the colder days ahead. We also needed to find employment. We eventually decided to try out Buxton in Derbyshire.

Alison has known, let's call them Alice and Fred, for years. After a career in teaching Alice retrained for the clergy and is now the vicar for this Parish. Fred does something exciting with chemicals and precious metals and confesses that one of the highlights of his job is being frisked every day. They have both been enormously welcoming, supportive and generous to a fault.

When we started on our adventures way back in March they foolishly offered us the opportunity to house and dog sit, and then probably spent the intervening 5 months desperately hoping we'd get a better offer. We didn't. So we enjoyed the tranquillity of a rural vicarage, that is when Alison wasn't hurriedly trying to clean up after my inevitable brushes with modern domestic living. The house was crammed full of in-built appliances and gadgets that even after a fortnight of living there were still a mystery to me. For example, the kitchen tap had a variety of settings that as far as I could tell were designed to drench one's midriff with a choice of scalding hot or ice-cold water. It had one of those bendy hoses attached whose function and operation are still completely unknown to me. One day while Alison was otherwise engaged walking Maddie I mounted a clandestine operation to unlock its enigmatic secrets. After much twiddling and prodding I managed to get a dribble of water out. Emboldened by this small victory I pressed a lever I hadn't tried and was rewarded by an uncontrollable fountain of steamy water that snaked around and gave the kitchen an abundant watering. When I eventually wrestled it into submission and turned around the only dry patch in the room was a Raymond shape on the floor where I'd taken the full force of the spray. Alison returned from walking Maddie to discover me mopping up and dripping from head to foot. Even the dog sighed.

I would have resorted to the dishwasher, but I could never find the blooming thing as all the kitchen appliances were hidden in identical cupboards for some inexplicable reason. When I made a cup of tea I'd open the fridge door to get milk to be met by half-finished laundry. Doing the washing one day I opened the freezer, realised my mistake and with a smug look triumphantly opened what turned out to be the dishwasher. I tried a couple more cupboards until I found the washing machine skulking behind a door I swear I'd already tried.

I grapple with all but the most familiar of appliances. I simply have no space in my head that is the right shape for a novel gadget to fit into. I have plenty of other spaces that are spilling over with obscure and pointless facts and can easily add to this reservoir of information if it concerns music or, at a pinch, current affairs. On our way back from a shopping trip a song came on the radio by an artist called Karl Blau. *'Oh'*, I casually remarked, *'this is a Tom T. Hall song. Tom is distributed by the Drumfire record label in the UK, the same one as Phil Burdett and Ags Connolly, although Karl himself is signed to Bella Union, which is run by Simon Raymonde, the same Simon Raymonde who was in the Cocteau Twins. Incidentally Simon is almost exactly a year older than me and was born in Tottenham where both of my parents were born...'* This last sentence gradually faded under Alison's stare, worryingly so since she was driving at the time. *'How come you know all this stuff but can't remember how to work a tap?'* she asked, not unreasonably I suppose. I simply shrugged and pointed out the truck coming towards us, which took her mind off the less urgent matter of obscure Americana artists. We survived our journey back to the tranquillity of Braughing and the sloppy warmth of Maddie, who greeted us as she always did, like a lively bar of soggy milk chocolate in a furry wrapper.

The house we were minding sits on the edge of the village in a new development just past The Square, a triangle (I know...best not mention it to the locals) of grass with a water pump and pleasant views to the church. The village straddles the River Quin, rising gently from two fords and a footbridge to the main settlement on the east, which includes the medieval St Mary the Virgin church, the charming red brick and beamed Old Boy's School, various thatched cottages along The Street and two old public houses. On the west of the river is another pub, a small Post Office and a shop.

A narrow footpath called Fleece Lane runs between Green Lane on the west side and the church on the east via a small tree shaded footbridge. This lane looms large in local folklore as it was on this path on 2nd October 1571 that a pallbearer slipped on the autumn leaves and dropped the coffin of local farmer Matthew Wall. Embarrassingly and presumably to some alarm and consternation among the mourners the fall woke Matthew from what was most probably a coma. When he finally did pass away in 1595, doubtless after his wife and family had thoroughly checked the old rascal was actually deceased this time, he left provision in his will for Fleece Lane to be swept annually. This ritual, known as Old Man's Day, is still observed on 2nd October every year with school children sweeping the lane, the church bells ringing and a short service held at his graveside.

All of which I find faintly puzzling. Presumably the poor pallbearer's slip saved Matthew's life, in fact saved him from the awful fate of being buried alive. Therefore it seems slightly ungracious to bequeath a sum for eliminating the very conditions that rescued him and denying others the chance of a bumpy autumnal resurrection. Still, upon such deeds customs and folklore are built and it seems a nice touch to keep these traditions alive.

The village is surrounded by arable fields interwoven with a network of well-maintained and signposted footpaths. These were our gateway to explore the neighbourhood under Maddie's expert navigation. The area is alive with wildlife, from tiny beetles and scorpions to abundant wildfowl and songbirds and the majestic Red Kites that soar over the fields in search of carrion. There are also plenty of deer and badgers to fly the flag for the mammals. The fields had recently been harvested so the sense of space on the gentle sloping countryside was heightened, the fields large with low hedges and some wooded areas, including 'The Bone' a tunnel like track flowing through a hollow between fields. It's enclosed by mature trees on both sides making it particularly becoming in the early morning. The angle of the rising sun casts restless shadows on the ground as it slices through the maze of branches, fingers of yellow light piercing the gloom, ever changing as the track switches back and forth over the dry river bed. It's usually about there that the dog will have a dump and my appreciation of nature's boundless splendour is enhanced by hauling a bag of her poo around for the next hour.

My usual route home took us through the playing fields where the youths of Braughing gather to conduct awkward teenage courtship rites. When I was their age the main opportunity to meet girls was the youth club. It was on a Thursday evening so I'd rush home from football training, stuff my grubby kit into my bag for next time, throw on a shirt and jeans, douse myself in Brut 33 or my dad's Old Spice if I was feeling particularly rakish, pull on my Green Flash tennis shoes and as the crowning sartorial glory slip on my denim waistcoat and mooch up the road, a heady mix of sweat, cheap perfume and desperation. Once inside the club we'd hang about in groups, swap records and tease the girls. As a mating ritual it was useless but I got to hear some great music and never caught anything more irritating than a cold, so there was some compensation. As a young and spotty teenager I fretted about the usual things, girls, food, girls, girls and girls. Actually, just girls, I added food to make me appear like a well-rounded human being. In an effort to try and understand this odd species I took to stealing copies of Buntie, Twinkle and Jackie from the doctor's waiting room. I thought maybe reading was an easier way to understand girls than taking them apart, a technique that had served me well with my bike and radio but was less successful with the gerbil. I came to appreciate that girls saw the world through a soft focus lens; they liked safe boys like David Cassidy who as far as I could see was just like me except rich, handsome, could sing and was blurry around the edges. Why didn't girls feel attracted to a lump of greasy BO like me for goodness sake? It just wasn't fair. I tried squeezing out the acne but apart from the minor satisfaction of hitting the bathroom mirror from 5 yards it just turned my face into a sea of angry red lumps. Coincidently angry red lump was an apt description of my mother when I forgot to wipe the bathroom mirror.

* * *

We had the use of a car for our stay in Braughing. This made travel much easier than negotiating Mavis around the twists and turns of rural Hertfordshire. Well, easier once we'd got over the not inconsiderable hurdle of adding us to Alice's car insurance. Alison's was relatively easy, just 30 minutes of increasingly intrusive questions. When it came to me I thought I'd declare that I had a part time job. It's only 5 or 6 days a year and pays precious little more than expenses but hey, it means that technically I'm employed. The trouble really started when they tried to slot it into one of their available tick boxes. I was recorded variously as an NHS Consultant, Management Consultant, Aerobics Instructor, Dog Trainer and God of Thunder. None of these adequately described my role but we settled on Management Consultant on the understanding that it was the closest, assuming of course that you disregarded all the known facts. After an hour of battling the system we were quoted a figure just short of the national debt of Greece for the both of us. We settled on Alison being the sole driver.

My motoring pedigree really does let the side down outside of a very specialist circle. I really cannot begin to describe the trauma of growing up the son of a Reliant owner. Not just that but one who actually joined a club of likeminded enthusiasts, The Reliant Owners Club (ROC). There comes a point in a child's life when they realise that mummy and daddy are human beings after all, with all the idiosyncrasies and failings that are inherent in human nature. For me it occurred one sunny afternoon in the back seat of our Reliant Rebel. For anyone not familiar with the Rebel it was a rare excursion by Reliant into conventional four wheeled cars rather than the three wheelers they were known and ridiculed for. Whatever chapter of the ROC my father belonged to were invited to take part in a carnival so their cars were all decorated and displayed badges, shields and other shiny adornments to enter into the festive spirit - except one. The only car with four wheels in the parade wore nothing more than its dull beige paint.

On a signal from a marshal my father snapped his driving gloves into place, clutched the steering wheel and indicated left to follow the stream of Reliants into the parade. For the spectators lining the route it looked like someone in an obscure light brown car had taken a wrong turning and wound up in the middle of a procession of cheerfully decorated three wheelers. Goodness I was embarrassed. I slunk as low as I could into the back seat and have no recollection of the rest of the day; I think I've repressed it. What I do recall though was him once winning a ROC treasure hunt. I have a picture of the cup being presented to him, a monochrome moment in time. My father's slight figure, a ghost from my past, smiling and accepting a cup from some dignitary, both facing slightly away from the camera, and standing in front of a startled man in an ill-fitting suit and odd bootlace tie. It's as if they've been caught furtively awarding cups in a police sting operation. I was in the back seat of his Reliant Robin as my parents followed clues and recorded waypoints en-route to their victory. It was all good innocent fun from a time when going for a drive was a regular Sunday afternoon activity. I have no idea how we won, my mother couldn't navigate. On long journeys she was charged with reading out a lengthy list of instructions my father had received in the post from the AA. It wasn't uncommon for her to turn two pages over together, sometimes missing out whole counties. Somehow, out of the fracas that followed we'd end up in approximately the right place, although not necessarily on the same day that we'd left.

While housesitting Alison and I celebrated our 1st wedding anniversary by going back to the Church in Cambridge where we'd got married, and we spent the rest of the day reminiscing about our wedding, the year we'd had and how important it is to try and live your dreams; then much to Maddie's disgust we went to the pub without her for a slap-up meal.

On our last night we packed up with mixed emotions. We'd loved our stay in Braughing; the house was lovely, the village warm and welcoming, the countryside inviting and Maddie the perfect host. We are indebted to Alice and Fred for their generosity, which we've repaid by giving them silly pseudonyms and stealing a bag of frozen peas from their freezer (I don't wish to incriminate anyone but it wasn't me...just saying). In a reverse of the norm we felt like two weeks in a house was a holiday and we were itching to hit the road again so after a brief reunion with Alice and Fred on the Friday morning we left them to unpack, settle back into normality and hunt for their missing peas while we left Hertfordshire and made our way through torrential rain to our next stop.

CHAPTER 24

Goodbyes and House Hunting

Bungay is one of Britain's rarest surnames, with fewer than 460 examples recorded in the country. That's around 12 people per million. I mention it because in May 2012 two football teams comprised entirely of people with the surname Bungay lined up against each other. The subs, referee and linesmen shared the same surname, as indeed did the mascot and doctor. Not coincidently the match took place in Bungay in Suffolk. It's that sort of place.[vii]

We arrived in Bungay amidst an ominous storm to a site perched suspiciously close to the flood plain of the rapidly rising river that snaked around it. The sun eventually broke through and a dank humid heat descended like a warm blanket. We'd been re-familiarising ourselves with Mavis and after a few polite *'excuse me's'*, faintly grumpy shuffling out of each other's way and *'no, no, its fine, I'll wait'* moments we settled back into our on-board routines.

The site we'd chosen was close to the River Waveney. It so happens that at Middle School I was in Waveney House, which meant I got to wear a cheap green badge and collect points for my house. At the end of the first term we all eagerly gathered in the hall as the headmaster spouted forth about pride, team work and suchlike until he eventually counted down to reveal that out of the four houses we were pipped at the post by Alde. (Red badge I think). Their elation was short lived when it was revealed that their reward was to have their house name engraved on a cheap cup and to have the satisfaction of knowing they'd won, which rather wiped the smug look off their faces. *'Bugger that'* we all thought and a hall full of disappointed children filed back down drab corridors and into lifeless classrooms vowing never to bother again. Every so often we'd be awarded house points for doing something worthy, like winning the 200 metres, excelling at a test or in my case remembering my name. If we could be bothered they'd be begrudgingly added to the tally. A friend of mine once earned an extra house point for remembering that he'd earnt a house point.

Back in the present day and we inspected the site facilities, which were basic and from an era when the most one expected was a door on the toilet and curtains with vivid orange flowers on them around the windows. Nevertheless they were clean and the showers hot and refreshingly free of gadgets, knobs, buttons, shiny dials and gizmos to steam your genitals; just the one button for on and off. I liked them immensely.

As the sun was now out we sat outside reading and drinking tea. The only blot on the landscape came in the form of the camp bore. Every site seems to have one, a regular visitor who wanders around with a proprietorial air and a bottomless reservoir of unexciting tales to deliver to the unsuspecting. Bungay's version wore orange camouflage trousers, which I cannot imagine were concealment against any terrain or flora on earth. He was towed along by a dog that was a cross between a Westie and a Staffie. We know this because poor Alison wasn't fleet-footed enough to avoid him and thus heard all about the dog, the deteriorating condition of his wife's legs, where he and his wife used to holiday and a lot more information than absolutely anyone needs to know, and I include him in that sweeping generalisation. I've found the best way to handle a camp bore is to stand with a fixed smile on my face letting him or her drone on until another unsuspecting victim happens along, whereupon I make eye contact with the new arrival, greet them warmly as if we've been best friends since primary school, make an introduction to Mr. Boring of Bungay or whoever and then depart post-haste, leaving a bewildered stranger to face his barrage of tedium.

Bungay itself is a most becoming place. The town centre radiates from the Butter Cross, which means that while ambling around you discover quaint shops round unpromising corners and stumble across interesting buildings in unlikely places. It has an old fashioned timeless feel to it, some of the shops close for lunch and Thursday is still half day closing. Writing in The Guardian in 2013 Tom Dyckhoff described it as '...*a town that's fallen down the back of the sofa.*' For all its antiquated feel though I formed the impression that it's struggling. A couple of large town centre pubs are closed and boarded up, some of the shop fronts are shabby, the stock faded behind grubby windows and the busiest trade seemed to be in the charity shops that occupy every other premises.

Honourable mentions go to the Old Bank, for its quaint tea shop on the ground floor and for transforming the former bank vault into a gallery; and also to The Chocolate Box, which was like a reverse Tardis, it's large shop front promising all manner of stationary, toys and confectionary but inside the merchandise was stacked floor to ceiling in a space about the size of a phone box. An additional commendation for Bungay Castle because although there isn't much left to admire it cost us the princely sum of 50p each to wander around in the afternoon sun. Even my father would have stumped up the paltry entrance fee for an opportunity to read the information signs and clamber over the remains. In 1165 Hugh Bigod began building his home on the site and in 1294 Roger Bigod got a royal licence to 'crenelate his house' and so retained most of the original keep and added curtain walls. Presumably no one thought to check but his magnificently crenelated house looked very much like a castle when he'd finished tarting it up.

The history of the town is quite exciting; the devil disguised as a black dog, a great fire and Roman and Saxon occupations. All this and more is summarised in the history section of the town's pleasingly succinct website. By the way, Bernie Ecclestone of Formula 1 and tax avoidance fame was born 3 miles away from Bungay in the hamlet of St Peter, South Elmham.

I had one last duty to perform before we left town and headed off to Cambridge for what would be an emotional couple of days. Regrettably though, Alison vetoed my plan to see if Mr Camouflage Trousers' caravan would float on the Waveney, so we left him to grind down the poor sap who was taking our place on the site.

* * *

I'd pretty much finished sulking by the time we arrived in Cambridge. We were there to pack up Alison's son for his move to London. The first task was to load up Mavis with his belongings. I stacked and crammed, then re-stacked and stuffed, and then I remembered we'd have a passenger in the back seat so I had to start over. Finally I stood back to admire my handiwork. *'How is it secured?'* Alison asked?

'Secured my precious?' I said and made to leave but found my elbow was gently but firmly held by Alison, who now posed her next query in a more assertive tone.

'What I mean is...when I brake, what will prevent approximately 3 tonnes of boxes, shelving and kitchenware from shooting forward ... and while we are on the subject, what will stop the ironing board from decapitating my only child?'

So that, gentle reader, is why when we arrived at his new room in London my first task was to remove a spiders web of Gaffer Tape from the van where I'd stuck everything to everything else, and quite a bit to myself. While I busied myself carrying in boxes and picking up supplies from a nearby supermarket Alison helped him unpack and make his room homely. She picks up the story below:

'When I moved to Colchester in 2013 the hardest thing for me was to leave behind my family and friends, and the most difficult of all the goodbyes was the one I made to my son. He said to me once that "I grew up and you left home" which I suppose strictly speaking is true but the decision to remain in Cambridge was his to make for himself. At 19 he was a

grown-up and he wanted to stay with his friends; he had a job and after the purchase of a flat in a small Cambridgeshire village, he had a home of his own. He took on the responsibility for the flat very well and had a real pride in his home, but earlier this year he decided that he wanted to return to college and pick up his education. So here we were dropping him off at his new digs, this son of mine who at 22 is a grown man, who has lived independently for the last 3 years, who has street smarts and a quiet confidence, but somehow, leaving him in London in a room in a shared house, not knowing another soul, was harder than leaving him that first time. At least in Cambridge he had family and friends close by, but here I was leaving him completely alone. We made the best of the room for him and took him out for dinner, all the time being positive and upbeat about the new opportunities and the excitement of living in London. Inside I was a bit of a mess. Driving away was so hard but my tears were mixed with a fierce pride. I knew he was going to be fine but no matter how independent your children are saying goodbye is never easy.'

And so we drove out of London and allowed ourselves to be swallowed up by the busy streets. Bright lights and stop start traffic ushered us out of the city and onto the motorway. We drove in silence, holding hands when traffic allowed and then we gently started speaking our private thoughts, all our hopes, fears and apprehensions. Knowing that the price of an independent fulfilling life can be high, that loneliness, homesickness, doubts and fears are natural emotions that we've all experienced and are a necessary part of growing up doesn't make them easier. Knowing that people we love dearly will experience them is none the easier for the knowledge that they'll build character and are an essential part of life. We ruminated on how far Alison's son had come and how he alone made the decision to move to London, away from his friends and dead-end jobs, a decision to better himself and to find his own path. We concluded that we are immensely proud of our children and pulled up at Alison's parents' house late at night in a tiny cloud of smugness.

* * *

After the emotional turmoil of the day before and an overnight stop in Cambridge we scooted off to Buxton in Derbyshire. We've always been attracted to the elegant Georgian spa town, known to the Romans as Aquae Arnemetiae, or *Waters of Arnemetia'* after a shrine dedicated to the Goddess Arnemetia. Doubtless they were attracted to the site by the warm springs, which bubble out of the ground at 28 degrees Celsius. The spa and the clear natural mineral water has brought visitors to the town ever since. Filtered through the surrounding hills the Buxton water still pours out of an ornamental tap in the town, from which people come from far and wide to fill their water bottles. The old water works in the town has been demolished and Buxton Water is now a subsidiary of the giant Nestlé Corporation and comes from a new plant nearby.

According to the official town website Buxton '*at 300m above sea level...is the highest town of its size in England*' which strikes me as a nebulous and somewhat pointless claim for a town with so much more to offer. Unless two towns occupy exactly the same amount of land or have exactly the same number of inhabitants (the site doesn't make it clear what they mean by size) then surely every town in the UK is the highest, or lowest town of its size in the country. Maybe at the time of writing this I was just in an awkward and pedantic mood.

We came to Buxton with the aim of buying a flat to winter in, intending to let it when we go back on the road, but things didn't quite go the way we'd planned. For all its allure we would end up leaving Buxton in a sombre mood.

First though we parked Mavis at a Caravan Club site situated in an old quarry just outside the town. It was an enchanting position with a jagged wall of rock behind us, fields nibbled by sheep rolling up towards the stark moorland of Axe Edge in front. To our left above the quarry were Bronze Age burial mounds and crowning the highest point the folly of Solomon's Temple. We walked into Buxton and spent much of the morning looking in estate agents' windows and arranged some viewings for the following morning. We walked back via the country park leading up to Solomon's Temple. We made way for a bus load of Chinese tourists to descend from the sylvan paths, delicately picking expensive footwear through the leafy floor and filing into the gift shop, ignoring the increasingly impatient pleas of their tour guide to re-board the bus. Once they'd dispersed we left the harangued guide to round up her flock and made our way up steep uneven steps and along a path that wound round the hillside, ever rising under the canopy of tall trees. The light from the sun was pale, diffused through autumn leaves, the path mulchy with rotting vegetation that was still moist from yesterday's rain and the air lay still with a humid woody aroma.

Up we rose, through mature woodland of Beech, Ash, Elm and Sycamore. I looked that up by the way, I can't tell one tree from another. Apparently there are lots of birds and other wildlife in abundance but all we saw was a dog. We reached open sky and entered an uneven pasture of grass kept short by constantly grazing cows. The hillside was once the domain of 'pudding pie' kilns where limestone was burnt to make lime for mortar and fertilizer, and stone was quarried on the summit. The land is pitted with the scars of old workings. Rising up from the centre of a Bronze Age burial mound is the tower known as Solomon's Temple.

The present building was erected in 1896 as a replacement for an earlier one constructed by Solomon Mycock a local farmer, landowner and inspiration for many juvenile puns on his surname. It's a round, two story tower that looks like one corner of a child's toy castle. Its function seems to be ornamental but the view from the top is, well, much like the view from the ground but slightly higher up. From the bleak looking Axe Edge to the South, you can gaze around 360 degrees, taking in a landscape disfigured by quarrying, undulating fields stretching away to a hazy horizon, ugly modern works, lonely farms, a railway viaduct, the sprawl of Buxton with its domes and spires, hills grazed bare, sparse woodlands, remote stone farmhouses, the old drovers road to Macclesfield slicing between hills pocked with old mine workings, the River Wye cutting a deep channel through the rocks and then back around to lush green hillocks and up again to Axe Edge in its stark purple beauty. Satisfied, we walked back to Mavis, full of anticipation for tomorrow's viewings.

We met our guide for the day and were given a walking tour of Buxton in charming and candid company, viewing four flats along the way; one possibly habitable under duress and three increasingly squalid hovels, the last of which shook under the constant flow of traffic grumbling up the steep A6 right outside the front door. We walked back into town with the agent and he was a mine of interesting information, pointing out where old shops had been, old roads, where it's liable to flood and such like. We nodded and said *'Ooh'* and *'gosh, really?'* in all the right places but inside we were lost in our own thoughts, mentally trying to fit ourselves into any of the apartments we'd just visited. We left our host in town and took refuge in a tea shop and sifted through our options. Over a cuppa we decided that Buxton probably wasn't going to be for us, the whole point was to avoid having a mortgage and if all we could afford was damp rooms with tiny kitchens and extortionate service charges then we'd have to think again.

* * *

We left Buxton in a despondent frame of mind and drove past the cottage at Flash where we'd honeymooned, and into the town of Leek in Staffordshire. We decided to have a look around and liked what we saw. We bought a picnic lunch and ate it looking out over fields on the outskirts of Leek and decided to explore the opportunities that the town had to offer. After an assault on every estate agent we could find we set up some viewings and spent an evening soul searching, deep in our thoughts about what may lie ahead and if Leek's more encouraging house prices were too good to be true.

Having spent a peaceful night nearby we arrived at an impressive four story former silk mill for our first viewing. The apartment we saw was stunning, big windows letting in lots of light and framing panoramic views over Leek and to the hills beyond. In the company of our sales representative and his amiable wife we were then given a tour of Leek, learning much about the area as we looked around a detached bungalow that had once been a butcher's shop and an apartment in the former cottage hospital that came with a view of the old mortuary. Dragging Alison away from Mrs Sales Representative before they had a chance to exchange addresses we then took ourselves off on an unescorted viewing at a small terraced house in the company of the owners and their three remarkably quiet young children. So discreet and unobtrusive were they that I longed to ask their parents if they'd drugged them. Sadly I didn't get the opportunity as Alison spotted that the shed was painted purple and hauled me away to look.

Wandering arm in arm through the rain slick streets of Leek we bounced ideas around, considered the pros and cons of what we'd experienced over the last few days and shared our thoughts. Taking refuge from the rain in a tea shop, of which Leek has more than its fair share, we chatted away and realised that we'd both come to the same conclusion and were waiting for the other to declare first. With that out of the way we drained our cups and stamped off through the drizzle.

CHAPTER 25

Flatlands

We really didn't have any plans for a few days so through some process I don't rightly recall but may have involved alcohol we booked ourselves into a site at Sutton-on-Sea in Lincolnshire.

The journey was through the wastelands of the Lincolnshire Fens. The last time we'd passed through they were golden with corn or green with, I don't know what exactly, barley or strawberries or something. Anyway they were at least colourful. Now, after the harvest they were dull; a flat and monotonous sea of brown punctuated by scrawny trees and uninviting settlements; the sort of places with suspiciously few surnames in the phone book. We passed lots of brown signs imploring us to visit a *'Historic Market Town'* and other nebulous attractions. At least the bypasses saved us from the lure of local museums with their displays of knotted corn, badly dressed mannequins and obscure exhibitions, like a collection of bus tickets I once saw, *'kindly donated by Mrs Vera Pantyhose in memory of her late husband Burt'*. I think we all suspect Vera murdered Burt because he was the sort of tedious tit who collected bus tickets.

I've always thought that the A14 is one of the world's most boring routes but the A16 gives it a good run for its money. Its only saving grace is the opportunity to see a spectacular traffic accident. The road is heaving with lorries ferrying produce from the surrounding farms, which gives the locals an opportunity to play leap frog with them. We were overtaken regularly, nearly always on bends. At one point a Smart Car whipped past and just managed to squeeze itself in front of a horsebox as 30 tonnes of articulated death thundered towards it. Presumably the 'Smart' in Smart Car referred to the cocoon of underpowered plastic and metal and not the sack of barely sentient meat behind the wheel.

Beyond Spalding, whose main attraction appeared to be the Springfields Shopping Village that also caters for weddings,[viii] the landscape became more interesting, although the bar wasn't set very high. We drove by lightly rippled fields looking like they'd heard about hills but didn't really understand the concept of height, crossed over the River Welland and into countryside of brassica rich greenery. It's a sign of how boring the rest of the journey was when a field of cabbages becomes interesting. At least the Lincolnshire Wolds were more inviting, an area of Outstanding Natural Beauty that we were completely unfamiliar with but from what we saw is worth a proper exploration one day. The road here was shaded by trees and even the traffic seemed more serene and happy to trundle along.

We rolled up at the Sutton site in time to sit out in the sunshine and watch it sink behind the trees. It was good to be back on the road, settling into our routines, cooking familiar staples in Mavis and generally pottering about.

* * *

Most of the coastal communities around Sutton seemed to be composed of bungalows. Perhaps if you've been born and raised in Lincolnshire life over one story high brings on altitude sickness. We wandered through streets of modern brick ones with ugly faux leaded windows and prim striped lawns and into a street lined with 50's style chalets, a patchwork of the well-kept and the ramshackle. At the edge of town we climbed onto the sea wall promenade to an expanse of featureless sand gently lapped by a grey sea; if the landscape of Lincolnshire is flat and featureless then the seascape matched it perfectly, mile upon mile of sand and sea with occasional scrubby sea grasses poking out from windswept dunes.

We were heading to Mablethorpe, a distance of around 3.5 miles on a promenade with an almost unbroken line of beach huts stretched along it. These were mostly boarded up for the winter, bleak and unloved in the autumn sunshine. Some had names; 40 Winks was quaint, and as it was between huts 39 and 41 it made sense. Others though just showed the owners' lack of imagination or sense of humour; Sea Breeze, Dun-Workin' or Shiver-me-Timbers. That last one made me want to scream 'you're not a fucking pirate, you're a retired accountant from Lincoln. The closest you've come to skulduggery is once short changing the coffee fund by 5p because you didn't have any more change.'

And on we trudged all the way to Mablethorpe, with its drab façade of a town centre and a High Street of fast food, cheap tat and poverty. Apart from a bright Co-Op every shop was closed or just clinging on by selling cheap holiday clothes or shoddy rip off designer wear, food past its sell by date or unsightly ornaments. The people looked hard and bitter, grim faced and in no particular hurry to be anywhere.

Mablethorpe may come alive in the summer but it looked wretched to us out of season. The neglect didn't set in the minute the last charabanc left after the summer holidays either, this is serious, endemic despair, generations deep and it's hard to see it turning around any time soon. If it has a saving grace it is at least an inexpensive place to live. I'd like to be more generous and see the upside but it was difficult. For all its brash and bawdy atmosphere, when we visited Hemsby it at least had spirit and was trying to re-invent itself as a traditional resort. Mablethorpe was once much loved; Alfred, Lord Tennyson visited regularly, and D.H. Lawrence set the Morel family's first holiday there in his 1913 novel Sons and Lovers.

We walked back through the outskirts of the town through the endless tide of dismal bungalows. There were examples of unbearable tweeness, little wooden wishing wells and neat beds of shingle and concrete signs with legends like *'Nanna's Garden'* on. Others chose a nautical theme featuring ropes and lifebuoys; some were overrun, neglected, with just a sad overgrown path leading to a peeling front door. This was a suburb of contrasts, wise investors who'd scrimped and saved next door to those with dwindling pensions stretched from one week to another on cheap food and a drink in the British Legion on a Friday night if the budget allows.

It's a place where the Union Jack flutters in the constant breeze and where Brexit won with an overwhelming majority (nearby Boston recorded the highest pro-Brexit vote in the country); a place where every face we saw was white and every accent British. Yet as much as many people may like to lay the blame for the town's decline on immigration, the town is, frankly, dying on its fat white arse, unlike more diverse and vibrant communities elsewhere. I don't know the answers, I'm not even sure I know what the questions are, but it'll take more than a little love and attention to turn Mablethorpe around.

Strangely if I saw a beacon of hope it was the previously mentioned Co-Op. They've taken the decision to build a shiny large store in a depressed town. Maybe people will travel in to it rather than away to the bigger towns. Maybe young people can get jobs, other shops will follow its lead, smarten up and people will invest in the place. I hope so.

We wondered why its neglect shocked us so much. We didn't reach any conclusions except that it was a stark reminder that on our twee little adventure around the UK we were closeted from the gritty margins of society; places where hope is a fading memory and where a simple life isn't an option for middle class couples like us to brag about but an everyday reality; living hand to mouth and depending upon ever dwindling tourists, caught in a spiral of decline and fucked over by successive governments whose interest lies in quick returns to guarantee them re-election. To restore pride and develop self-esteem people need more than a bullying job centre robot in a polyester suit. Mablethorpe and communities like it all over the UK need help. It's no wonder they distrust the political class and vote for extreme parties, blame Europe, immigrants and anyone else for their plight. Why should they trust the Westminster elite and why should they trust themselves to change? When no one believe in you it's hard to believe in yourself.

* * *

After that depressing interlude we decided to be up bright and early the next day to make the most of the sunshine. That's why at the crack of 11.24 am we shuffled sheepishly out of the site as most of the caravaners were returning from their morning constitutionals in time for afternoon tea and a gossip about the lazy sods in the motorhome. The printed leaflet about the walk we were on promised us an educational saunter around the Lincolnshire countryside where we'd get to see all manner of delights. Now, I hate to take issue with it but once we left the cover of the tree lined old railway, which as Alison pointed out had the duel benefit of shade and screened us from the rest of Lincolnshire, we entered a featureless desert where the most interesting highlights were roadkill.

The old railway line we started out on was closed in 1970 because the drivers regularly fell asleep and woke up in Belgium with a trainload of angry wet passengers. Actually I made that up, but it's more interesting than the truth that the line died out because people didn't use it. Our route took us up a B-road, alongside some young inquisitive foals in a field and we eventually took a left turn along the bank of a drainage ditch, freshly dredged and stagnant. After a while we turned left again and down a track that took us passed farms that look like farms everywhere else; a tumbling outbuilding, defunct apparatus rusting in a corner, barns with miscellaneous machinery under dusty tarpaulins and a tidy farmhouse with children's toys scattered about the garden with washing fluttering on a sagging line.

We crossed between fields, freshly ploughed and smelling of parched earth. We could feel the crushing weight of the vast open sky and featureless landscape stretching away to an indistinct horizon in every direction. Breaking up the monotony were two tall radio masts and to the north elegant wind turbines rotated gently in the breeze. Mablethorpe was home to two of the first commercially operating wind turbines in the country way back in 2001, located at a water treatment works. Today there are vast arrays of turbines off these shores in the choppy North Sea. Some people objected, as they do everywhere else, because writing angry missives to the local rag is something to do and is easier than actually researching renewable energy and thinking for yourself I suppose. Aside from the usual parade of climate change deniers, head buriers, not entirely unreasonable concerns for bird and marine life and some downright lies about subsidies and carbon footprints, people were objecting to the view. I wanted to reply with ...'*object to the view...why? This is Lincolnshire, it IS the view you numptie!*'

But I didn't because they were built ages ago and my intervention was entirely imaginary and served only to relieve the tedium of the countryside. A countryside which was enlivened no end when we skirted around a roadside bungalow to be confronted by a gentleman trying to repair a puncture on his penny farthing bicycle. We should have been more surprised but this was Lincolnshire so we took it in our stride, watched as he gave up and with a shrug tottered off forlornly pushing his machine beside him.

The last leg of our walk was along the sea front where we braved the sand for a while then walked along the seemingly endless promenade, passing beach huts of a bygone era and into Sandilands and refreshment. While partaking of fine coffee I read a leaflet about one of the UK's premier tourist attractions that we'd missed, close to the furthest point of our walk, the Anderby Drainage Museum. Located in a 1945 pumping station that was built to drain 9,200 acres of land it is open for 2 Sundays a year so that visitors (I'm probably being generous using the plural, but who knows) can admire it's...'*two Ruston 10HRC twin cylinder oil engines. These engines then drive Allen Gwynnes 42" centrifugal pumps which are capable of pumping 4,500 litres of water per second.*' Alison was particularly relieved to know that we were not staying in these parts on one of the Sundays when it opened.

I don't wish to seem ungrateful to the engineers and farmers of the fens. Ever since the Earl of Bedford and his Gentleman Adventurers' set about draining the fens in 1630 these dry flatlands have become valuable arable land and the source of much needed staple crops for the UK. It's a magnificent feat of engineering and not one we should take for granted. It's just that in the same way that carnivores don't want to take the grandchildren for a day out at the abattoir[ix] I don't feel I need to understand the workings of the farms or visit drainage museums that supply our crops. Nevertheless, if you're the sort of person who likes looking at 10HRC twin cylinder oil engines, be they built by Ruston or not, then it's probably a treasure trove of oily delights.

Back in Mavis rain fell as darkness descended and we drifted into a gentle sleep, lulled by the pitter-patter rhythm on the roof. I eventually climbed down the ladder from our bedroom around 9am the following morning, creaking and groaning away like a Ruston 10HRC twin cylinder oil engine in need of a good service. After the usual packing up routine we set sail for Stamford.

* * *

Stamford is just inside the border of Lincolnshire and was the perfect antidote for the waste lands we'd found to the east of the county. It was a charming and pretty place, and on a sunny Sunday the soft limestone buildings, multitude of churches and ornate civic buildings were a delight to wander lazily around. Thanks to becoming the first town in the country to create a conservation area, back in 1967, it is largely unspoilt and has even been a bit of a TV star of late, with Middlemarch and Pride and Prejudice filmed there. It lies just off the A1, once the Great North Road, approximately half way between London and York, where it served as a mail coach interchange and was a prosperous wool town. Today its prosperity seems to be from tourists who come to wander its streets, poke about in expensive shops, slurp coffee and eat in one of its many pubs and restaurants.

As we were wandering back towards Mavis the now familiar cry of 'Alison...Co-eee' went up and a lady who had once worked with Alison came bobbing out of a coffee shop. I settled in to my familiar role of nodding sagely, desperately trying to remember who she was, in what context she was known, whether I'd met her before and if so to speculate about whether I did anything embarrassing or awkward that I should be suitably contrite for. I eventually occupied myself on a nearby bench by reading a brochure that had fallen out of the Sunday paper and offered all manner of attire for the debonair chap. I mulled over a fiesta of man-made fabrics, cardigans whose main attraction was diamond shaped detailing around the nipple area, tartan pyjamas, jeans with elasticated waists, faux fur lined slippers and cargo trousers that went up to a 56" waist. Frankly, I thought, if you have a 56" waist you don't need cargo pants, you are cargo.

Alison returned from her impromptu reunion just as I was about to purchase a plastic re-sealable condiment set with matching bathrobe and hurried me up because we were supposed to be in Suffolk.

CHAPTER 26

East

To reach Suffolk we spent more time on the A14 than is good for the human soul – which is any time over 20 seconds. It really is an interminably dreary journey. It runs for 127 mind numbing miles from the Port of Felixstowe in Suffolk, skirting around interesting places like Ipswich, Bury St Edmunds, Newmarket, Cambridge and Huntington then across a bleak wilderness marked *'here be dragons'* on the map before avoiding Kettering, passing the site of The Battle of Nasby and finally, if you're still conscious, you'll end up at the Catthorpe Interchange junction of the M1 and M6 motorways close to Rugby. The route is synonymous with traffic congestion, thundering lorries and accidents. Travelling along it on this particular day, some of the tedium was relieved by the vibrant autumnal colours of the trees along the roadside, although on the A14 that's like saying watching magnolia paint dry is slightly better than watching white paint dry. It was a reminder though that we could at least take notice of the splendour of the trees and the colours of nature. I passed this way, and on many other roads more gifted in scenery while commuting or driving for work, and although I noticed the backdrop in a casual way my head was always busy with other matters. Now though we were free to appreciate the views and absorb the magnificence of Mother Nature in her full splendour.

Talking of splendour, the jewel in the dismal crown of the A14 is The Orwell Bridge, although even then it shares it with its close friend the A12 which joins it for the crossing. And what a bridge it is; 1,287 metres of graceful sweeping concrete ferrying up to 60,000 vehicles a day over the wide River Orwell. The central span of the bridge is high enough to let ships pass underneath but retains its elegant flowing profile as it rises and curves across the river. It cost in the region of £24 million to build and it opened for traffic in December 1982, just in time for my father to ferry me home from college for the Christmas holiday. We were bitterly disappointed that the barriers prevent motorists in ordinary cars, and you couldn't get more ordinary than my father's Mazda, from seeing the views.

Today we turned off before the bridge and planted ourselves in sleepy Rattlesden, a tranquil spot in Suffolk that we holed up in for a while. Along with a 13th century church and some comely homes around the river Gipping it boasts a splendid local shop with a post office and well stocked store run largely by volunteers. We presented ourselves in the shop mid-afternoon expecting the adjoining post office to be open but we were kindly informed that it closed at 1pm. As we were about to pay for our other goods the post mistress, who happened to be in the shop, interrupted and offered to send our recorded delivery items anyway and assured us it really was no bother. This was simply marvellous service and better than I received when I made a lone sortie later in the week. The volunteer assistant got terribly confuddled using the till, and wasn't sure of the difference between the price and the sell by date. *'Why yes, of course I want to buy a small cheese and onion flan for 07/10/2016 pence'* I longed to say, but stopped myself; this wasn't the time for sarcasm I decided as we gently added up the total together. The final tally came to an eye watering figure completely unrelated to my meagre shopping which caused much checking of the till roll and inspecting of labels until we settled on a figure in the right ball park and he gave me a fist full of random change, wiped the sweat from his brow and settled back to his book, exhausted from scaling the giddy heights of commerce.

We'd both had colds to contend with so after a day of abstinence from anything more strenuous than pressing play on the DVD controller we decided on a short walk to recuperate and take in some fresh Suffolk air. Woolpit is a town approximately 3 miles away from where we were staying via paths across open countryside. Leaving Rattlesden we climbed a small hill and took off in a straight line between fields of sugar beet, a crop widely grown in these parts for the huge sugar refinery at nearby Bury St Edmunds. As we were just getting into our stride a cheery bespectacled face popped out from a strand of trees, checked we didn't have a fierce dog in tow and duly satisfied, encouraged her tubby Terrier to follow her. We (by which I mean Alison) engaged our new friend in conversation. She was a sprightly older lady, born and bred in a nearby village. Still living locally she was most welcoming and very impressed that we were walking all the way to Woolpit, where she assured us... *'you'll find everything you could need'.* With the lure of this Pandora's Box of earthly delights awaiting us we strode on with renewed vigour. The air was fresh; the early rain had heightened the scents and colours and the sun occasionally peaked out from the cloud. Sadly we didn't discover everything we could need awaiting us in Woolpit. We did however find a couple of empty pubs, a bakery, fish and chip shop, a Tardis like Co-Op and a gift shop full of what Alison refers to as fripperies; nick-knacks, ornaments, mugs and all manner of expensive trinkets. Happily for us they also served tea and cake, so we made ourselves welcome among the wooden ducks and in-sympathy cards and chatted away to our charming host, who again seemed most impressed with our hiking. So much so that when her replacement came in she told her all about her adventurous customers and they gathered behind the counter to congratulate us. I expect we'll feature in the next Parish Magazine and eventually become local legends.

Talking about local legends the Woolpit village sign features two children known as the Green Children of Woolpit. The story goes that in the 12th century locals found 2 children in a hole in the ground. They appeared to be green, or at least had a green tinge to their skin, and spoke in a language no one recognised. The boy was taken ill and died soon after they were discovered but the girl grew into a healthy, and if some versions of the tale are to be believed, a somewhat wanton woman who went on to get married and live a regular life. That's it really. Over the centuries the story has been embellished in the re-telling with various adaptations surfacing along with attempts at explanations, none of which I'll bother you with here because frankly we'll probably never know if they even existed in the first place. There's a copy of the legend in the Church written by a medieval commentator if you are interested.

We could see the steeple of St Mary's church on our way here. It proved a handy navigation point on our walk, especially when the sun hit it and it appeared to be glowing white like soft marble rising out of the surrounding trees. Inside the church sports a *'magnificent double hammer beam roof, angel carvings, fourteenth century porch and carved pew-ends, which makes it one of the finest village churches in East Anglia'* according to the village website. We were entranced by the pew end carvings, mostly of dogs and dragons. These were smooth and shiny from the hands of countless worshipers. They've witnessed christenings, marriages, funerals, lively sermons, dull homilies, packed congregations, empty pews and who knows what manner of unusual and bizarre occurrences; maybe even two green children.

Early on the next morning we stood outside the pub in Rattlesden watching the local dogs go through agility training on the recreation ground while we waited for the bus. From our brief wait I'd say that the pooches of Rattlesden have quite some way to go before they reach Crufts standards. We had an appointment to meet a friend in nearby Bury St Edmunds for lunch and so the bus made perfect sense rather than dragging Mavis through the narrow country lanes.

The bus routes are supported by the local authority. The subsidies they can afford are constantly under pressure and many former routes in these parts have been cut. It's a dilemma of course. How much public money do you plough into poorly used services? And the answer is that there is no correct answer. If by poorly used you just count passenger numbers it may be easy to target a route that carries only a handful of people. If you look deeper or actually use a bus once in a while you'll see young people going to minimum wage jobs, pensioners with no other lifeline from their shop-less hamlet, workers and shoppers leaving their cars on the drive and doing the responsible thing for the environment by sharing public transport and adults with a learning disability given a slither of independence by using the bus into town. We picked up a collection of passengers en-route to our destination; a young woman proudly sporting her supermarket uniform, an ample chap who skipped empty seats in favour of squeezing in beside a demure lady who clutched her handbag tighter to her chest and refused to engage in his attempts at conversation. There were young friends with learning disabilities who got on at different villages a couple of miles apart, but without the bus they might as well have lived a million miles from each other. A gentleman sporting a fine pair of lime green corduroy trousers with a sports top and cowboy hat climbed aboard, helloed everyone and kindly sat up front so that he could share his BO with the entire bus. It mingled with the fruity scent of the young lady in front of us. I'd wager it was from Lush but I'm not ruling out something from the Bodyshop's Dewbury range.

In a rural county like Suffolk the bus service really is a life line, although the way we rocketed along the narrow lanes and braked from 40 – 0 as cars appeared from around blind bends I did begin to worry if we'd actually survive long enough to find out how useful the service really is. Along the winding route we flew through obscure villages, some little more than a farm masquerading as a hamlet because cartographers get embarrassed by too much blank space on a map. We passed the impressive red brick pile of Gedding Hall, where local legend has it that Ronnie and Reggie Kray fled after killing Jack 'the Hat' McVitie in 1967. The Krays apparently knew Geoffrey 'The Godfather' Allen who owned it at the time. The Hall changed hands in 1968 when it was purchased by Bill 'the one who played bass guitar' Wyman of the Rolling Stones.

Our rendezvous was fun and we took the opportunity to pop into a garden centre. Nowadays these places seem to be more like day centres for the ambulant retired with a pension burning a hole in their nylon pockets. This one had clothes, cards, ornaments, gifts, jams, books, a cafe and a whole department of sweets in retro bags which as far as I could tell just means that they make them look old and charge twice as much for a bag of flavoured sugar. You could purchase all manner of shiny things and maybe if you looked hard enough some plants too. We left with a few trinkets and after a serene bus trip back started packing up Mavis in readiness for our next stop in an area of outstanding natural beauty, a few miles from the east coast in an area that I knew well.

✼ ✼ ✼

DOWNWARDLY MOBILE

Today the village of Blythburgh is rather reduced from the Domesday Book entry which showed that the place was taxed 3000 herring each year. A fire in 1676 seems to have driven many locals away and the present village's spread-out footprint reflects the fact that many properties were never re-built. By 1754 there were only 21 households and a population of 124. Over the years it's been home to a 12th Century Augustine priory and to a narrow-gauge railway that joined nearby Halesworth to Southwold on the east coast. Operating between 1879 and 1929 this 9-mile branch line reached its peak in 1900, carrying 10,000 passengers, 90,000 tons of minerals and 600 tons of general merchandise, according to the Southwold Railway Trust's website.

This really is a most bewitching area of the country and particularly so on an early morning walk when the air is crisp, fresh and untainted. The River Blyth flows into a large tidal creek here, which dominates the area. Across the shimmering waters sit the white specks and spires of Southwold in the distance. Walking east, clouds stack up from the tree line, glowing orange from the rising sun. Pheasants squawked wildly and thundered aloft as we approached, songbirds trilled in the hedgerows as the short lane we followed fell away into Walberswick Nature Reserve. Here reeds rose from the marshy shores and the canopy of trees sparkled with silver dew and cast shadows across the sandy path. From here the track follows the old railway line towards Walberswick where it joins the Suffolk Coastal Path to cross the river via the old railway bridge and into Southwold.

I always took the large creek to be a natural feature but apparently it is the result of deliberate flooding in 1940 as a precaution against invasion at the start of WWII, a story that my father relayed to me on one of our many excursions this way but that did not really sink in at the time. Eventually we moved to live nearby in Saxmundham, a market town that had known glory as a transport hub, with its coaching inn, railway line, bus station, A12 trunk road and bustling livestock market. During our time the town grew in population but sank in importance and went through something of a slump as the livestock market finally closed, the bakery and the greengrocers warehouse shut, garages uprooted and the town centre market faded from a cheerful parade of colourful stalls to a few sad displays of out of date provisions, fabric remnants and never in fashion clothes.

Not that I cared. As a bored teenager adrift in what I considered the arse end of nowhere the only pastimes of any interest to me were cycling, a pursuit that had the benefit of being entirely solitary, and making model aeroplanes, an interest that mostly ended up with hideous sticky mutated aircraft with wings at jauntily irregular angles, a pilot glued to the tail and a clump of dog hair stuck to the nose. My only other interest was music. I was glued to the radio, literally if I'd recently been allowed back near the Airfix adhesive. I turned 14 and spent my birthday money on a budget Bill Haley record. Halfway through side one I started a lifelong addiction.

Bill Haley gradually became Jerry Lee Lewis who morphed into Status Quo and Black Sabbath. I discovered pirate radio and worked at the local chip shop to fund my growing music habit. I had Bowie, T Rex and Pink Floyd scrawled on my pencil case. My best friend had the Confederate flag and Showaddywaddy on his. I like to think I won.

Living in Suffolk we were surrounded by American airbases, which delighted the inner nerd in me. *'So that's what an A-10 Tankbuster is supposed to look like'* I'd sigh, stamping another failed model into the bin. It exposed my youthful self to American service families with exotic record collections. Lou Reed, The Stooges, MC5 and Funkadelic were taped and exchanged for copies of my Deep Purple, Black Sabbath and Hawkwind. I tried to emulate my musical heroes, the drawback being that every instrument I tried I failed to wrestle into submission. I could read music but hammered at keyboards like my fingers were made of lead shovels and plucked at guitars like Robin Hood loading an arrow. I tried the drums at school and found that although I could move each limb independently when walking, I couldn't do so with sticks in my hand or pedals under my feet.

After a couple of years of on and off frustration and having to content myself by taping the radio to make my own shows, something reached our sleepy backwater that was to permanently change my outlook on music and, more importantly, on life. Suddenly, thanks to a few scruffy oiks swearing on The Bill Grundy TV Show, punk burst forth in a maelstrom of tabloid hysteria. In the space of a year my world exploded into a thousand musical fragments, every one more exciting than the last. Now it was permissible not to be a classically trained musician or ex-public schoolboy, or to understand chord progressions and such harmonious niceties; attitude became more important than ability. A grey generation who were growing up under the shadow of the cold war and nuclear annihilation became a multi-coloured, switched on vibrant mess of furious spitting music, imperfectly played under snarling words that railed against every injustice we could imagine. It was often an inaudible squall, challenging and wilfully obtuse, but brilliant all the same.

From then on, my musical interests ranged from heavy rock to punk. I discovered the music press, especially Sounds and The New Musical Express and devoured them from cover to cover every week. I embraced anything that would transport me out of this shabby little town. I joined a band in a desperate attempt to participate and over the period of two shambolic rehearsals went from guitar to bass on the grounds that I could probably do less damage with four strings than six. After one gig I admitted that perhaps four strings was pushing it a bit, by a factor of about four, and tried the drums again, this time on a bass drum we 'appropriated' from school and painted yellow together with a single snare. It was maybe my finest 10 minutes on stage; a five-minute tune up while the singer grappled with the audience for control of the microphone, a 30 second burst of feedback, approximately one minute of heart pounding bewildering noise and a further 30 seconds while we all finished the song in our own good time. Imagine a guitar, a bass, drums and a singer who between them had attended two music lessons, were drunk and had only rehearsed twice, and at one of those the guitarist forgot to bring his instrument, and you have only just begun to know how awful we were. We were followed by two bands who knew what they were doing, one of whom were the nucleus of soon to be local legends who had proper record deals and were on Top of the Pops.

Saxmundham survived the arrival of punk rock and went through something of resurgence, gradually becoming quietly gentrified, with a busy high street and growing economy. We drove past my old family house, which we saw had been undergoing some modification after the new owners eventually wore down the planners over its listed status restrictions, a hazard my cautious father felt keenly and my pragmatic mother largely ignored. For all my misery in the early 1970's at finding myself transported from central heating to coal fires, from a modern semi to a cold, creaky house overlooking a grave yard, in time it grew on me and having to sell it when my mother moved into a residential home broke our hearts. One of the last items I carried out of the house was that Bill Haley record. Nothing could make me part with it and, if you look closely, you can still see a finger mark that looks suspiciously like it's made by Airfix glue.

* * *

After visiting Saxmundham more nostalgia awaited when we visited Snape. The Snape Maltings Concert Hall was advertising a vintage market. This proved mildly diverting, with plenty of stalls selling what was essentially the content of our parents' homes circa 1960 for extortionate prices. The concert hall was much more interesting to me as I worked there on and off during my late teens as a general dogsbody/stagehand/programme seller/café assistant/janitor. I started out assisting my father, who in 1973 bravely traded corporate accounting with BP in Harlow for a bookkeeping position with the Aldeburgh Festival Association, who owned and ran the concert hall. The advert asked for a full-time book-keeper (male) aged 30 to 45. He qualified on the book keeping requirements and although he was slightly beyond their cut off age he managed to prove he wasn't too old and jittery to keep their books in good order. I'm assuming they took his word on his gender.

Visiting the venue today I was delighted to see the main foyer and auditorium were just as I remembered them. There was the statue of the bull, next to which I would sell programmes along-side one of my father's army of over perfumed volunteers; ladies of a certain age with a propensity for heavy face powder and ruby lips. The stage was exactly as I recalled it, deep and worn to a lush matt finish with the same faded white tape on the front of the stage. During festival season I'd arrive about 5am to sweep the stage and shine the floors with an industrial polisher that had a mind of its own. It would gently thrum away like a purring kitten until I released the break and whoosh, we were off, waltzing around the floor, down aisles, under seats and occasionally up steps and once into the orchestra pit. That took some explaining and a mild rebuke from my boss, once he'd stopped laughing. Somewhere around 9am the caretaker would track me down with a pile of toast and coffee fortified with whisky. Then I'd start clearing the dressing rooms with renewed vigour and a slightly wobbly gait, on more than one occasion discreetly closing the door on slumbering couples surrounded by the detritus of an impromptu liaison. During the morning rubbish would accumulate in a dank corner of an old outbuilding ready for me to deal with. Armed with whatever food and drink I managed to snaffle from the green room I'd trundle wheelbarrows full of refuse out to an incinerator overlooking the marshes, and after a few minutes Barbara Hepworth's iconic The Family of Man sculpture would be obscured by pungent black smoke and I'd chomp my may through stale smoked salmon sandwiches and swig flat champagne. Today my old spot has been replaced by an overspill car park, although The Family of Man is still there, three custodians of a grand view over the reeds and broad swathe of the River Alde, Iken Church poking through the trees and the hazy outline of distant Aldeburgh.

We had a browse in the shops, admiring exotic groceries, obscure preserves and expensive confectionary, cookware you never thought you needed and will use twice before confining to the back of a cupboard and all manner of glittery fripperies with price tags longer than their lifespan. Mind you the shops help to bring people and money in when the concert hall isn't in use. When I worked here as a spotty teenager the concert hall was ridiculously snobbish and the curious were brusquely turned away at the door. Happily today we were able to walk unchallenged into the foyer, peek into the main hall and visit the café unhindered by curt staff.

On our way out we passed the ghost of an awkward teenager shyly avoiding eye contact with customers and fumbling to make change. Standing in the shadows watching everything with a concerned eye is a pale, skinny man in a dinner jacket and an oversized bow tie, a mop of fine blond hair and a gaunt slightly worried face. He carries a black case stuffed with money bags, change, cash books and plenty of sharp pencils. Before the final curtain falls he will have collected all the takings and be seated in the empty restaurant counting every penny, meticulously recording each transaction until he is satisfied that everything tallies and he can stow it all away in his case. As the last punters crunch over the gravel to the car park and the bar shutters clunk into place a father and son who love each other but don't know how to say so make their way to the last remaining car in the courtyard. The headlights sweep the decaying red bricks of the empty yard one last time as they leave, side by side in silence, to be swallowed by the waiting night.

CHAPTER 27

Reunion and Racism

The biggest distraction on our long and otherwise featureless journey to Dorset was the colours. The A40 was particularly blessed by autumn, strands of trees shaded in rich auburn, russet, golden green and pale lemon, studded with the occasional deep green conifer. Larger clumps of trees on the hillsides were spectacular, reflecting the colours of the surrounding ploughed fields, dark browns and yellows at their edges and deeper greens within the dense woodland yet to feel the full chill of the autumn air.

We arrived at a pleasant site, clean and with views over open meadows. The occasional parp of a train's horn was the only distraction to an otherwise tranquil little spot on the outskirts of the village of Wool. It sits inland from popular Lulworth Cove and just south of the River Frome, which flows under a lovely 16th Century 5-arch stone bridge and past the austere Woolbridge Manor. The Manor was the fictional setting for the honeymoon of Angel Clare and Tess in Thomas Hardy's book Tess of the D'Urbervilles. I don't wish to spoil the plot but their nuptials were ill-fated. According to Alison, Angel really was a bit of an ass.

We took a walk around the village and found it an interesting mix. The west was mostly newer buildings, faceless offices and the old Ship Inn, which apparently has links to smugglers. This is not a claim of great significance though as most old pubs and ancient buildings around here boast of some nebulous past involvement in cheating the tax man. We walked along a road of anonymous bungalows and tidy houses, past the library and sports field and into the older part of the village with its pretty thatched cottages, squat Holy Rood Church and imposing Black Bear pub. Spring Street, so named I assume because the name Wool comes from the Saxon for Well, has a bubbling little brook running beside it, so the cottage gardens are accessed over miniature bridges. Further along the road divides and Church Lane leads gently up to the church, past plenty of examples of thatchers' art as the lane twists and narrows to a farm track on the edge of the village. Along here it is easy to imagine the world of Thomas Hardy, who lived and wrote extensively about Dorset. Well, easy if you remember you are not up to your knees in mud and horse shit, the cottages now have heating and inside plumbing and you've a good chance of surviving childhood but, you know, all that aside it's very Hardyesque.

I'm no Hardy scholar; I think I might have owned a copy of The Mayor of Casterbridge once in a vain attempt to look serious. It probably sat on the bookshelf beside a load of other classics I had no intention of reading. Alison though is more familiar with his works and tells me he was something of a serious social commentator, raising issues and injustices of the day through his writing in a way that didn't win him many friends at the time, at least not among the class of people he was criticising. Good for him I say.

Okay, this next passage may not be for the squeamish. Access to the shower block on the site was controlled by an entry code, which for convenience I kept in my phone case. After a shave one evening I went for, let's call it a 'sit down', followed by a shower. Unrobing in the shower cubicle I couldn't locate my phone, so I put my trousers back on and retraced my steps, with increasing urgency as it wasn't anywhere to be found. I appeared to be the only person in the shower block at the time and had clearly had it with me to gain access. On my fourth retracing of my steps I became aware of a curious weight in the pants department as I bent down to search behind the toilet bowl. I had a flashback to being 3 years old at nursery and having one of 'those' accidents. I was just investigating this curious phenomenon when someone else came in, someone who may still be traumatised by the sight of a topless middle-aged man scurrying into a shower cubicle with one hand down his trousers and holding something in his underpants that turned out to be the missing phone. Still, a minor compensation was exiting the shower block to see a perfect rainbow arched right over the site, one end illuminating the ancient stone walls of Woolbridge Manor, the other rather less poetically the railway footbridge.

Shortly afterwards, and eager to escape any attention that may have followed my 'toilet' incident earlier, we were picked up by my sister and brother-in-law and whisked away to an evening of fine food, good beer and convivial chat. My sister and I had been separated by distance, and to some extent misunderstanding, for many years. Having chosen different paths early on in life we seldom saw each other outside of family weddings and funerals. People make choices for reasons, and the separate paths we took were the result of many influences, not all negative; there is quite an age gap between us too. Over dinner, the time over which resentments and misunderstandings had built up fell away like tissue paper wrapped around our lives. In one short evening we discovered much in common neither of us realised we had. It was a cathartic, emotional reconciliation of two people who didn't realise how close they really were. Climbing into bed that night I reflected on a life spent steadily dealing from a pack of cards neatly sorted into a particular sequence. I always knew what to expect. Finding the pack has been reshuffled going forwards may be unsettling and scary but ultimately more rewarding as I experience the cards being dealt in a new and exciting order. Such is our life on the road and in our relationships too. Distance may break fragile bonds, but it can also cement the stronger ones. It's a good feeling having a big sister back in my life. As a bonus I didn't seem to embarrass myself too much, which is unusual when food and I get together, especially if food's cousin alcohol joins us at the table.

* * *

Waking late we had a leisurely breakfast in Mavis and pondered the state of the world, as one does. Part of our motivation for this was a couple of comments some mindless numbskulls made in the media that we were reading over breakfast. Exhibit A concerned comments under a heart rending piece on the deteriorating situation in Syria and the awful injuries and losses children were suffering there. The comments in question were along the *'what about the children in America, we should help them first'* lines, to which the obvious retort is, *'you live in the richest nation on earth, a country that has over 200 brands of breakfast cereal on the supermarket shelves and you think you cannot afford to help people in Syria? By help I don't mean buy them a colouring book or give them a better choice of candy bar. I mean save their lives. Let's spell that out; I mean stop them from dying in appalling pain in the streets, writhing in agony because the grown-ups are bombing the fuck out of the country.'*

Exhibit B concerned the sad events when an Eritrean man was run over and killed by a British holiday maker in Calais. Apparently, the man was erecting a road block at the time. I have no idea of his status, whether he was a refugee, economic migrant, fleeing persecution or whatever. He may have been up to no good, he may have been desperate; the point is whatever way you look at it, it's a tragedy. Through a desperate or foolish act a mother has lost a son, a man has been killed. At that point surely a civilised response, the response of a mature first world nation, is to stop name calling and persecution, to pause, reflect and to mourn the loss of a life.

Instead the baying mob of Daily Mail on-line commenters went into full-on gloating mode, celebrating the death of a human being with a tirade of gleeful posts: *'Good, pity it's only one,'* *'wife's alive? Good, make her pay for a new bumper'* and *'run them all over....'* It's this mob mentality that so divides the world. One doesn't have to condone irresponsible behaviour to be moved by its consequences. The irony is that a lot of these keyboard warriors consider themselves Christians. The line of The Mail is that this is a Christian country and our Christian values need protecting and preserving. It's a perverted self-serving version of scripture though, one that is not even remotely based on love and compassion. Baying for the blood of perceived 'enemies' is not the mark of a civilised faith or patriotic country, it's the rhetoric of a de-humanising fascist 'Might, White and Right' ideology.

In an odd case of serendipity one of the old photos we took to show my sister showed my parents and me visiting my gran, aunts and cousin. I was wearing a Rock Against It badge – a homemade rip-off of the Rock Against Racism (RAR) badge I was forbidden from wearing at school. According to the school authorities, rocking against 'It', whatever 'It' was, was acceptable, but specifying racism wasn't okay, because, as I was told at the time *'one has to consider both sides Raymond. If we allow the wearing of RAR merchandise we have to allow racist badges, and you wouldn't want that now would you?'*

I was a meek child and allowed this to go unchallenged, my passive resistance being the fashioning of the aforementioned badge. Today I want to scream at him...*'No, you don't have to allow racist badges. We have to have some lines in the sand to preserve our democracy you pointless wet middle class excuse for a teacher. If I wore a Rock against Rape badge would you ask me to remove it lest someone wore a Rape is Fun one? Rape is wrong, there's no counter argument, no justification; its rape. Likewise racism is wrong. There is no defence. Our fathers fought for a democracy that has rights and freedoms; with them comes the burden of responsibility. Sometimes that responsibility needs to be reinforced and people reminded of it. I shouldn't need to make my anti-racism position clear but sadly the fascists are gaining traction again and well-meaning tits like you are allowing them room to breed. It is time to stand up and be counted.'*

Of course I wasn't anything like as eloquent as that at the time (if indeed that was eloquent, which I doubt), but that was the gist of my argument, filtered through the intervening years. The world is still chaotic and troublesome, we have many issues to grapple with that require intervention, many injustices that we must face, and we should face them with heart, compassion and reasoned debate. Let's not revisit the dark days of Mosley's black shirts (incidentally lauded at the time by none other than The Daily Mail) or the National Front, that prompted the formation of RAR. Nor should we tolerate todays quasi-fascist parties or the revolting keyboard warriors who fuel the click-baiting Mail on-line. When we devalue a human life to the point of ridicule the only people who benefit are the enemies of democracy.

Goodness that was a bit of a tirade. Now that's out of my system lets return to what passes for normality around here. To lighten the mood I can report that we visited my sister and brother-in-law again, met up with a niece I haven't seen for years, were made very welcome and had a super time. And Alison fell over a dog. I only mention it because it the sort of thing that usually happens to me.

Ray Canham

* * *

Goodbyes exchanged we made the most of a sunny gap between showers to meander our way along the highways and byways from Wool to the rather plush Henley-on-Thames. It happens that Henley is where my sister and brother-in-law spent a lot of time in their courting days, so it was a nice link to our stay with them. The Catherine Wheel public house where they spent more than a few evenings was still busy. Now a Wetherspoons, it was a handy refuge for us when we'd walked in from the nearby Henley Caravan Club site. Once stuffed full of cheap and cheerful grub we wandered around the town centre. It was very comely in a twee well-to-do kind of way. The prices in the estate agents' windows made our eyes water but the views along the Thames were splendid and the sight of a vivid rainbow sinking into the autumnal trees on the opposite bank was truly breathtaking.

Every so often we'd see Red Kites gliding above the town's chimneys and spires, oblivious to the townsfolk scurrying home from work and the ceaseless parade of high end cars squeezing through the bunting lined streets. It was easy to see the appeal of this quaint area of The Thames Valley. Henley itself has a lot to offer the casual visitor if prim shops, cosy eateries and olde world pubs are your kind of thing. I was quite interested in visiting the rowing museum until Alison explained away that it wasn't, as I'd hoped, a monument to squabbles and quarrelling but all about paddling in little boats, so I happily allowed myself to be steered away to a tea shop instead. Henley is of course synonymous with the famous Regatta, which was first held in 1839 and has been an annual fixture ever since, except during the two World Wars. It attracts huge crowds to the town every July; although I suspect few of those are rowing enthusiasts and bother to watch the racing. The event doesn't have any commercial sponsorship; about 85% of the £3million it costs to stage comes from subscriptions paid by members of the Stewards' Enclosure. Henley isn't a poor parish. In fact one thing it has in abundance is money. It's one of the most expensive places in the country to live and goodness knows where the many people who work in its shops, clean its streets and mow its lawns live. Interestingly though it's twinned with Borama in Somaliland, a self-declared republic, internationally recognised as an autonomous region of poverty-stricken Somalia. From a little light research Borama seems to be rebuilding itself positively in the aftermath of an awful civil war in the region. I hope that a fraction of Henley's spare change has helped them in their attempts to rebuild the town. It certainly seems more commendable than some other twinning associations that appear to be little more than opportunities for local bigwigs to enjoy subsidised holidays somewhere sunny with cheap beer.

Enchanted as we were by Henley we had to move on. The area surrounding it looked most inviting, from the broad Thames plain and Chiltern Hills to cosy villages and enchanting towns. As we drove through the winding Thames valley we were both silent, lost in our private thoughts. We were on our way to an overnight stop, one that would bring with it mixed emotions. In less than 48 hours we would be reunited with our cats, but before that we would be sitting down to a final meal and our last night of the season in Mavis.

As we rounded a corner a Kite took off from disembowelling its lunch and swooped aloft to watch us pass, the last rays of the sun turned the hills to amber, the Thames sparkled, and an Audi overtook us on a blind bend to the accompaniment of much tooting of the horn and a severe rebuke from Alison in language that would be sure to get us ejected from the Regatta.

'How are you feeling darling?' I enquired tentatively.

'Much better now thank you.' She said. *'What do you fancy for our last dinner of the year in Mavis?'*

And so with our minds firmly fixed on our stomachs we left the tranquillity of the Chilterns and allowed ourselves to be engulfed by the M25.

CHAPTER 28

Work and Pyrotechnics

We headed to Greenwich. Well, the site was actually in Abbey Wood, South London but as it's within the Royal Borough of Greenwich I guess that name makes it more appealing for tourists. It was a very attractive site, set in hilly woodland and secluded from the surrounding urban sprawl. The only sound we heard from outside was the occasional aeroplane. The autumn trees had carpeted the ground in soft orange and yellow leaves. When we arrived a warden was busy re-distributing them with a noisy leaf blower, a fruitless exercise considering that they just whirled around and settled behind him, but he did get to wear lots of exciting safety gear and a helmet with a visor so I'm guessing he felt a surge of machismo every time he caught his reflection in a caravan window.

The area is named after Lesnes Abbey, or The Abbey of St Mary and St Thomas the Martyr at Lesnes to give it its full title. It was founded in 1178 by Richard de Luci when he was Chief Justiciar, the monarch's chief minister, which was a role similar to today's Prime Minister. Some sources say he may have founded the abbey as penance for his part in the murder of Thomas Becket which was interesting to us because our very first stop on this tour was in Canterbury where poor old Thomas met his end. We didn't venture out to look at the Abbey ruins though, or the Bronze Age barrows in the parkland or indeed anything else because we were happy to just be in Mavis. During our brief discussion about our 'last supper' we'd decided that fish finger sandwiches were our favourite on-board dinner and so that is what we settled down to as the stars came out over the rapidly thinning trees and we prepared for our last night in Mavis.

Back in March we'd sold the house in Colchester and bought Mavis. We quit our jobs, hugged loved ones and with no fixed agenda set off. We had covered just over

10,000 miles and now it was time to settle down again. During our time on the road we'd decided that we liked the Peak District and Staffordshire Moorlands area. The scenery was gorgeous, it was comfortably near to family and friends, the property prices were reasonable, and it wasn't Mablethorpe. We had been offered work there with our friends in the retreat centre near Stafford which included some temporary accommodation and, as an added bonus, our cats could join us.

In another serendipitous moment, as we hit the road for the last time the next morning we joined stationary traffic just as we had done on our very first journey to Canterbury. After a delay of an hour we trundled north with two surprisingly settled cats and arrived in Staffordshire to a warm welcome.

Our accommodation for the next few months would be a large basement room with a separate kitchen and bathroom. We had a couple of days to settle in before starting work so we set about organising everything into a cosy home.

The cats explored every nook and cranny and rubbed their cheeks against the furniture and us. I read somewhere that when cats rub their head against you, they're marking you as one of their own with the concentrated scent glands in their cheeks and head. I don't think so. I was once severely reprimanded by Alison for rubbing my glands against guests and I think that cats should be expected to meet the same standards. The theory that when cats bring dead animals into the house they do it because they consider you family is nonsense too. They're actually trying to teach you that unless you cede to their every demand that half pigeon could well be you. It's the feline equivalent of waking up to find a horse's head in bed beside you. Cats are prima donnas; selfish, arrogant and demanding but somehow we still love them and enjoy their company.

* * *

On our first evening we wandered out of our basement home to watch fireworks being let off a couple of days before the November 5th festival of bangy and whizzy things.

Consider this. Late in November 2014 the Conservative government of the United Kingdom banned any pornography produced in the UK from showing spanking. To the best of my knowledge no one has been harmed from watching a consensual slap on the rump. Reflect then that every year around 1,000 people in the UK are treated in hospital for injuries caused by fireworks and of those about 5% are regarded as serious, potentially life changing injuries. Unlike films showing spanking, you can buy fireworks at your local supermarket along with your tinned peaches and toilet roll. You can purchase a bag of sparklers that burn at a temperature five times that of cooking oil to hand around to the children. You can shove a few 150 mph rockets into the trolley next to a bottle of whiskey to keep the chill away while you set them off.

Somewhere in China around the 7th Century someone mixed some potent ingredients like potassium nitrate, sulphur and charcoal together and made crude gunpowder. Hey presto, fireworks were invented. One report I've read suggests this was completely by accident while they were searching for the secret to eternal life. However, it came about, thanks to some startled alchemists wandering around without eyebrows and waiting for the smoke to clear we can now buy all manner of colourful projectile explosives. And we really do love them; the UK spends around £15 million on fireworks every year. A lot goes on organised displays, but it's probably not a surprise to learn that most accidents requiring hospital treatment happen in the nation's back gardens or in the streets when they fall into irresponsible hands, sometimes literally.

I used to take my boys to a delightfully inept display in a small village near to us. Sparklers could only be used in the designated area, so hordes of over excited children in nylon coats were corralled elbow to elbow into a roped off pen where they singed each other's hair and melted their neighbours coat while trying to write their names in the air in sparkly light. During the main display a stray missile would inevitably end up in a hedge or lodge in a tree where it rained bright embers down onto the puzzled organisers. One year a hedge caught alight and everyone went ooh and aah thinking it was part of the display. Reluctant Catherine Wheels were encouraged to spin by prodding, first with long poles, then a stick and finally a push with bare hands. The climax to the evening would be a sign made from fireworks that spelt out Thank You. Or at least we think it did. When first lit it glared so brightly you couldn't look at it, then a thick plume of acrid smoke would drift over to blot out the whole display. We'd all clap then drive home to tend to our burns. It was great fun. We first went along because its what dads did with young children on bonfire night, but we continued well into their teens just to watch the burning foliage and interesting accidents. We only stopped going when it became safe.

Actually, the best bit was the announcer. Speaking through a network of tinny loudhailers nailed to trees that had somehow survived previous displays he would deliver an echoing running commentary that went something like this:

'Ooh that's a bright green whizzbanger going up...(loud bang)...to Rob and Josie's youngest...(bang)...green and red there...(series of loud explosions)...7pm tomorrow night in the village hall...(bang)...with...(bang)...and...(bang)...of the...(bang)...and a nice firm...(bang)...ooh...(burning tree)...well Roger has that under control nicely now, we'd like to thank...(wail of ambulance siren)...and not forgetting...(loud bang)...for the tea...tea...tea...(long pause)...are you sure this blasted think is turned off?...(loud farting noise)...'

The best thing we ever heard him say was *'woops a daisy'* when a deafening mortar burst at ground level yards from hastily retreating spectators, showering them with a rainbow of white hot sparks. We loved him dearly, whoever he was, a true stolid gent of the highest order, calm, unflappable and determined to carry on even though his job was patently absurd. For all that, I don't recall any incidents that weren't solved by the onsite first aider or a parental kiss. Nevertheless, around the country as we playfully celebrate burning people alive, emergency services and hospital A&E departments will be needlessly stretched treating burns and injuries. Still it's nice to know that year after year no one dies or is scared for life from watching couples playfully spank each other.

Back in our underground lair we spent much time sorting out, resorting, remembering things that we'd left in Mavis necessitating some more sorting, and generally, sorting. The place gradually began to look and feel comfortable. To add to the excitement the first duty on our first day of work was ... to help at a bonfire night and firework display!

I'm happy to report that it was a safe and grand affair.

CHAPTER 29

The Queen of the Moorlands

What do darts champion Eric Bristow, the vocalist with heavy metal legends Demon, the founder of the Arts and Crafts movement William Morris and James Ford, one half of electronic duo Simian Mobile Disco and producer of artists including Artic Monkeys and Florence & the Machine have in common?

Well, they all live in or have close ties to a town of approximately 21,000 people that calls itself The Queen of the Moorlands; Leek in Staffordshire. Of course a chubby bloke who throws pointy things, a couple of musicians barely known outside of their own front door and a revolutionary socialist designer of flowery wallpaper do not make Leek the epicentre of culture, but it's something.

Back in October we were in a bakery on Leek High Street when the call came in that our offer had been accepted on a sunny 2 up 2 down terraced house with a purple shed. The young lady serving us tea and cake offered congratulations and advice about a reasonable local solicitor before we skidded down the wet street and into the estate agents to check that we'd heard them correctly.

We passed through Leek several times during the year. It has long been a transport hub. The major roads had lucrative turnpikes and it was connected to the canal system as a branch of the Caldon Canal, which closed in the 1940s. The railway lasted until the 1960s when Dr. Beeching got his grubby hands on it and there is a bus station, hidden behind an ugly parade of 1960s shops well past their prime. At the foot of the High Street is the Nicholson War Memorial. Built in 1925 and clad in pale Portland stone it stands an impressive 90 feet high with a large clock face on each of its four aspects. Over the road from the memorial the High Street crowns the hill Leek sits upon, with an ancient market square at its apex. Granted a charter to hold a market on Wednesdays during the reign of King John at the beginning of the 13th century the market is still a regular local fixture. The High Street came second in the Telegraph's High Street of the Year in 2013, losing out to Deal in Kent. I'm not sure it would do so well now, it's not gentrified like Southwold or touristy like nearby Buxton, but its charms are still there in the details; original wooden hitching posts along the street, the cobbled market square, independent shops and cafés, a surfeit of busy pubs and echoes of the arts and crafts movement heralded by William Morris. Look up as you walk along and you'll see there are fine stained-glass windows in unexpected places, examples of elaborate plasterwork above anonymous shops and little architectural gems down narrow alleys and side streets. Some streets close to us are still cobbled, abandoned silk mills pop up around street corners, some converted into offices and warehouses, some are apartments and others sit abandoned and derelict, casting sinister shadows over the surrounding houses.

I think the thing that most endeared us to Leek was the fact that it's an honest town, its people unpretentious and friendly. The first time we were called 'duck' I crouched in anticipation of falling masonry. Then it became quaint, a linguistic anachronism. Now it's normal; we miss it if a shop assistant doesn't greet us like long lost friends while she scans our groceries and bids us farewell with a hearty *'ta-ra duck'*. The town seems proud of its heritage but wise enough to know it came at a cost. It has been shaped and bent around the silk industry but the scars don't so much disfigure the town as lend it character and depth. After all, where else could you wander past an Oatcake shop on a cobbled street on your way to Waitrose? We think that we are going to be very happy in Leek, although we cannot pretend that the house is anything but an investment and winter refuge; life on the road holds far too much appeal.

* * *

We were discovering that parts of our new work provided altogether too much fun, with some of my time spent on a mini tractor in the grounds of the retreat centre while Alison was in organisational heaven merging three book collections into one library. These were just a couple of our myriad duties, from cooking for guests to serving them in the bar, picking up leaves to cleaning rooms, helping run a craft day to building a bonfire. Speaking of bonfires, I absolutely loved that particular responsibility. Standing in the crisp autumn air nursing the embers into life was an absolute joy; a gentle manly pursuit, the love of which I think I've inherited from my father. He looked at his most relaxed trundling a wheelbarrow full of brown leaves towards incineration on a smouldering heap that he'd prod, poke and fork at regular intervals. If he wasn't feeding it he'd be leaning on his fork staring at the flames, lost in his own smoky world.

Once a year we'd have a visit from my dad's childhood friend Stan and his wife Margery. Stan was an enigmatic man of few words and even fewer opportunities for pyromania as they lived in a smokeless zone; torture to a man like him. Thus while Margery was ensconced inside chatting to my mother Stan would be given sole responsibility for the bonfire while my father and I scurried around desperately trying to find more debris to feed his passion. He'd hover over the fire with a proprietorial air, like Beelzebub with a pipe. Keeping it smouldering all weekend was a duty he took remarkably seriously. One weekend I returned very late and slightly drunk from a party, the sun was just creeping up when I came face to face with Stan in his dressing gown, walking up the garden path holding the garden fork and smelling distinctly of bonfire. He calmly removed his pipe, greeted me with a grave *'good morning Raymond...I've just been tending to the fire',* tapped out his pipe on the heel of his slippers and held the door open for me. It was never mentioned again but I think from then on we shared a silent understanding.

* * *

I began writing the above passage at around 02.45 one morning. I'd had to do something to calm myself as 15 minutes before we'd been startled out of our slumbers by the most unholy screeching and growling imaginable. I sat bolt upright and let loose a guttural howl along the lines of:

'ArrrrurggwhatthefuckisthatwhereamIwheresthelightstopthatunholyracketugg...' until Alison put the light on. Curiously the cats were spooked but having confirmed that they were inside we then heard the cat flap clunk shut. Various theories on our nocturnal visitor were proffered, including a fox, badger or leprechaun. It turned out to be a neighbour's cat who I caught fleeing the scene of the crime again the following evening. Frankly I was rather disappointed that our two cats hadn't dealt more decisively with an interloper who wore a pink collar with a bell on it. Especially since moving there they had discovered the delights of hunting; we were getting at least a couple of presents a week of the squeaky rodent variety. Walking to the bathroom in the dead of night, an all too frequent outing for a gentleman of my age, now had the additional hazard of stepping on an oozing bag of squelchy fur cooling on the carpet.

That aside it was wonderful having the cats for company. While we were waiting for the house purchase in Leek to complete we had made our little basement into a lovely comfy home with some of our own furniture, familiar pictures on the walls and those odds and ends that make a place into a home. It was taking a while to fully settle though. We'd really taken to life on the road. One of the biggest challenges was adapting to not living 'in the moment' in the way we had grown accustomed to. Our easy-going summer in Mavis really taught us both the value of being alive to the possibilities of the day, to allow ourselves to be spontaneous and to relax into whatever we chose to do.

CHAPTER 30

10,093 Miles

Way back in March 2016 we swapped our computer screensaver of a sunset for over 200 real ones. We traded our suburban semi for a motorhome and pointed it at whatever took our fancy. We've seen sights we never expected to see, met wonderful people, worked at some amazing festivals and had unforgettable experiences; we've observed the seasons changing, seen abundant wildlife, watched the sun rise and set around the country, felt the peace of total silence under the stars, walked over hills, up mountains and down dales, covered 10,093 miles, played kazoo's with a biker gang and generally had a blast. We celebrated our first wedding anniversary on the road, a year that we have spent over half of travelling and living in a space smaller than most bathrooms, cooking on two gas rings, sleeping with our noses a few inches from the ceiling and rarely had hot running water. We've opened our front door to over 60 different views, from Devon to The Isle of Skye; and we have laughed every single day.

Our trip may have been conceived as an opportunity to see the country, meet people and find somewhere to put down fresh roots but it has also been a personal journey for both of us. We've discovered things about ourselves and about each other that will bind us forever. At times it has been a spiritual journey, an opportunity to reflect and consider; my relationship with my late father, whose presence has been a not unwelcome companion during the journey, Alison's son moving on in his life, watching him mature as he has grappled with life's complexities and settled into a new phase. From our insulated little motorhome we've witnessed momentous decisions, Brexit and the American presidential race for example, and debated these and many more topics with friends old and new the length and breadth of the country as we've wrestled with matters of faith and social justice.

After all the bitterness of the Brexit fallout, the American presidential election campaign and the constant flow of fleeing war-ravaged refugees it's tempting to conclude that we are a remarkably foolish species. We seem able to complicate our lives to such a degree that the colour of our skin, our private beliefs or where we happen to have been born seems to matter more than love, compassion and mutual respect. We acquire possessions, trinkets and fripperies by the dozen, line the walls of our houses with tat and then watch children starve on our 42" Plasma TV's while we sup on wine and graze on snacks to keep us going until the pizza is delivered.

But we've been inspired on our journey by people who live on the fringes of society, and those who are firmly embedded in it, people who stand shoulder to shoulder against prejudice and injustice. There are many people who don't accept the status quo, people who are fighting for justice and lasting change. From the pulpit to the punk concert there is a groundswell of hope.

* * *

We expected our journey to be a little relief from the day to day, a chance to sit back and watch the world go by. I'm sure friends and family saw it as a mid-life crisis, even if they were too polite to say so to our faces. But it became so much more than that. My relationship with my father wasn't just a recurring opportunity to squeeze in a few jokes at his expense, although I guess it started out that way. Finding that I could actually relax properly, probably for the first time since...well since I can remember, meant that there was mental space for those thoughts and feelings that I'd kept suppressed to surface. In many ways Glastonbury was a cathartic experience for me, even without the festival or anything more mind-expanding than Halloumi. I loved my father dearly and regret that I'm only able to say that now. He wasn't perfect and sometimes made decisions that we find hard to fathom now, but they were his to make. I can't go back, I can't repair the past, the most I can do is seek to understand it and strive to be an understanding father to our children.

Our love survived a season on the road; if anything it is stronger now because of the things we've shared, the trials and tribulations, the joys and the pleasures. I've teased Alison in this book and gone on to dominate the story with my own recollections and observations. Since completing the first draft we've played a game where I'll try and credit her as co-author and she will bat it back saying that I did all the work. Which isn't true, the adventures were ours, we took the decisions together and neither of us would be where we are without the other. I will though happily take the blame for any inaccuracies, errors, omissions and for any opinions that cause you to spit out your tea in disgust, especially if you live in Mablethorpe or read the Daily Mail.[x]

Writing this passage in a tiny two up two down terraced house in a humble Midlands town I don't miss any of the trappings of our previous outwardly successful life. We've no mortgage, no debt, food on the table and opportunities for further adventure. Occasionally I still catch myself halfway through a repetitive ritual, gathering my food onto the fork in a particular way for example, but it's a reminder that for all our wonderful experiences stress is still a part of real life. We don't have less, but we do have much better ways of coping. Our priorities have changed, and we are so much happier. '*Getting downwardly mobile opens your eyes to really living.*'

EPILOGUE

March 2017

We're not really sure quite how it came about. I was supposed to be researching vets at the time but somehow an email was sent to the general manager of a castle on the Scottish Hebridean island of Mull. Some correspondence was exchanged, one thing led to another and one sunny Sunday afternoon in March we loaded the final bag into Mavis and set forth for Scotland and the ferry to Mull. Ahead of us was a crash course in Scottish history and a summer of adventure in one of the most beautiful parts of the country.

After our adventures on the road we hadn't really settled down. We didn't get to use our house very much as we spent most of our time in our apartment at work and after much agonising we'd concluded that another carefree summer on the road just wasn't practical either. We needed an alternative, something that would satisfy our wanderlust and provide us with a modest income, or indeed with an obscenely large income should the opportunity arise.

So, after a winter standing idle Mavis was back on the road...and you can read about our further adventures in volume 2, coming soon.

* * *

That's all folks...time to plan your own adventure!

ACKNOWLEDGMENTS

To live our dream we have relied on the companionship and support of people who have opened their lives to us, given us advice, shelter, offered us hospitality, shared our passion and worked alongside us; friends and family who have contributed to our experiences in ways they may or may not be aware of to give us the courage to leave the rat race behind.

The list of people to thank is too long and we'd be mortified if we overlooked anyone, so if you're reading this please take it as a thank you for being you. Whoever you are, you are very special and we love you.

Likewise everyone who has encouraged us to keep writing the blog, for indulging our flights of fancy and for taking the time to comment, we are indebted to you. To those people who urged us to write a book, this is it. You only have yourselves to blame.

Ray would like to add:
Hello to Linda; I love having a big sister.

A special extra big thank you to Alison who encouraged me to write and didn't try to put me off, even when she realised the cost of doing so was having to read everything I wrote, edit it and explain why she'd changed it without once hurting my feelings. Her patience, tact and grace are only superseded by her editorial skills. She's also quite gorgeous but I promised her I wouldn't embarrass her by mentioning that here.

Alison would like to add:
A special mention and big thank you must go to my parents. We are indebted to you for welcoming us on countless occasions, allowing us to park on your drive and providing us with home cooked meals, laundry facilities, comfort and unfailing encouragement and support. We would like to award you with the 'Mavis Trip Advisor Special Award for Hospitality 2016.'

To access the exclusive material visit **www.downwardlymobile.weebly.com** and on the **ABOUT** page click on the word **Tequila** at the end of Alison's biography.

DOWNWARDLY MOBILE

NOTES:

[i] Andy Flannagan – The Reason, from the album Drowning in the Shallow.
[ii] www.dysgraphiahelp.co.uk
[iii] Levellers - Battle Of The Beanfield.
[iv] The The – Armageddon Days.
[v] Ibid.
[vi] A political theory that government is created by, and subject to, the will of the people.
[vii] Final score 6-6 in case you were wondering.
[viii] If that doesn't amuse and depress you in equal measure then you are probably from Spalding.
[ix] The gift shop would be amazing though, little Johnny and Jessica could take home souvenir pencil erasers in the shape of their favourite offal, Dad could pick up a replica stun gun for the mantelpiece while mum considered the wonderful choice of sinew and blood soaps available.
[x] If you live in Mablethorpe and read the Daily Mail I suggest that you take a long hard look at your life.

Printed in Great
Britain
by Amazon